DANIELLE M. CONWAY

State and Local Government Procurement

Section of State and
Local Government Law

AMERICAN BAR ASSOCIATION

Cover design by Monica Alejo/ABA Publishing.

The materials contained herein represent the opinions and views of the author, and should not be construed to be the views or opinions of the law firms or companies with whom the author is in partnership with, associated with, or employed by, nor of the American Bar Association or Section of State and Local Government Law, unless adopted pursuant to the bylaws of the Association.

Nothing contained in this book is to be considered as the rendering of legal advice, either generally or in connection with any specific issue or case. Readers are responsible for obtaining advice from their own lawyers or other professionals. This book and any forms and agreements herein are intended for educational and informational purposes only.

Printed in the United States of America.

16 15 14 13   5 4 3

Library of Congress Cataloging-in-Publication Data

Conway, Danielle M.
    State and local government procurement / Danielle M. Conway.
        p. cm.
Includes bibliographical references and index.
    ISBN 978-1-61438-508-0 (print : alk. paper)
    1. Government purchasing—Law and legislation—United States. 2. Public contracts—United States. I. Title.
    KF849.C6665 2012
    346.7302'3—dc23

                                                                    2012012700

Discounts are available for books ordered in bulk. Special consideration is given to state bars, CLE programs, and other bar-related organizations. Inquire at Book Publishing, ABA Publishing, American Bar Association, 321 North Clark Street, Chicago, Illinois 60654-7598.

www.ShopABA.org

For my son, Ema
And my husband, Emmanuel

Summary of Contents

Contents

Preface

The magnitude of state and local government procurement is staggering, with annual spending by state and local governments projected at nearly $2 trillion. Equally astounding is the degree to which state and local government procurement has become complex, dynamic, and constantly the focus of efforts at reform and transformation. Although facing a dynamic and changing landscape, the common mandate for government procurement is to timely meet user minimum needs with the delivery of best-value products or services, while ensuring the highest standards of integrity in order to maintain the public's trust and fulfilling state and local government public policy objectives. Thus, state and local government procurement professionals are faced with massive responsibilities to assist their departments and agencies in accomplishing their missions while simultaneously guarding expenditures of taxpayer dollars. The increased responsibilities shouldered by state and local government procurement professionals are attributable to, among other things, the massive spending power controlled by state and local governments; the strategic uses of procurement to accomplish public policy goals and objectives; the federal government's policy of passing more responsibilities to the states by imposing unfunded mandates; and the ever-present requirement to ensure their citizens have access to necessary and essential government services.

State and Local Procurement is not the first book to discuss state and local government procurement. Certain books focus on best practices to be followed by procurement professionals while others provide general outlines of state procurement codes and rules. Each of these books has a purpose and fills a definite need in the procurement community. *State and Local Procurement*, however, is the first to address comprehensively state and local government procurement law, policy, and best practices to provide the reader authoritative guidance in the identification and analysis of legal and policy standards for procurement actions in the context within which they arise. This book seeks to expand on both the 2000 Model Procurement Code and the 2007 Model Code for Public Infrastructure Procurement by presenting explanations of provisions in action as illustrated in court decisions and opinions, attorney general opinions, agency policy statements, and private organization commentary. *State and Local Procurement* is the first to provide detailed treatment of the theory, analysis, and best practices of state and local government procurement law and processes. It strives to be comprehensive by discussing procurement topics from A to Z. For example, this book covers state and local fiscal issues in conjunction with procurement issues. In addition, it covers public private partnerships, acquisition planning, alternative dispute resolution, labor standards, and procurement of intellectual property, to name a few topics that are routinely excluded from other manuscripts covering state and local procurement.

This book offers more than mere citations to state codes and cases; rather, it guides readers through the analysis and reasoning of specific topics and presents a firm analytic foundation for those who will need to perform more in-depth research on any of the given procurement topics for their specific jurisdiction. *State and Local Procurement* will be useful to those who consider themselves procurement professionals and will be an indispensable resource as the work is updated to address the evolution of the field of state and local government procurement.

Acknowledgments

This book project has been six years in the making with support and encouragement from so many wonderful, caring people. As with any process, there are people along the way who prepare you for the various challenges and undertakings that come with practicing law, teaching, and producing scholarship. A phenomenal mentor, Professor David Callies, lobbied on my behalf to the American Bar Association's State and Local Government Law Section to grant me the opportunity to write and publish this important work. Professor Callies, a prolific author in his own right, is a champion of my scholarship and teaching. I have stayed the course in the legal academy due in large measure to Professor Callies's active participation in advancing my career. I am personally and professionally indebted.

I must also acknowledge the institution that set me on the path to practice and teach public procurement law. Judge Frederick Lees served as my academic advisor and mentor 15 years ago when I studied in the Government Procurement Law and Environmental Law Programs as an LL.M. candidate at George Washington University Law School. Since then, the faculty at GW Law, especially Professors Steven L. Schooner and Christopher Yukins, have made significant contributions to my development as an expert in public procurement law. I am grateful for the world-class education I received at GW Law and for the constant recognition I receive from its faculty.

The Board Members of the Hawai'i Procurement Institute (HPI) and the partners and associates of Alston Hunt Floyd & Ing have been integral partners in promoting the principles of competition, transparency, and integrity in Hawai'i's procurement community. I am extraordinarily lucky to have Terry Thomason, a partner in the Labor and Employment Group of the firm and the education director of HPI, as a friend and mentor. Mr. Thomason makes procurement law fun with his amazingly entertaining procurement stories that are too bizarre to be imagined. Mr. Thomason is one of the most effective teachers of the practice of procurement law to grace the procurement bar.

Dean Aviam Soifer and the faculty at the William S. Richardson School of Law are enthusiastic financial and intellectual supporters of my scholarship. I am fortunate to be a member of an academic community that rewards hard work and commitment to scholarship in diverse areas of law and legal practice. In addition, I must recognize my lead research assistant on this book project, Mr. Thomas Villalon, for his personal investment in this project and his exceptional commitment to seeing it completed. Mr. Villalon made significant contributions to this book by providing accurate and timely research and legal memoranda, which formed the foundations of several of the book's later chapters. I am immensely grateful to Mr. Villalon for delivering his work to my home to accommodate me during the last trimester of my pregnancy. In addition, Mr. Villalon proved to be an effective manager of several very talented research assistants who also made important contributions to this book. For their hard work, I would like to recognize Mr. Barron Oda, Ms. Courtney Sue-Ako, Mr. Michael (John) Howell, Ms. Shannon Sinton, and Ms. Samantha Sneed. I am deeply grateful to my cadre of research assistants who worked long hours on what sometimes amounted to tedious assignments. As well, I wish to thank my faculty support specialist, Ms. Princess Soares, for always anticipating my administrative needs.

I dedicate this book to my newborn son, Emmanuel Kweku Quainoo III, who came along for the ride and made writing the complete draft of this book a swift yet exciting process. I also dedicate this book to my loving husband, Emmanuel Quainoo, who dashed home from work every night so that I could steal away to write just one more section. Finally, I dedicate this book to my mom, retired Judge Gwendolyn Conway, who temporarily moved to Hawai'i to help us care for Little Ema during the first year of his life.

In conclusion, I am grateful to the governing members of the ABA's State and Local Government Law Section for placing trust in me to complete this book. I also must thank Leslie Keros for her enthusiasm and gentle, yet effective prodding to get this work written and published.

About the Author

Danielle M. Conway is the Michael J. Marks Distinguished Professor of Business Law and director of the University of Hawai'i Procurement Institute at the William S. Richardson School of Law. Professor Conway teaches courses in intellectual property law, licensing intellectual property, international intellectual property law, indigenous peoples and intellectual property law, Australian intellectual property law, Internet law and policy, and government contract law. Named Outstanding Professor of the Year in 2003, and awarded the University of Hawai'i Regents' Medal for Excellence in Teaching in 2004, Professor Conway completed a 2006–07 Fulbright Senior Scholar post in Australia. In academic year 2007-08, Professor Conway held the Visiting E.K. Gubin Professor of Government Contract Law Chair at the George Washington University Law School; as well, she was selected as the 2008 Godfrey Visiting Scholar at the University of Maine School of Law. In 2008, Professor Conway was selected to hold a Chair-In-Law position at La Trobe University Faculty of Law and Management in Melbourne, Australia.

Professor Conway coauthored the treatise *Intellectual Property, Software, and Information Licensing: Law and Practice* (2006 & 2007–2011 Supps.) and the casebook *Licensing Intellectual Property: Law and Application* (2d ed. 2011), both with Robert W. Gomulkiewicz and Xuan-Thao Nguyen. Her writings have also been published by Oxford University Press, *Southern Methodist University Law Review, Howard Law Journal, University of Richmond Law Review, Santa Clara Law Review, Asian-Pacific Law and Policy Journal, Washington University Global Studies Law Review, Computer Law Review and Technology Journal, The Army Lawyer, Texas Wesleyan Law Review, Michigan Journal of Race and Law,* and the *American Law Institute–American Bar Association Business Law Course Materials Journal.* She has lectured in the United States, Europe, the United Kingdom, China, Japan, Ghana, Palau,

Micronesia, Australia, New Zealand, and Mongolia on topics including globalization, government contract law, intellectual property law, intellectual property licensing law, and indigenous people's rights.

Professor Conway serves as a Lieutenant Colonel in the U.S. Army Reserve. For eight years she was assigned to the Contract and Fiscal Law Department (ADK) at the Judge Advocate General's Legal Center and School and served as a professor of law in ADK for six years and then as Assistant Chair of ADK for two years. She is currently assigned to the United States Pacific Command (USPACOM), Camp H.M. Smith, serving as an Assistant Staff Judge Advocate. While on active duty, Professor Conway was an Assistant Counsel for Procurement at the Headquarters, U.S. Army Corps of Engineers in the Office of the Chief Counsel's Honors Program in Washington, D.C. She has been of counsel to the law firm of Alston Hunt Floyd & Ing, LLP in Honolulu since 2003.

Professor Conway earned a B.S. from New York University, Stern School of Business, a J.D., *cum laude*, from Howard University School of Law, and a dual LL.M. from the George Washington University Law School. Professor Conway is a member of the American Law Institute.

1

An Overview of Government Contract Law

This chapter provides a general overview of the scope and power of state and local governments to develop an infrastructure that supports a properly functioning procurement system. State and local government procurement presents challenges for lawyers, procurement professionals, and contractors alike because oftentimes the laws, regulations, rules, and judicial opinions are not accessible. This chapter attempts to provide a starting place for identifying procurement laws and codes of the 50 states and several U.S. territories, but by no means is it meant to be comprehensive. Additionally, this chapter canvases the topics dealing with procurement oversight, the contracting power of procuring officials, the authority of government personnel, and the type of authority required to bind state and local governments.

State Procurement Organizations

Implementing effective procurement policy requires an infrastructure that will support and promote transparency, competition, and flexibility. State procurement is in a period of renaissance. States are making purchases of supplies and services that are complex yet necessary for economic growth within state borders. In order to sustain and support such growth during a period of complex purchasing, states have established state procurement offices with policymaking or operational responsibilities or both. The American Bar Association's (ABA) 2007 Model Code for Public Infrastructure Procurement (MC PIP)[1] and its 2000 Model Procurement Code (MPC) set forth the basic organizational concepts for establishing procurement policy and conducting procurement operations.[2]

Researching State Procurement Codes

Many states and localities have passed laws and regulations on public contracting procedures. These laws are not uniform across the states. State procurement laws may be found in the various state codes, which may also be referred to as state statutes or other, similar terms. Typically, state laws on procurement fall into a few general categories of legislation; for example, California has a public procurement code, but the state has also enacted statutes governing contracting and procurement in other codes, including, among others, the California Government Code, the California Public Utilities Code, and the California Code of Regulations. Some states have passed detailed, comprehensive Procurement Codes, based on the ABA's 2007 MC PIP and/or 2000 MPC. In these states, detailed procedures are included for nearly all aspects of public contracting, from types of specifications to contract administration. This chapter's appendix offers a starting point for researching state procurement statutes and codes in specific jurisdictions. For a comprehensive compilation of state procurement laws and statutes, refer to the American Bar Association's *Guide to State Procurement: A 50-State Primer on Purchasing Laws, Processes and Procedures.*[3] For more detailed citations to local government codes in which municipalities may have their own procurement and purchasing procedures, refer to the Municode Library, a free service of the Municipal Code Corporation providing access to an online library of municipal codes to casual users.[4]

Control and Oversight of Procurement

Any expenditure of public funds to procure goods, services, or construction automatically invokes the requirement that state and local governments exercise control and oversight over such purchases. The authority to exercise this control and oversight is generally articulated in state and/or local procurement codes. For example, Louisiana's Public Bid Law;[5] Professional, Personal, Consulting, and Social Services Procurement law;[6] and the Louisiana Procurement Code[7] all become applicable when there is an expenditure of public funds.[8] Similarly, the Utah Procurement Code provides, in pertinent part, that it applies "to every expenditure of public funds irrespective of their source, including federal assistance, by any state agency under any contract."[9]

Procurement codes, statutes, and ordinances of the state governing the letting of public contracts exist to support a strong public policy of fostering honest competition, to assure prudent and economical use of public monies, and to facilitate the acquisition of high-quality goods and services at the lowest possible cost. The purpose of these laws, in addition to the protection of taxpayers and the public treasury by obtaining the best work at the lowest possible price, is to guard against favoritism, improvidence, extravagance, fraud, and corruption in the awarding of public contracts. Inasmuch as these laws were intended for the benefit of the taxpayers and not to help enrich the corporate bidders, they are to be construed and administered as to accomplish such purpose fairly and reasonably with sole reference to the public interest.

Even when a formal procurement code has not been adopted, as is the case with the Virgin Islands and American Samoa, similar goals to protect the integrity of their procurement systems are invoked. For example, the statutory requirements pertaining to contracts with the government of the Virgin Islands were created "to protect the local treasury from fiscal mismanagement, unauthorized expenditures, and generally to insure the functions of the legislature in dispensing local revenues from encroachments by the executive branch."[10] To allow enforcement of agreements with the government despite statutory violations "would destroy the life and vitality of the statutes."[11] Policy concerns underlying the statutory requirements pertaining to contracts with the government of the Virgin Islands apply with equal force whether or not federal or local funds are to be disbursed at the discretion of the territorial government.[12]

The Government's Power to Contract

A contract is the basic method by which the government procures needed supplies, services, and construction from the private sector. The power of state governments to enter into contracts and to seek their enforcement emanates from the inherent authority of states as "sovereigns." This authority may also be affirmed by express authorization by state constitutions or statutes.[13] Moreover, departments of state governments are typically delegated to exercise the states' contract powers. For example, in Ohio, the Department of Administrative Services may purchase supplies and services for use by state agencies.[14] In addition to these powers, the Department of Administrative Services is required to exercise the power, among others, to "prepare, or contract to be prepared, by licensed engineers or architects, surveys, general and detailed plans, specifications, bills of materials, and estimates of cost for any projects, improvements, or public buildings to be constructed by state agencies that may be authorized by legislative appropriations or any other funds made available therefor, provided that the construction of the projects, improvements, or public buildings is a statutory duty of the department."[15]

The power of local and municipal governments to enter into contracts is dependent upon whether Dillon's Rule or home rule applies. Dillon's Rule is a canon of statutory construction from common law that calls for the strict and narrow construction of local governmental authority.[16] Dillon's Rule provides that a municipal corporation possesses and can exercise only the following powers: (1) those granted in express words; (2) those necessarily or fairly implied in or incident to the powers expressly granted; and (3) those essential to the accomplishment of the declared objects and purposes of the corporation—not simply convenient, but indispensable.[17] Today, home-rule authority reverses Dillon's Rule; however, the rule remains the most important factor in deciding the powers of non-home-rule local governments.[18] Home-rule units of local government may enact regulations when the state has not specifically declared its exercise to be exclusive; non-home-rule units of local government are governed by Dillon's Rule, under which non-home-rule units possess only the powers that are specifically conveyed by the state constitution or statute.[19] One state still operates entirely under this regime, while a few other states incorporate aspects of this regime into their delegation of municipal powers, and another state grants, pursuant to the state constitution, the privilege of autonomous rule over municipal affairs.[20]

An example of the government's power to contract is *Digital Biometrics, Inc. v. Anthony*.[21] In *Digital Biometrics*, the court upheld the decision of an administrative body with quasi-judicial functions to refuse to exercise general jurisdiction over contracts for the procurement of electronic data processing and telecommunications goods and services.[22] The refusal was based on the administrative body's recognition that it did not have broad jurisdiction and authority over supervising the procurement of goods and services. Instead, the administrative body determined, and the court agreed, that California's General Services Administration had general supervisory authority over the procurement of such goods and services as specifically provided for in section 12100 of California's Public Contract Code.[23] Specifically, the court concluded that if "after the selection of an awardee a disappointed bidder can protest to the Board of Control and raise matters relating to the earlier stages of the process that could and should have been presented to General Services," it "would encroach upon the jurisdiction committed to General Services and would be contrary to the Legislature's declaration that General Services's decision on such matters shall be final," meaning that the matter at issue in this case was correctly handled by General Services and that for a court to rule on the matter would be a usurpation of the powers delegated to General Services.[24]

A Tennessee case recognizing the power and authority of a government purchasing agent to contract for goods and services is

Metropolitan Air Research Testing Authority, Inc. v. Metropolitan Government of Nashville and Davidson County.[25] According to Metropolitan Charter §§ 8.109, 8.110, 8.111, the responsibility for procuring goods and services for most of the city's departments rested on the purchasing agent.[26] Upon receipt of a requisition for goods or services costing more than $1,000, the purchasing agent prepares the specifications[27] and issues the advertisements or invitations to bid.[28] After the bid opening, the purchasing agent requests the requisitioning agency to review the bids[29] and obtains a certification from the finance director that funds for the contract are available.[30] Thereafter, the purchasing agent "with the approval of the mayor" makes all determinations with regard to the award of the contract.[31] In concluding that the purchasing agent held the authority to contract, as opposed to a government official on hand at a meeting to give opinions about contract award, the court explained that "procuring goods and services is the type of routine activity that is best left to governmental officials," and that "public procurement authorities have wide discretion with regard to accepting bids or any of the other details of entering into a contract," and "in the absence of fraud, corruption, or palpable abuse of discretion, the courts will ordinarily not interfere with [those] governmental procurement [decisions]."[32]

The Authority of Government Personnel

The authority to contract is not unfettered. State agencies and their personnel are restricted in their contracting actions by legislative oversight through appropriations laws and through the requirement of actual authority to enter into and enforce state contracts. With respect to local governments and municipalities, home-rule provisions may provide authority for personnel to contract to the extent that the procurement is strictly local; however, home rule may be limited by state legislatures when contract actions impact statewide interests.[33] Accordingly, state personnel must have actual authority to contract; as well, local and municipal government personnel must also adhere to home-rule limitations as well as actual authority.

In Wyoming, all purchases or all encumbrances on behalf of any municipality shall be made or incurred only upon an order or approval of the person duly authorized to make such purchases except encumbrances or expenditures directly investigated, reported, and approved by the governing body.[34] Similarly, in *District of Columbia v. Greene*,[35] the court reiterated a basic principle of state procurement law: That, in accordance with District law, a contracting official cannot obligate the District to a contract in excess of his or her actual authority.[36]

In addition to stating the rule requiring actual authority, *Greene* also restates the well-settled general principle that one who makes a contract with a municipal corporation is bound to take notice of limitations on both the government entity's and particular officer's authority to make the contract. That is, persons dealing with a municipal corporation through its agent are bound to know the nature and extent of the agent's authority in accordance with long-existing and well-settled general rules obtained in the law of agency generally and applying to dealings with both artificial and natural persons. Accordingly, a person making or seeking to make a contract with the District is charged with knowledge of the limits of the agency's (or its agent's) actual authority.[37]

In *Greene*, Verizon South asserted its reliance on the action of the contracting officer, making what amounted to a claim of estoppel against the District. In rejecting the estoppel claim, the court reaffirmed that a party contracting with the government is "on constructive notice of the limits of the [government agent's] authority," and cannot reasonably rely on representations to the contrary.[38]

Delegation of Actual Authority

It is a general principle of procurement law that only those specifically delegated actual authority may bind a state government. In *ARA Health Services, Inc. v. Department of Public Safety and Correctional Services*,[39] a contractor argued that a state department had waived its sovereign immunity against suit for additional contract payments.[40] The Department of Public Safety and Correctional Services, as "a principal department of the State Government,"[41] challenged and stated that it continued to enjoy the protective cloak of sovereign immunity. It cited § 12-201(a) of Maryland's State Government title, which provided,

> Except as otherwise expressly provided by a law of the State, the State, its officers, and its units may not raise the defense of sovereign immunity in a contract action, in a court of the State, based on a written contract that an official or employee executed for the State or [one] of its units while the official or employee was acting within the scope of the authority of the official or employee.[42]

The court concluded that although § 12-201(a) indeed constitutes a partial waiver of sovereign immunity, its application is limited to actions where: (1) the contract upon which the claim is based was reduced to writing; and (2) the state employee or official acted within the scope of his or her authority in executing the contract.[43] The Court of Special Appeals concluded that neither requirement was satisfied and held that the contractor's claim was barred as a result.[44]

The court also noted that the original contract afforded the contractor "no relief in that its plain terms indicated that reimbursement was due only for hospital-related AIDS services."[45] In addition, Modification H to the contract was "similarly unhelpful in that its effective date was subsequent to the period relevant to the dispute."[46] The basis of the contractor's claim, "therefore, [was] the contract as modified by the parties' conduct during the initial 18-month term of the contract. In order for the waiver of immunity in § 12-201(a) to apply, therefore, the modification by conduct must satisfy the requirements set forth in the statute."[47]

An express requirement of § 12-201(a) was that "the claim must be based on a contract executed within the scope of authority of the State employee or official."[48] In determining whether the Department of Corrections "would have acted within the scope of its authority if it modified by conduct the payment terms of the contract with the contractor," the court found it "necessary to examine the procurement procedures with which the [Department of Corrections] was required to comply."[49]

The court determined that the "terms of the contract clearly stated that the parties to the contract were the contractor and the State of Maryland, 'acting through'" the Department of Corrections.[50] In executing the contract on the State's behalf, the Department of Corrections "acted merely as an agent of the State and, in this capacity, enjoyed only limited powers."[51] Specifically, the Department of Correction's authority to modify the contract with the contractor "was circumscribed not only by the contract terms, but also by the statutes and regulations applicable to State procurement."[52]

The court further stated that the legislature has empowered the Board of Public Works (the Board) with control over procurement by State agencies.[53] Under the applicable statute, procurement is broadly defined, in relevant part as "buying or otherwise obtaining supplies, services, construction, construction related services, architectural services, engineering services, or services provided under an energy performance contract," and a procurement contract is "an agreement in any form entered into by a unit for procurement."[54] The Board has the "statutory authority both to 'require prior Board approval for specified procurement actions,' as well as to dispense with the requirement of Board approval."[55] Furthermore, the statutory and regulatory scheme that governs State procurement contemplates Board approval "of not only initial procurement contracts, but also of modifications to these contracts."[56]

Based on the court's interpretation, the Board has "delegated contracting authority to various governmental units. Often included in these delegations is the authority to execute contract modifications, provided certain conditions are met. For example, the Department of Public Safety and Correctional Services has the authority to execute modifications to contracts for construction and construction-related services that, among other things, do not exceed $50,000 or materially change the scope of the original contract."[57]

The court concluded that "where there has been no delegation of authority, . . . the procurement regulations expressly provide that Board approval must precede the procurement action."[58] The court determined that the Board "ha[d] not delegated to the Department [of Corrections] procurement authority with respect to the service contract at issue in the instant case," and that "[t]he absence of this delegation necessarily means that the Department must obtain Board approval prior to executing such a contract or any modification thereto."[59]

The court found that the modification at issue was "purportedly accomplished by the parties' conduct. Moreover, while Board approval was procured for Modification H, the modification by conduct that forms the basis of the contractor's claim did not receive Board approval."[60] As a result, the Department of Correction's "failure to follow the requirements of the statutory and regulatory scheme with which it must comply amounted to an *ultra vires* act" and failed to "satisfy the second requirement of § 12–201(a)."[61]

The court reiterated that "the scope of a State official's authority is co-extensive with his or her actual authority."[62] As the court observed in the context of municipal corporations in other cases, "[a]lthough a private agent, acting in violation of specific instructions, yet within the scope of a general authority, may bind his principal, the rule, as to the effect of a like act of a public agent, is otherwise."[63] The court explained the general procurement principle that "those who contract with a public agency . . . are presumed to know the limitations on that agency's authority and bear the risk of loss resulting from unauthorized conduct by that agency."[64] Accordingly, the "scope of authority" to which reference was made in § 12–201(a) was "synonymous with the State agent's actual authority."[65] "It matters not that the [Department of Corrections], though lacking in actual authority, might have acted with apparent authority to modify the contract. Public policy demands that the State cannot be bound by the unauthorized acts of its agents."[66]

The Requirement to Comply with Limits on Authority

The power of the government and its personnel to contract is limited by the requirement of actual authority.[67] State courts have analyzed the enforceability of public contracts under the *ultra vires* doctrine. A contract is said to be *ultra vires* when it is wholly beyond the scope of the public agency's authority under any circumstances and for any purpose.[68] Where contracts are let in a manner that contravenes the purpose of competitive bidding, courts have declared them to be void and illegal *ab initio*. For example, in *Platt Electric Supply v. City of Seattle*,[69] a contract was awarded to a bidder after the contracting officer privately negotiated with him to lower his bid. The court held that the award was void.[70] Similarly, when a contract, which by statute required competitive bidding, was let without seeking bids, the contract was void.[71] However, a contractor who performs under such a void contract may be permitted to recover in *quantum meruit*.[72] Similarly, where an agency has the general authority to award such a contract, but the award is technically or procedurally flawed such that it violates a statute, a contractor may be permitted *quantum meruit* recovery so long as the award is not marked by fraud or bad faith and does not manifestly contravene public policy.[73] Accordingly, a private party acting in good faith may recover to the extent necessary to prevent manifest injustice or unjust enrichment, thus recovering the reasonable value of performance.

On the other hand, when actual authority does exist, the contracting agency has discretion in awarding contracts. In *Heritage Pools, Inc. v. Foothills Metropolitan Recreation and Park District*,[74] the court determined that a contracting officer acted within the scope of actual authority by conducting negotiations with prime contractors regarding their ability to work with certain subcontractors. In *Heritage*, the subcontractor argued that the district forced the contractors to select another subcontractor in violation of § 18-8-307 of the Colorado Revised Statutes. This provision stated, in pertinent part,

> (1) No public servant shall require or direct a bidder or contractor to deal with a particular person in procuring any goods or service required in submitting a bid to or fulfilling a contract with any government. . . .
>
> (3) It shall be an affirmative defense that the defendant was a public servant acting within the scope of his authority exercising the right to reject any material, subcontractor, service, bond, or contract tendered by a bidder or contractor because it does not meet bona fide specifications or requirements relating to quality, availability, form, experience, or financial responsibility.[75]

In this case, the district had called in each of the four low-bidding general contractors separately and asked if it would have any problem working with a subcontractor other than Heritage if the district decided to select another subcontractor with greater experience. Each agreed it could work with one of the other subcontractors.[76] The next lowest-priced subcontractor was proposed. According to the court, the district did not require that the general contractors accept a particular subcontractor, nor did the district require the general contractors to absorb any additional cost because it preferred a different subcontractor.[77] This type of negotiation and modification did not "constitute a designation of supplier to fulfill a government contract, but rather" was considered "an exercise of the District's discretion in rejecting a particular subcontractor on the basis of experience."[78]

Legal Significance of Actions by Government Employees without Actual Contract Authority

Arguments have been raised that a chief procurement officer or purchasing agent, having actual authority, may ratify conduct in violation of a procurement law as long as the ratification is in the best interest of the state.[79] The majority of state courts interpreting state statutes and codes do not agree. In *McMahon v. City of Chicago*,[80] the plaintiff, a prospective contractor, asserted that he was party to an oral contract made by a state employee on behalf of the State. Specifically, the plaintiff alleged that a city employee asked him for a proposal, told him he had been awarded the contract, gave him a purchase order number, wrote a memorandum under the city employee's supervisor's signature stating that certain city departments (none of which was the purchasing or procurement department) approved of the department's choice of plaintiff, and arranged for the plaintiff to gain access to restricted vantage points to work on his sketches.[81] The court found that the plaintiff had not alleged that either city employee he dealt with was a procurement officer or purchasing agent under the statute.[82] Although the plaintiff stated that he was given a purchase order number, he did not "allege that an authorized official expressly approved the purchase order or assigned the purchase order number. In fact, issuing purchase order numbers" was not "among the enumerated powers and duties of a municipal purchasing agent."[83]

Purchasing and public works contracts with Illinois municipalities are governed by Article 8, Division 10 of the Illinois Municipal Code, which "consists of a municipal purchasing act applicable to cities with populations of 500,000 or more."[84] The Municipal Code "substantially limits the contracting power of municipal employees," stating,

> No department, office, institution, commission, board, agency or instrumentality of any such municipality, or any officer or employe[e] thereof, shall be empowered to execute any purchase order or contract [involving amounts in excess of $10,000] except as herein specifically authorized, but all such purchase orders or contracts shall be executed by the purchasing agent in conformity with [this statute].[85]

"Municipalities are limited to only those powers that are given to them by constitution and statute, and a municipality cannot be bound by a contract that does not comply with the prescribed conditions for the exercise of its power."[86] "A purchase order or contract that does not comply with the Illinois Municipal Code 'shall be null and void as to the municipality.'"[87]

The Chicago Municipal Code provides that the city's chief procurement officer has the powers and duties mandated by the Illinois Municipal Code.[88] "No contract shall be binding upon the city, nor shall any work contracted for be commenced . . . until the contract . . . has been duly executed."[89] "A municipality's power to contract is limited by statute and the city cannot be bound unless statutory requirements are followed."[90]

Based on the governing codes and statutes, "a prospective contractor who deals with a municipal corporation is presumed to know the limitations of the power of the city officials to enter into contracts."[91] This expectation is also explained in Eugene McQuillin's treatise on municipal law: (1) a prospective contractor must confirm that his or her contract complies substantially with the city ordinance and is authorized by the controlling law; (2) when a municipality exceeds the law, the person dealing with the municipal official does so at his or her own risk; and (3) if the contract is not authorized, the would-be contractor is deemed a mere volunteer.[92] Accordingly, the court determined that when a plaintiff, as the one in *McMahon*, "relies on the statements of an unauthorized official, the reliance has been held to be unwarranted because the statute has put the party on notice that the official's authority is limited."[93]

Relying on agency law, the plaintiff also contended that the city employees with whom he dealt "had either actual or apparent authority to enter into the contract with him," and that, because the city employee obtained a purchase order number, the employee "must have been authorized to enter into contracts."[94] In particular, the plaintiff argued,

> [t]he Purchasing Statutes do not grant absolute immunity from the entry of certain of its employees into well documented (as the case at bar) oral contracts—to bind the City. Courts must carefully consider the facts of each individual case, with an eye towards whether actual authority, implied authority or ratification arose during the transaction—all of which were ignored by the Court below. While the statutes limit the circumstances under which authority can arise, they do not eliminate the existence of authority altogether.[95]

The court articulated that the plaintiff "relied on principles of agency law" to argue that the city employee "was authorized to enter into the contract based on the theories of delegation, apparent authority, implied authority or ratification."[96] The plaintiff offered several arguments to support his theory, saying that

> the city is allowed to delegate its authority to contract; a city may cloak its employees with the apparent authority to enter into agreements on the city's behalf; a contract is valid where a city knowingly ratifies or fails to interfere with a contract made by unauthorized employees; a city commissioner's knowledge that work is being done for the city's benefit may be imputed to the city; even where a statute expressly limits the authority of an official, the inconsistent acts of the city act as a waiver on the limitations; and a third party can hold a defendant liable for

the acts of its agent where the defendant created the appearance of authority.[97]

The court concluded that the plaintiff's reliance on principles of delegation, apparent authority, implied authority, ratification, and agency law was "misplaced within the municipal law context."[98] The court agreed with the city's argument that

> implied contracts are not recognized in cases involving municipalities: a contract cannot be implied if the statutory method of executing a municipal contract has not been followed. Implied contracts with municipalities that are *ultra vires*, contrary to statutes, are unenforceable. Unless the power to bind the city in a contract is expressly delegated to someone other than the statutory authority, only the statutorily designated authorities may execute contracts.[99]

"A municipal contract which is legally prohibited or beyond the power of the municipality is absolutely void and cannot be ratified by later municipal action."[100]

According to the court, "under both state statutes and city ordinances, only the city's procurement officer or purchasing agent has the authority to contract."[101] The plaintiff "did not allege that the authority to contract had been expressly delegated. Instead he alleged, without factual support, that the city employee must have had implied authority. This fails because implied authority results in *ultra vires*, unenforceable contracts."[102]

The plaintiff also raised a "fairness argument," asking the court "not to immunize the city from liability for its informal contracts because the city must be held to standards of honesty and fair dealing."[103] The court concluded that it did not "see how honesty and fair dealing would be promoted by holding the city to unauthorized informal agreements," because "the municipal purchasing statute circumscribed municipal contracting," in order to guard against "favoritism, improvidence, extravagance, fraud and corruption, [and to help] secure the best work or supplies at the lowest price practicable."[104] Accordingly, the enforcement of the statute, not informal contracts, achieves those aims.

Similarly, in *Shampton v. City of Springboro*,[105] the court summarized the rule that lack of actual authority to contract results in a null and void contract. Specifically, the court stated that people "seeking to enter into a contractual relationship with a governmental entity are on constructive notice of the statutory restrictions on the power of the entity's agent to contract."[106] Reinforcing this principle is *Shipley v. Cates*,[107] in which the court held that a government contract is "void where the public official did not have constitutional or statutory authority to enter into the contract."[108] The court went on to say, however, "[t]hough . . . a person entering into a contract with the government is charged with knowing the government agent's authority to contract, he or she is not charged with knowing whether the authorized contract is somehow defective because of the agent's misinterpretation or misapplication of law."[109] Regardless, the court concluded that all persons dealing with government officers are charged with knowledge of the extent of their authority and are bound, at their peril, to ascertain whether the contemplated contract is within the power conferred.[110] Finally, *Nichols v. Jackson*[111] cements the principle that contracts of public officials entered without constitutional, statutory, or other authority are void.

Binding the Government through Conduct of Its Agents

This section deals with the scope of a government employee's authority as opposed to whether authority to contract is present. The doctrine that the government cannot be estopped or bound by the unauthorized acts or conduct of its agents or its employees has been widely applied in a variety of contexts. For example, it is well settled that "only those with specific authority can bind the government contractually; even those persons may do so only to the extent that their authority permits."[112] This judicial reluctance to bind the government by its agent's unauthorized conduct is based upon numerous considerations, including sovereign immunity, separation of powers, and public policy.

For example, in *Service Management, Inc. v. State Health and Human Services Finance Commission*,[113] the court determined that an "erroneous misconstruction of the contract by a State employee" did not "change the contract's explicit terms" and the State was not bound by the act of its officer in making an unauthorized payment.[114] Thus, the general rule is that a government entity cannot be estopped by the conduct of one of its officers that exceeds the authority conferred upon him or her, and anyone dealing with a government agency assumes the risk of having ascertained whether the official or agent is acting within the bounds of his or her authority.[115]

Conclusion

State and local procurement systems are challenging to navigate because of the various levels of government and the many layers of authority to contract. It is vital to understand that, more often than not, purchasing and procurement authority is dispersed at each level of government—state, local, city, and municipal. Accordingly, lawyers, procurement professionals, and contractors should be aware of the laws, regulations, and rules governing authority for any given procurement.

Appendix

State Procurement Codes

State	Main Citation	Related Citations
Alabama	ALA. CODE ANN. 1975, Title 41, Ch. 16, Arts. 1–7, §§ 41-16-1 through 41-16-144	Chapter 16A; ALA. ADMIN. CODE, Ch. 355-4-1; ALA. DEPT OF FINANCE, FISCAL PROC. MAN., Ch. 4
Alaska	AK ST. ANN. Title 36, Chs. 10–90	STATE PROCUREMENT CODE, §§ 36.30.005 et seq.; AK ADMIN. CODE, Title 2, Ch. 12
American Samoa	AM. SAMOA ADMIN. CODE, Title 12, Ch. 2	http://www.asbar.org/Regs/asac10_02.htm#PR10_0201
Arizona	AZ ST. ANN. Title 41, Ch. 23, §§ 41-2501 et seq.	ARIZ. ADMIN. RULES & REGS., A.A.C. R2-7-101 et seq.; Local Government Code (Construction) A.R.S. Title 34; Local Government Code for Non-construction, A.R.S. Titles 9 (Cities) and 11 (Counties)
Arkansas	AR ST. ANN. §§ 19-11-101 et seq.	AR ADMIN. CODE 006.27; *State of Arkansas Vendor Manual*, http://www.dfa.arkansas. gov/offices/procurement/Documents/vendorManual.pdf

Note: This table is not comprehensive; rather, it is offered as a starting point for researching a jurisdiction's laws, codes, and/or regulations dealing with procurement. The table identifies a state or territory. Next, the table offers a citation to the primary state level procurement statute. Finally, where space limitations permit and when jurisdictions have significant additional governing codes, the table provides a reference to these codes under the related citation heading. A number of jurisdictions will likely have codes addressing local government procurement that should be consulted when dealing with procurement actions at the local level.

Jurisdiction	Citation	Notes
California	WEST'S ANN. CAL. PUB. CON. CODE § 100	While contained mostly in the Public Contract Code, statutes governing contracting and procurement also reside in other codes including the California Government Code, the Military and Veterans Code, the Civil Code, Education Code, Public Resources Code, Streets and Highway Codes, Vehicle Code, the Water Code, and Welfare and Institutions Code. In fact, there are laws governing one or more aspects of contracting and procurement in nearly every one of California's 29 codes. See California Law, http://www.leginfo.ca.gov/calaw.html
Colorado	CO ST. ANN. §§ 24–101–101 et seq.	24 C.C.R. §§ 24–101–101 et seq. (State Procurement Rules); *State of Colorado Procurement Manual*, http://www.colorado.gov/cs/Satellite?blobcol=urldata&blobheader=application%2Fpdf&blobheadername1=Content-Disposition&blobheadername2=MDT-Type&blobheadervalue1=inline%3B+filename%3D1017%2F641%2FProcurement_Manual.pdf&blobheadervalue2=abinary%3B+charset%3DUTF-8&blobkey=id&blobtable=MungoBlobs&blobwhere=1251698161633&ssbinary=true
Commonwealth of the Northern Marianas Islands	C.N.M.I. Title 70, Ch. 70–30, Subch. 70–30.3	The Department of Finance Regulations and relevant subsections of the Commonwealth Administrative Code are currently under review. Once the review is complete, the code and regulations will be posted at http://www.cnmidof.net/procure/
Connecticut	C.G.S.A., Ch. 58, §§ 4a–4e	CONN. ADMIN. REGS. §§ 4a–52–1 through 4a–63–5; *State Procurement Contracting Manual*, http://das.ct.gov/cr1.aspx?page=15
Delaware	Title 29, Ch. 69 of the Delaware Code	*Selling to the State Guide*, http://gss.omb.delaware.gov/contracting/documents/selling_to_the_state_guide.pdf
District of Columbia	D.C. ST. ANN. §§2–351.01 et seq.	D.C. St. Ann. Title 2 Ch. 3B, Other Procurement Matters; D.C. Municipal Regulations, Title 27–100 et seq., http://ocp.dc.gov/DC/OCP/e-Library/27+DCMR?nav=3&vgnextrefresh=1

State	Main Citation	Related Citations
Florida	Fl St. Ann. Title 19, Chs. 287 & 255 (Capital Projects)	Commodities, Insurance, and Contractual Services, §§ 287.001–287.1345; Means of Transport, §§ 287.14–287.20; Ch. 120, Florida Statutes, which is the Florida Administrative Procedures Act, contains provisions governing bid protests, specifically § 120.57(3); Florida's Public Records Act, Ch. 119, Florida Statutes, and Florida's Code of Ethics for Public Officers and Employees, Part III, Ch. 112, Florida Statutes, also contain provisions relevant to state and local procurement in Florida. Ch. 255 (Construction Projects) Ch. 337.11 (Highway Construction/Maintenance).
Georgia	Ga. Code Ann., §§ 50-5-50 et seq.	GA St. §§ 50-5-100 et seq.; GA St. § 36–80–7; *Georgia Vendor Manual*, http://doas.ga.gov/StateLocal/SPD/Docs_SPD_Official_Announcements/GVM-A1-2010.pdf
Guam	GU St. Ann. Title 5, Div. 1, Ch. 5, Arts. 1–13	Adopted the 1979 Model Procurement Code with amendments consistent with Guam's organizational structure, http://www.guamopa.org; Guam Proc. Regs. Title 2, Div. 4, Chs. 1–12, http://www.justice.gov.gu/CompilerofLaws/GAR/02gar.html
Hawai'i	Division 1, Title 9, HRS § 103D	Division 1, Title 9, HRS § 103F; H.A.R. §§ 3-120–132; H.A.R. §§ 3-140–149
Idaho	Idaho Code Ann. §§ 67–5714 through 67-5748	Idaho Admin. Code 38.05.01; *Introduction to Idaho Public Purchasing*; *Vendor's Guide to Doing Business with the State of Idaho* (both manuals available at http://purchasing.idaho.gov/publications.html)
Illinois	30 ILCS 500	Ill. Admin. Code Title 44 §§ 1.1 through 1.7030; local government contract rules and regulations are spread across living wage ordinances, debarment rules, dispute resolution regulations, and protest procedures, http://www.cityofchicago.org/content/city/en/depts/dps/provdrs/comp.html

State	Statute	Regulations / Resources
Indiana	IND. CODE §§ 5-22-1-1 et seq. (second version)	IND. ADMIN CODE Art. 1.1; *Indiana Procurement Contracts Manual*, http://www.in.gov/idoa/2342.htm
Iowa	IOWA CODE Title I, Subtitle 4, Ch. 8A; the Iowa Code chapters relating to procurements Ch. 8, Ch. 8A, Ch. 72, Ch. 73, Ch. 73A, and Ch. 307	IOWA ADMIN. CODE 11, Ch. 105. Procurements by counties, municipalities, and utilities are governed by other sections of the Iowa Code, including IOWA CODE Chs. 331 (County Home Rule Implementation); 362 (Cities—Definitions and Miscellaneous Provisions), 364 (Powers and Duties of Cities); 384 (City Finance); and 473 (Energy Development and Conservation).
Kansas	KS ST. ANN. §§ 75-3735 through 75-3744	KS Admin. Regs. Agency 48 and Agency 50. The Code of Ordinances for each municipality may contain purchasing rules or polices; see municipal code library for the State of Kansas, http://www.municode.com/library/KS. An example is Wichita Code of Ordinances Purchasing Policy Title 2, Ch. 64.
Kentucky	KY REV. ST. ANN. §§ 45A.005 through 45A.990	KY REV. St. Chs. 46, 47, 48; K.A.R. Title 200, Ch. 5, http://www.lrc.state.ky.us/kar/TITLE200.HTM
Louisiana	L.S.A. REV. ST. ANN. §§ 39:1551 through 39:1755.	RS 38:2211–2296 (Public Contracts); RS 39:196–200 (Data Processing); RS 39:1761 (Lease/Purchase); RS 42:1101–1170 (Code of Ethics); RS 43:1-34 (Printing); RS 43:111–211 (Advertisements); RS 44:1-41 (Public Records); LA. ADMIN. CODE Tit. 34; *Louisiana Vendor Guide: How to Do Business with the State of Louisiana*, http://doa.louisiana.gov/osp/vendorcenter/docs/vendorguide.pdf
Maine	5 MRSA §§ 1741 et seq.	18-554 C.M.R. Ch. 1, §§ 1–4 and Ch. 110, §§ 1–3; *Maine Policy Manual*, http://www.maine.gov/purchases/policies/index.shtml; *Doing Business with the State of Maine*, http://www.maine.gov/purchase/venbid/doing_business/index.shtml
Maryland	MD. CODE STATE FIN. & PROC., Div. 1, Title 11-19 §§ 11-101 through 19-120	Title 17, State and Local Subdivisions; COMAR Title 21
Massachusetts	M.G.L.A. Part I, Title 3, Ch. 30B, §§ 1–22	801 C.M.R. 21.00; *The Chapter 30B Manual*, http://www.mass.gov/ig/publ/30bmanl.pdf

State	Main Citation	Related Citations
Michigan	MI COMPILED LAWS ANN. Ch. 18, Arts. 1–2, §§ 18.1101 through 18.1299	General Gov't Act, Public Act 191 of 2010, Sec. 810; State Printing Law, Public Act 153 of 1937 (MCL 24.62); Freedom of Information Act, Public Act 442 of 1976 (MCL 15.231–15.244); Standard of Conduct for Public Officers and Employees, Public Act 196 of 1973 (MCL 15.341–15.348); Qualified Service-Disabled Veteran-Owned Preference, Public Act 91 of 2005 and 133 of 2008 (MCL 18.1261)
Minnesota	MN ST. ANN. Ch. 16C, §§ 16C.02 through 16C.35	MINN. ADMIN. RULES Ch. 1230; *Minnesota Authority for Local Purchase Manual*, http://www.mmd.admin.state.mn.us/pdf/alpmanual.pdf
Mississippi	MS ST. ANN. Titles 29 and 31, primarily §§ 29-17-1 through 31-31-41	*State of Mississippi Procurement Manual*, http://www.dfa.state.ms.us/Purchasing/ProcurementManual/ProcurementManual.pdf; State of Mississippi Purchase Law Summary, http://www.osa.state.ms.us/downloads/purchase-law-update07.pdf; State of Mississippi State and Local Government: Information on How to Purchase, http://www.dfa.state.ms.us/Purchasing/PurchasingGuidelinesQuickReference.pdf
Missouri	MO ST. ANN. §§ 34.010 through 34.375	1 C.S.R. 40 (Rules of Office of Admin., Purchasing and Materials Management, Procurement); *State of Missouri Vendor Manual*, http://oa.mo.gov/purch/vendorinfo/vendormanual.pdf
Montana	MONT. CODE ANN. Title 18, Chs. 1–11, §§ 18-1-101 through 18-11-112	MONT. ADMIN. Rules 2.5.101 et seq. and *Montana General Services Division Policy Manual, Procurement Procedures*, both at http://gsd.mt.gov/ProcurementServices/montanaprocurementlaw.mcpx
Nebraska	NE CODE §§ 73-501 through 73-509	Local Government Procurement, Neb. Code Chs. 13, 14–17, 18–19, and 22; Neb. D.A.S. Title 9, Chs. 1–5; *State of Nebraska Vendor Procurement Manual*, http://www.das.state.ne.us/materiel/purchasing/vendorinfo.htm
Nevada	NV Title 27, Ch. 333, §§ 333.010 through 333.820	NRS Ch. 332, Purchasing: Local Governments; NRS Ch. 333A, State Performance Contracts for Operating Cost-Savings Measures; NRS Ch. 334, Purchasing: Generally

New Hampshire	N.H. Rev. St. Title I, Ch. 21, §§ 21-I:1 through 21-I:86	RSA § 28:8, Competitive Bidding on Purchases (county purchases); RSA § 48:17; City Purchasing Departments (city purchasing departments); Title III, Ch. 31:59a–d, Town Central Purchasing Department; N.H. Admin. Rules, Adm. 600 et seq (Plant and Property Management Rules); City of Manchester, New Hampshire Procurement Code, http://www.manchesternh.gov/website/portals/2/departments/purchasing/Current%20Procurement%20Code.pdf
New Jersey	N.J. St. Ann. Title 52, Subtitle 5, Chs. 32–35, §§ 52:23-1 through 52-52:35–12	Local Public Contract Law, N.J.S.A. 40A:11-1 et seq.; NJ Admin. Code Ch. 17:12
New Mexico	N.M. St. Ann. Ch. 13, Art. 1, §§ 13-1-1 through 13-1-199	N.M. Admin. Code 1.4.1.1 through 1.4.7.9, Procurement Code; *State of New Mexico Request for Proposals Procurement Guide*, http://www.gsd.state.nm.us/spd/rfpguide.pdf
New York	N.Y. Cls. St. Fin. §§ 160 et seq.	N.Y. Comp. Codes R. & Regs. Tit. 9, §§ 250.0 et seq., Purchasing Regulations
North Carolina	N.C. Gen. St. Ann. §§ 143-48 through 143-64	N.C. Gen. Stat. §§ 143-129 through 143-135.9, Local Government Procurement; 1 N.C. Admin. Code Ch. 5; *N.C. Agency Purchasing Manual*, http://www.pandc.nc.gov/documents/wholeapm.pdf
North Dakota	N.D. St. Ann. §§ 54-44.4-01 through 54-44.4-14	N.D. Admin. Code §§ 4-12-01 to 16; N.D. Cent. Code § 11-11-14, County Procurement Authority; N.D. Cent. Code § 40-05-01, Municipality Procurement Authority; Public improvement Bids and Contracts, N.D. Cent. Code § 48-01.2; Architect, engineer, construction management, and land surveying services under N.D. Cent. Code Ch. 54-44.7
Ohio	Ohio Rev. Code Ann. §§ 125 et seq.	Ohio Admin. Code 123:5, Division of Purchasing; *State of Ohio Procurement Handbook for Supplies and Services*, http://procure.ohio.gov/pdf/PUR_ProcManual.pdf
Oklahoma	74 OK St. Ann. §§ 85.1–85.44C through 227	19 OK St. Ann. §§ 1500–1507 (county purchasing); 61 OK St. Ann. §§ 101–137 (state construction); OK Admin. Code §§ 580:15-1-1 through 580:15-13-6

State	Main Citation	Related Citations
Oregon	OR REV. ST. ANN. § 279A–C	*Attorney General's Public Contract Manual*, http://osbgovernmentlaw.homestead.com/files/TOC.pdf (Table of Contents only; book available for purchase at http://www.doj.state.or.us/oregonians/pubs.shtml)
Pennsylvania	62 PA CONSOL. ST. ANN. §§ 101 et seq.	*PA Dep't of General Services Procurement Handbook*, http://www.votespa.com/portal/server.pt/community/procurement_handbook/14304
Puerto Rico	22 L.P.R.A. § 41	"The Commonwealth public works and joined services connected therewith, such as the buying of materials and so forth, which are the subject of §§ 412, 413, 417–423 of Title 3 and §§ 1-5 and 41–46 of this title shall be done by contract awarded after public bidding in accordance with the provisions hereof."—Political Code, 1902, § 420.
Rhode Island	R.I. GEN. LAWS 1956 §§ 37-2-1 et seq.	R.I. GEN. LAWS §§ 45-55-1 et seq.; R.I. PROC. REGS. §§ 1–12
South Carolina	S.C. CODE ANN. Title 11 Ch. 35–10 et seq.	S.C. CODE REGS., Ch. 19, Art. 4; Local Government Procurement S.C. CODE ANN. §§ 11-35-50 and 70
South Dakota	S.D.C.L. §§ 5–18A–D et seq.	S.D. ADMIN. R. §§ 10:02:05:01–03; *Doing Business with the State of South Dakota*, http://www.state.sd.us/boa/opm/downloads/SDVendorManual.pdf
Tennessee	TN CODE ANN. § 12-3-101 et seq.	TN CODE ANN. Title 5, Ch. 14 (county purchasing); Title 6, Chs. 19, 35, and 56 (cities and towns); TENN. CODE R. & REGS. R 0620-3-3-.01 and .03; *Department of General Services Purchasing Division, Purchasing Policy Manual*, http://tn.gov/generalserv/purchasing/documents/topsman.pdf; *Purchasing Guide for Tennessee Municipalities*, http://www.mtas.utk.edu/KnowledgeBase.nsf/bfbd8572d38db86185256 9ca006e7708/467676aed07ba76b8525757500544ee6/$FILE/Purchase%202008.pdf
Texas	TEXAS GOV'T CODE, Chs. 2155.001 through 2155.510, 2156, 2157, 2158	TX ADMIN. CODE Title 34, Part 1, Ch. 20; Texas Local Gov't Code, Title 8, Chs 252 and 271; *Texas Procurement Manual*, http://www.window.state.tx.us/procurement/pub/manual/

State	Statute	Additional References
Utah	UT St. Ann. Title 63G-6-101 et seq.	UT Admin. Code R33-1 et seq.; *Guide to Doing Business with the State of Utah*, http://purchasing.utah.gov/vendor/documents/Vendorgd.pdf
U.S. Virgin Islands	V.I. St. Title 31, Ch. 23, §§ 231–251	Procurement-related documents and forms, http://pnpvi.org:2005/pnpvi/documents.php
Vermont	VT St. Ann. Title 29, Ch. 49; Title 3, Part 1, Ch. 14, §§ 341 et seq.	State of Vermont Agency of Administration, Bulletin No. 3.5, Contracting Procedures, http://aoa.vermont.gov/sites/aoa/files/pdf/AOA-Bulletin_3_5.pdf
Virginia	VA Code Ann. § 2.2-4300 et seq.	*Virginia Agency Procurement and Surplus Property Manual*, http://www.eva.state.va.us/aspm-manual/aspm-manual.htm
Washington	RCW 36.32.235, .240, .250, .260, and .270	RCW 43.19.190, *Washington Purchasing Manual*, http://www.ga.wa.gov/pca/manual.htm; Washington Admin. Code Ch. 236–48 et seq.
West Virginia	W.V. Code Ann. §§ 5A-3-1 et seq., and § 7-1-11; W.V. Code Ann. § 7-1-11	W.V. Code Ann. § 8-12-10 (Municipalities); W.V. Code Ann. § 5-22A-11 (Design Build Procurement Act); 148 C.S.R. 1 et seq. (Purchasing Division); 148 C.S.R. 11 et seq. (Design-Build); *West Virginia Purchasing Division Procedures Handbook*, http://www.state.wv.us/admin/purchase/handbook/2007R14/default.htm; *Vendor Procurement Guide*, http://www.state.wv.us/admin/purchase/vrc/VPG/default.html
Wisconsin	Wis. St. Ann. §§ 16.70 et seq.	Wis. St. Ann. § 66.0131 (Local Government Purchasing); Wis. Admin. Code Chs. 5-10, 20-21, and 50; *State of Wisconsin Procurement Manual*, http://vendornet.state.wi.us/vendornet/procman/index.asp
Wyoming	WY St. § 9-2-1027	WY St. § 16-4-107 (Local Government Procurement); WCWR 006-160-001 through 009 (State Purchasing Rules); *Wyoming Purchasing Procedures Manual*, http://ai.state.wy.us/generalservices/procurement/PDF/PurchasingPolicyAndProcedures.pdf

Notes

1. 2007 MODEL CODE FOR PUBLIC INFRASTRUCTURE PROCUREMENT (2008).
2. THE 2000 MODEL PROCUREMENT CODE FOR STATE AND LOCAL GOVERNMENTS (2d ed. 2006).
3. MELISSA J. COPELAND, GUIDE TO STATE PROCUREMENT: A 50 STATE PRIMER ON PURCHASING LAWS, PROCESSES AND PROCEDURES (2011).
4. Municode.com, *available at* http://www.municode.com/Library/Library.aspx (last visited Feb. 1, 2012).
5. LA. REV. STAT. ANN. §§ 38:2211–2296 (2011).
6. *Id.* §§ 39:1481–1526.
7. *Id.* §§ 39:1551–1755.
8. *See id.* §§ 39:1482, 1554.
9. UTAH CODE ANN. § 636-6-104(2) (Lexis 2011).
10. Smith v. Dep't of Educ., 751 F. Supp. 70, 73 (D.V.I. 1990), *aff'd*, 942 F.2d 199 (3d Cir. 1991).
11. *Id.*
12. *See id.*
13. With respect to local governments and municipalities, home-rule provisions provide authority for personnel to contract to the extent that the procurement is strictly local. *See In re* Title, Ballot Title and Submission Clause, and Summary for 1999–2000 No. 104, 987 P.2d 249 (Colo. 1999); Worth County Friends of Agriculture v. Worth County, 688 N.W.2d 257 (Iowa 2004) (other than to levy taxes); *In re* Dakota Telecommunications Group, 590 N.W.2d 644 (Minn. Ct. App. 1999); Munroe v. Town of East Greenwich, 733 A.2d 703 (R.I. 1999).
14. OHIO REV. CODE § 125.02 (LexisNexis 2011).
15. *Id.* § 123.01(A)(1).
16. *See* Eugene McQuillin, *The Law of Municipal Corporations, Legislative Control of Municipal Corporations, Delegation of Powers by Legislature-Municipal Powers Under Dillon's Rule,* 2 MCQUILLIN MUN. CORP. § 4:11 (3d ed. 2011).
17. *Id.*
18. *Id.*
19. *Id.*
20. *Compare In re* Extension of Boundaries of City of Sardis, 954 So. 2d 434 (Miss. 2007) (operating entirely under Dillon's Rule) *and* Marich v. Bob Bennett Constr. Co., 116 Ohio St. 3d 553 (2008) (confirming primacy of general law when ordinance is in conflict) *with* Cawdrey v. City of Redondo Beach, 15 Cal. App. 4th 1212, 19 Cal. Rptr. 2d 179 (1993) (referring to California State Constitution, Art. XI, section 3, which permits a measure of home rule by allowing counties as well as cities to adopt a charter that shall supersede any existing charter and all laws inconsistent therewith).
21. 13 Cal. App. 4th 1145, 17 Cal. Rptr. 2d 43 (1993).
22. *Id.*, 17 Cal. Rptr. 2d at 48.
23. *Id.*

24. *Id.* at 48–49.
25. 842 S.W.2d 611 (Tenn. Ct. App. 1992).
26. *Id.* at 618.
27. *Id.*
28. *Id.*
29. *Id.*
30. *Id.*
31. Metropolitan Air Research Testing Authority, Inc. v. Metropolitan Government of Nashville & Davidson County, 842 S.W.2d 611, 618 (Tenn. Ct. App. 1992).
32. *Id.* at 619.
33. *See* Greater Cincinnati Plumbing Contractors Ass'n v. Blue Ash, 106 Ohio App. 3d 608, 666 N.E.2d 654 (1995); City of Chicago v. Chicago Fiber Optic Corp., 287 Ill. App. 3d 566, 222 Ill. Dec. 821, 678 N.E.2d 693 (1997) (holding that a home-rule city has authority to procure its contracts when based on a matter of local concern).
34. Wyo. Stat. Ann. § 16-4-107 (2011).
35. 806 A.2d 216 (D.C. 2002).
36. *Id.* (citing Coffin v. District of Columbia, 320 A.2d 301, 303 (D.C. 1974)).
37. Chamberlain v. Barry, 606 A.2d 156, 159 (D.C. 1992).
38. *See* Greene, 806 A.2d at 222 (citing *Chamberlain*, 606 A.2d at 159 and Office of Personnel Management v. Richmond, 496 U.S. 414, 419 (1990) (that "equitable estoppel will not lie against the Government as against private litigants" is well established)).
39. 685 A.2d 435 (Md. 1995).
40. *Id.* at 436.
41. *Id.* at 439.
42. *Id.* at 438.
43. *Id.* at 438–39.
44. *Id.* at 438. *See also* Dep't of Pub. Safety v. ARA Health Servs., Inc., 668 A.2d 960, 969–70 (Md. Ct. Spec. App. 1995).
45. ARA Health Servs., Inc. v. Dep't of Pub. Safety & Correctional Servs., 685 A.2d 435, 438 (Md. 1995).
46. *Id.* at 438–39.
47. *Id.* at 439.
48. *Id.*
49. *Id.*
50. *Id.*
51. *ARA Health Servs.*, 685 A.2d at 439.
52. *Id.*
53. *Id.* (citing Md. Code (1985, 1995 Repl. Vol., 1996 Supp.), State Fin. & Proc. Art., §§ 12-101(b)(1) *et seq.*).
54. 685 A.2d at 439 (citing Md. Code (1985, 1995 Repl. Vol., 1996 Supp.), State Fin. & Proc. Art., § 11-101(m), (n)).

55. *Id.* (citing MD. CODE (1985, 1995 Repl. Vol., 1996 Supp.), State Fin. & Proc. Art., §§ 10-204, 12-101).

56. *Id. See also* COMAR 21.02.01.04A-D (delegating authority to the Secretaries of the Department of Budget and Fiscal Planning, the Department of General Services, the Department of Transportation; the Maryland Transportation Authority; and the Chancellor of the University of Maryland System for the approval and award of certain contracts and contract modifications under limited conditions).

57. 685 A.2d at 439.

58. *See* COMAR 21.02.01.05A(1) (providing that "the Board shall review and approve the award of those procurement contracts not delegated under this chapter, before execution").

59. 685 A.2d at 439.

60. *Id.*

61. *Id.* at 439–40.

62. *Id.* at 440.

63. *Id.*

64. *Id.* (citing Schaefer v. Anne Arundel County, Md., 17 F.3d 711, 714 (4th Cir. 1994) (applying Maryland law and observing that "[people] who contract with the government do so at their peril when they fail to take notice of the limits of the agent's authority")).

65. *ARA Health Servs.*, 685 A.2d at 440.

66. *Id.*

67. *See* Earthmovers of Fairbanks, Inc. v. State, Dep't of Transp. & Pub. Facilities, 765 P.2d 1360, 1364 (Alaska 1988).

68. *See* 10 MCQUILLIN MUN. CORP., § 29.10, at 236 (3d ed. 1981).

69. 555 P.2d 421, 431 (Wash. Ct. App. 1976).

70. *Id.*

71. *See* Martin v. City of Corning, 101 Cal. Rptr. 678 (Ct. App. 1972).

72. *See, e.g.*, Edwards v. City of Renton, 67 Wash. 2d 598, 409 P.2d 153, 159 (1965).

73. *See* Noel v. Cole, 655 P.2d 245, 250 (Wash. 1982).

74. 701 P.2d 1260 (Colo. App. 1985).

75. *Id.* at 1263.

76. *Id.*

77. *Id.*

78. *Id.*

79. HRS § 103D-707; HAR § 3-126-38.

80. 789 N.E.2d 347 (Ill. App. Ct. 2003).

81. *Id.* at 348.

82. *Id.* at 351.

83. *Id.* (citing 65 ILL. COMP. STAT. 5/8-10-16 (West 2000); Chicago Municipal Code § 2-92-010 (amended September 4, 2002)).

84. *Id.* at 350 (citing 65 ILL. COMP. STAT. 5/8-10-1 *et seq.* (West 2000)).

85. *Id.* (citing 65 ILL. COMP. STAT. 5/8-10-18).

86. *Id.* (citing Ad-Ex, Inc. v. City of Chicago, 565 N.E.2d 669, 673 (Ill. 1990)).

87. *Id.* at 350 (citing 65 ILL. COMP. STAT. 5/8-10-21 (West 2000)); *see also* Stanley Magic-Door, Inc. v. City of Chicago, 393 N.E.2d 535 (Ill. 1979).

88. *McMahon*, 789 N.E.2d at 350 (citing Chicago Municipal Code § 2-92-010 (amended September 4, 2002)).

89. Chicago Municipal Code § 2-92-050 (amended July 19, 2000).

90. *McMahon*, 789 N.E.2d at 350; *see also* Roemheld v. City of Chicago, 83 N.E. 291 (Ill. 1907) (where a statute or ordinance specifies how a city official can bind the city by contract, that method must be followed); DeKam v. City of Streator, 146 N.E. 550 (Ill. 1925) (a contract expressly prohibited by a valid statute is void; there are no exceptions); Haas v. Commissioners of Lincoln Park, 171 N.E. 526 (Ill. 1930) (where a charter prescribes how a municipal corporation is to enter into contracts, that method is exclusive and must be followed); Chicago Food Management, Inc. v. City of Chicago, 516 N.E.2d 880 (Ill. 1987) (where a city's agents are restricted by law as to the method of contracting, agreements executed by officials lacking authority are illegal and void).

91. *McMahon*, 789 N.E.2d at 350 (*citing Ad-Ex*, 565 N.E.2d 669); *see also* Metropolitan Water Reclamation Dist. of Greater Chicago v. Civil Service Board of Metropolitan Water Reclamation Dist. of Greater Chicago, 291 Ill. App. 3d 488, 684 N.E.2d 786 (1997).

92. *McMahon*, 789 N.E.2d at 350–51 (citing 10 MCQUILLIN ON MUNICIPAL CORPORATIONS, § 29.04, at 250 (3d rev. ed. 1999)).

93. *Id.* at 351.

94. *Id.*

95. *Id.*

96. *Id.*

97. *Id.* at 351–51 (internal citations omitted).

98. *Id.* at 347, 352.

99. *Id.* at 352 (internal citations omitted).

100. *Id.* (citing *Ad-Ex*, 565 N.E.2d 669, 675 (Ill. App. Ct. 1990)).

101. *Id.*

102. *Id.* at 352.

103. *Id.* at 353.

104. *Id.* (citing Smith v. F.W.D. Corp., 106 Ill. App.3d 429, 431, 436 N.E.2d 35 (Ill. App. Ct. 1982)).

105. 98 Ohio St. 3d 457, 2003-Ohio-1913, 786 N.E.2d 883.

106. 2003-Ohio-1913 at ¶ 34, 786 N.E.2d at 888.

107. 200 S.W.3d 529 (Mo. 2006).

108. *Id.* at 534.

109. *Id.* at 535.

110. *Id.* at 539 (citing Aetna Ins. Co. v. O'Malley, 124 S.W.2d 1164, 1166 (Mo. 1939)).

111. 2002 OK 65, 55 P.3d 1044.

112. Gardiner v. Virgin Islands Water & Power Auth., 145 F.3d 635, 644 (3d Cir. 1998).

113. 298 S.C. 234, 379 S.E.2d 442 (Ct. App. 1989).

114. *Id.* at 444. *See also* Wisconsin Central R.R. Co. v. United States, 164 U.S. 190 (1896); Dep't of Pub. Safety v. ARA, 668 A.2d 960, 969 (Md. Ct. Spec. App. 1995) (noting the rule that those who contract with a public agency are presumed to know the limitations on that agency's authority and bear the risk of loss resulting from unauthorized conduct by that agency, and citing *Gontrum v. City of Baltimore*, 182 Md. 370, 35 A.2d 128 (1943), which has stated: "Although a private agent, acting in violation of specific instructions, yet within the scope of a general authority, may bind his principal, the rule, as to the effect of a like act of a public agent, is otherwise." 182 Md. at 375, 35 A.2d at 130); Schaefer v. Anne Arundel County, Md., 17 F.3d 711, 714 (4th Cir. 1994) (applying Maryland law and observing that "[people] who contract with the government do so at their peril when they fail to take notice of the limits of the agent's authority")).

115. *See* Metromedia, Inc. v. Kramer, 504 N.E.2d 884 (Ill. App. Ct. 1987) (in Illinois, a limited exception to the general rule exists only where the party invoking the doctrine of estoppel shows (1) some affirmative act by the government agency that induced his good-faith actions and (2) that without the relief requested he or she would suffer a substantial loss).

2

An Overview of Fiscal Law

This chapter provides a brief overview of appropriations law at the state and local government levels. State and local fiscal (or appropriations) law can be derived from several sources, including state constitutions, municipal charters, authorizing legislation, organic legislation, judicial opinions, and/or attorney general opinions. The aim of fiscal law is to establish rules that ensure taxpayers' funds are being used properly and in accordance with the law. To assess when an appropriation is available to a state official or agency for obligation, a state or local government will employ some variation of the time, purpose, and amount test. The objective of this chapter is to provide a basic introduction to fiscal law and its role in the procurement process.

State Appropriations Law

"Appropriation" means a designation of money raised by taxation to be withdrawn from the public treasury for a specifically designated purpose.[1] An appropriation is a process by which a legislative body may authorize, designate, allot, or set aside monies for a purpose authorized by law. Thus, an expenditure of public funds requires legal authorization. As a rule, money cannot be drawn from the treasury of a state except in pursuance of a specific appropriation made by law and a warrant drawn by the proper officer in pursuance thereof.[2] It is a general policy usually supported by statute that no public contract shall be entered into unless there has been an appropriation of funds and a certification by the proper fiscal officer that such funds are available. For example, California's appropriations statute states, "Money may be drawn from the Treasury only through an appropriation made by law and upon a Controller's duly drawn warrant."[3]

With respect to municipalities, similar limitations on expenditures of public monies may exist to protect the public purse; accordingly, documentation may be required to substantiate such expenditures and encumbrances. For example, Wyoming Municipal Uniform Fiscal Procedures section 16–4–108 provides,

> (a) No officer or employee of a municipality shall make any expenditure or encumbrance in excess of the total appropriation for any department. The budget officer shall report to the governing body any expenditure or encumbrance made in violation of this subsection.
>
> (b) The expenditure of municipality monies, other than employee contract payments, may be authorized by the governing body when the payee has provided the municipality with an invoice or other document identifying the quantity and total cost per item or for the services rendered included on the invoice or other document and the claim is certified under penalty of perjury by the vendor or by an authorized person employed by the municipality receiving the items or for whom the services were rendered.

States also establish guidelines for the time period for use of appropriated funds. Similar to the time, purpose, and amount requirements firmly rooted in federal appropriations law, states follow a similar rubric when setting the time for the life of an appropriation as well as establishing procedures for the return of unexpended monies.[4] For example, Alaska appropriations law sets the time for the expiration of an appropriation as June 30. If appropriated funds are not expended by this time period, the appropriation bill lapses, unless a valid encumbrance is obligated before the June 30 expiration date. Alaska appropriations law section 37.25.010, Unexpended balances of one-year appropriations, states,

> (a) The unexpended balance of a one-year appropriation authorized in an appropriation bill lapses on June 30 of the fiscal year for which appropriated. However, a valid obligation (encumbrance) existing on June 30 is automatically reappropriated for the fiscal year beginning on the succeeding July 1 if it is recorded with the Department of Administration by August 31 of the succeeding fiscal year.
>
> (b) A valid approved claim arising from a prior year for which the appropriation has lapsed shall be paid from the current year's appropriations if this claim does not exceed the balance lapsed.

Alaska also has separate statutory authority for appropriations for capital projects. Specifically, section 37.25.020, Unexpended balances of appropriation for capital projects, states,

> [a]n appropriation made for a capital project is valid for the life of the project and the unexpended balance shall be carried forward to subsequent fiscal years. Between July 1 and August 31 of each fiscal year, a statement supporting the amount of the unexpended balance required to complete the projects for which the initial appropriation was made and the amount that may be lapsed shall be recorded with the Department of Administration.

Standards Applicable to State Appropriations Law

Time

The general benchmark standards for protecting the public purse are three-fold. The standards require adherence to the principles of time, purpose, and amount. The first requires the state to comply with time requirements for expenditure of appropriated funds. As mentioned previously, time limitations are established for state appropriations. These time limitations are in place to ensure that the spending of public funds remains transparent, consistent with the legislature's intent to fund authorized projects, and ensure the public treasury is protected.

Illinois state law provides a useful and clear expression of the time requirement. For example, section 25 of Illinois's State Finance Act provides,

> (a) All appropriations shall be available for expenditure for the fiscal year or for a lesser period if the Act making that appropriation so specifies. A deficiency or emergency appropriation shall be available for expenditure only through June 30 of the year when the Act making that appropriation is enacted unless that Act otherwise provides.
>
> (b) Outstanding liabilities as of June 30, payable from appropriations which have otherwise expired, may be paid out of the expiring appropriations during the 2-month period ending at the close of business on August 31. Any service involving professional or artistic skills or any personal services by an employee whose compensation is subject to income tax withholding must be performed as of June 30 of the fiscal year in order to be considered an "outstanding liability as of June 30" that is thereby eligible for payment out of the expiring appropriation.

To be clear, an appropriation bill is not a law, in the ordinary sense. It is not a rule of action, it has no moral or divine sanction, and it defines no rights and punishes no wrongs. It is purely *lex scripta*, and it is a means only to the enforcement of law, the maintenance of good order, and the life of the state government. Such bills pertain only to the administrative functions of government.[5] Accordingly, budget bills may not contain substantive law because a budget bill, by its nature, appropriates funds for a finite time period—two years— while substantive law establishes public policy on a more durable basis.[6]

Purpose

The second benchmark is purpose. Purpose refers to the expenditure of funds for obtaining an object. Appropriation is the act by which the legislative department of government designates a particular fund, or sets aside a specified portion of the public revenue or of the money in the public treasury, to be applied to some general object of governmental expenditure or to some individual purchase or expense. The purpose of a law limiting the use of an appropriation is to bar the state from adopting an annual budget in which expenditures exceed revenues.[7] An appropriation is the setting aside from the public revenue of a certain sum of money for a specified object, in such manner that the executive officers of the government are authorized to use that money, and no more, for that object and no other.[8] Thus, the purpose can be general or specific. By way of illustration, the Illinois Compiled Statutes Title 30, section 105/13, provides,

§ 13. The objects and purposes for which appropriations are made are classified and standardized by items as follows:
(1) Personal services;
(2) State contribution for employee group insurance;
(3) Contractual services;
(4) Travel;
(5) Commodities;
(6) Equipment;
(7) Permanent improvements;
(8) Land;
(9) Electronic Data Processing;
(10) Operation of automotive equipment;
(11) Telecommunications services;
(12) Contingencies;
(13) Reserve;
(14) Interest;
(15) Awards and Grants;
(16) Debt Retirement;
(17) Non-Cost Charges;
(18) Purchase Contract for Real Estate.

When an appropriation is made to an officer, department, institution, board, commission or other agency, or to a private association or corporation, in one or more of the items above specified, such appropriation shall be construed in accordance with the definitions and limitations specified in this Act, unless the appropriation act otherwise provides.

An appropriation for a purpose other than one specified and defined in this Act may be made only as an additional, separate and distinct item, specifically stating the object and purpose thereof.

A case analyzing the purpose of an appropriation is *State v. Boncelet.*[9] In *Boncelet*, the defendant was convicted for violating the Local Budget Law. Specifically, the defendant, a member of the borough council and chairman of its finance committee, voted to incur liabilities chargeable to four line items in the budget in amounts that exceeded sums appropriated. In addition, the defendant voted thereafter to transfer funds from two other line item appropriations to make up already-incurred over-expenditures, thereby overexpending those two appropriations. The defendant argued that the over-expenditure prohibited by law was the over-expenditure of the total budget, as opposed to the specific line items, and thus he could not be found guilty because the transfers voted on and approved added sufficient funds to each over-expended account to make up for the alleged over-expenditure.[10] The court recognized that

[i]mplicit in th[e defendant's] argument [wa]s the contention that municipal obligations may be incurred and paid for notwithstanding that they result in the overexpending of the line item to which they are chargeable, in the expectation that at the year's end there will be unexpended sums in other line items which may be transferred to the overexpended accounts, or, alternatively, that illegality in the overexpenditure of a line item is cured by a subsequent transfer of funds from other line items.[11]

In response to the express and implied arguments put forward by the defendant, the court held that "the Local Budget Law was intended to control municipal expenditures by line item."[12] The court cited N.J.S.A. 40A:4-57, which provided that

> no officer, board, body or commission shall during any fiscal year (1) spend any money, (2) incur any liability, or (3) enter into any contract which by its terms involves an expenditure of money, [f]or any purpose for which no appropriation is provided, or in excess of the amount appropriated [f]or that purpose. The line item designates the purpose of the expenditure. A contract made in violation of this section of the statute is declared null and void and payment thereon is enjoined.[13]

The court concluded that the defendant violated the Local Budget Law, which was intended to control municipal expenditures by line item.[14]

Amount

While many of the cases upholding taxpayer standing to enjoin illegal expenditures have involved challenges to the legality of those expenditures' purposes, there is no law or rule precluding a suit that challenges a state entity's exceeding the amount of an appropriation. Thus, in *Granberg v. Didrickson*,[15] substantive provisions of the State Finance Act limiting the amount of appropriations from road funds for the benefit of state police could not be amended by implication through authorization of a higher appropriation in the state's appropriations bill. Such an attempt to expand the amount of the appropriation through the appropriations bill was found unconstitutional.[16]

An agency also cannot expand the amount of its appropriation with fees it collects when such fees, by law, must be returned to the general fund. Specifically, in *Billey v. North Dakota Stockmen's Association*,[17] the Stockmen's Association acted as an agent of the state when performing brand inspection and recording services. The association generated fees, which were considered public monies. By depositing the fees in the association's general fund, officers of the association violated the provision of the State Constitution requiring all public monies to be paid over to the State Treasurer and be disbursed only by appropriation by the legislature.[18] Thus, a purported "continuing appropriation" that wholly bypasses the state treasury does not comply with the constitutional mandate that all public monies be paid to the State Treasurer.

While many of the cases dealing with exceeding the amount of an appropriation revolve around general augmentation issues and where funds should be deposited, the general principle against misdirecting or augmenting appropriated funds absent legislative authority applies equally in the procurement context. Admittedly, violations of fiscal or budget laws with respect to the amount of an appropriation, whether relating to over-expenditure, misdirection, or augmentation, in the procurement context are rare because contracts typically contain clauses that make government performance contingent upon the availability of the right color of money to fund the contract work. Generally these fiscal contingency clauses read as follows: "The continuation of the contract is contingent upon the appropriation by the Legislature of funds to fulfill the requirements of the contract."

Conclusion

The purpose of fiscal (or appropriations) law is to provide mechanisms for safeguarding taxpayer dollars. Violations of fiscal law represent unjustifiable breaches of trust. Procurement professionals are admonished to heed budget laws and to use good judgment in the obligation and expenditure of appropriated funds. To this end, regular fiscal law training will ensure that procurement professionals dispatch their duties within appropriate fiscal bounds.

Notes

1. *See* County of Mercer v. Amundsen, 2005 WL 1630876 (Pa. Commw. Ct. 2005).
2. Fiscal operations in most states are governed by budget and finance sections of state constitutions and/or statutes. *See* Tenn. Const. art. II, § 24 (providing

that "[n]o public money shall be expended except pursuant to appropriations made by law"); K.R.S. § 45.244 (reiterating that officers in Kentucky may not obligate the government beyond appropriations and providing that any purported obligation in the absence of appropriations does not bind the government).

3. West's Ann. Cal. Const. Art. 16, § 7; *see generally* California State Employees' Ass'n v. State, 32 Cal. App. 3d 103, 108 Cal. Rptr. 60 (1973).

4. *See* K.R.S. § 45.251 (providing that "[e]xpenditures shall be limited to the amounts and purposes for which appropriations are made"); Colo. Const. Art. 10, § 16; *see also* State *ex rel.* Browning v. Brandjord, 106 Mont. 395, 81 P.2d 677 (1938).

5. *See* Apa v. Butler, 2001 S.D. 147 (2001).

6. *See* Retired Public Employees Council of Washington v. Charles, 62 P.3d 470 (Wash. 2003).

7. *See* Lance v. McGreevey, 2004 WL 1657735 (N.J. 2004); *see also* N.J. Const. Art. 8, § 2, par. 2.

8. *See* Bennett v. Napolitano, 206 Ariz. 520, 414 Ariz. Adv. Rep. 3 (2003).

9. 107 N.J. Super. 444, 258 A.2d 894 (1969).

10. *Id.* at 449.

11. *Id.*

12. *Id.*

13. *Id.* at 449–50.

14. *Id.* at 448.

15. 665 N.E.2d 398 (Ill. App. 1996).

16. Ill. Const. Art. 4, § 8(d); 30 Ill. Comp. Stat. 105/8.3.

17. 579 N.W.2d 171 (N.D. 1998).

18. Const. Art. 10, § 12; NDCC 36-09-18, 36-22-03.

3

Competition

This chapter discusses what could be deemed the pillar of any government procurement system: competition. Competition in the procurement process relies upon transparency and integrity. Those who do business with state and local governments must be sure that they will be treated fairly and dealt with ethically when competing head-to-head to win government business. By promoting competition through transparent solicitations, evaluations, and award decisions, state and local governments build trust in the contractor community and become the beneficiaries of healthy contractor pools that perpetuate the cycle of robust competition and the receipt of best value in exchange for taxpayer dollars.

The Requirement for Competition

Underlying the procurement process is the basic tenet that competition is critical to obtaining the best value for taxpayer dollars. The competition requirement also sends a very important message to taxpayers and those who do business with state and local governments that favoritism in the procurement process will not be tolerated.[1] In fact, by promoting integrity in the procurement process through vigilant application of competition requirements, state and local governments signal that they recognize their responsibility to guard the public's interest.[2] By demanding competition, state and local governments receive the best value in terms of price, quality, and contract terms and conditions.[3] Accordingly, several states' statutes include a "maximum practicable competition" requirement, ensuring that their contracts are awarded after a rigorous process of bidding or negotiation.

New Mexico law has a good example of such a provision. According to the code, "all specifications shall be drafted so as to ensure maximum practicable competition and fulfill the requirements of state agencies and local public bodies."[4] Of course, circumstances may arise when a procuring agency's minimum needs may restrict competition to a limited number of responsible bidders or offerors. Here, New Mexico law is instructive, stating that

> if, in the opinion of the state purchasing agent or central purchasing office, a proposed component is of a nature that would restrict the number of responsible bidders or responsible offerors and thereby limit competition, if practicable, the state purchasing agent or central purchasing office shall draft the specifications without the component and procure the component by issuing a separate invitation for bids or request for proposals or by entering into a sole source procurement.[5]

Significantly, certain sectors are statutorily exempt from following the procedures of the procurement code entirely. In New Mexico, for example, the procurement code is inapplicable when the purchase is necessary for the operation of a public or private hospital if the arrangement will likely reduce health care costs, improve quality of care, or improve access to care.[6]

Like New Mexico, Colorado also has clear maximum practicable competition requirements. The relevant state statute reads, "All specifications shall seek to promote overall economy for the purposes intended and encourage competition in satisfying the state's needs and shall not be unduly restrictive."[7] As one might expect, states modify the legislative language of such clauses, while maintaining essentially the same purpose. Arkansas, for example, holds that "All specifications shall be drafted so as to assure the maximum practicable competition for the state's actual requirements."[8] Similarly, Delaware's competition statute states that "All specifications shall seek to promote overall economy for the purposes intended and encourage competition in satisfying the agency's needs and shall not be unduly restrictive."[9]

Because competition is an ever-present theme of state procurement codes, it is not surprising that there exists ample case law concerning maximizing competition for the public good. Many of these cases involve bad faith dealings in which the state agency prepares solicitations or evaluates bids or offers in a manner that restricts competition. One such case in Hawaii illustrates the complexity of these issues.

In *Carl Corp. v. State of Hawaii, Dep't of Education*,[10] an aggrieved bidder filed a protest to an awarded contract, claiming that the process "was not an open procurement and that another vendor was predetermined from the outset."[11] The aggrieved bidder stated that the evaluation of bids was inaccurate and that he was not given an opportunity to demonstrate his system. He also claimed that the implementation schedule proposed in the RFP was "unrealistic and could only be achieved by a vendor who had received information not contained in the RFP."[12] The Supreme Court of Hawaii held that in order to determine whether ratification of an unlawfully awarded contract is in the state's best interest, consideration must be given to the state's interest in achieving the purposes of the procurement code.[13] In articulating these purposes, the court looked to the legislative history of the code, which stated that the procurement code would "foster broad-based competition among vendors while ensuring accountability, fiscal responsibility, and efficiency."[14]

As *Carl Corp.* would suggest, public perception is central to the procurement process. A wide array of cases deal with integrity of procurement law and the bidding process. In *State, Dep't of Admin. v. Bachner Co., Inc.*, for example, the Alaska Supreme Court analyzed a state statute concerning the appropriate remedy for defective procurement.[15] Before reaching the state supreme court, the superior court had reasoned that preserving the integrity of the procurement system "had priority" over a relevant state provision governing the remedies for errors committed in the procurement process. Here, the

Alaska Supreme Court recognized that "with respect to the integrity of the procurement process . . . cancellation [was] the preferred remedy."[16] However, because cancellation of the contract with the successful bidder would have resulted in significant financial impact to the department, the decision of the commissioner of the state agency was ultimately affirmed, and the decision of the superior court was reversed to the extent that it was in conflict.[17]

The Idaho Supreme Court also addressed the underlying purpose of the state procurement process in *SE/Z Constr., L.L.C. v. Idaho State University*.[18] At issue in *SE/Z* was the interpretation of a portion of the state code that held "an invitation to bid shall include a project description and all contractual terms and conditions applicable to the public works."[19] The bid documents at issue requested that each contractor submit a base bid, prices for five alternates, and individual "unit prices" for two "classroom package" audio-visual systems, referred to in the bidding documents as classroom packages Nos. 2 and 3. The bidding documents discussed at least ten rooms in which classroom packages Nos. 2 and 3 might be installed, but the bidding documents did not specify in which, if any, of the rooms the State would actually elect to install the classroom packages.

After the bids were opened, but before determining which bidder was the low responsible bidder, the State considered how many of the classroom packages it could purchase. Based on the unit prices and budget considerations, the State decided to purchase 14 audio-visual equipment packages, two classroom packages No. 2, and 12 classroom packages No. 3. Additionally, the State decided that the project budget would allow purchase of all five bid alternates. The bid documents stated that the State would determine the low bidder "on the basis of the sum of the Base Bid and Alternates accepted."[20] To determine which bidder was the low responsible bidder, the State totaled the bidders' base bids, the five bid alternates, and the price of the desired classroom packages. Based on this calculation, the lowest bid totaled $1,313,774 and SE/Z's bid totaled $1,317,726. The State determined that the lowest bidder would receive award.

SE/Z protested and argued that the State violated the competition statute by incorrectly considering the unit prices for the classroom packages when determining the low bid. SE/Z contended that only the base bid and five bid alternates could be considered in determining the low bidder. In affirming the lower court's decision that the competition statute was not violated, the Supreme Court of Idaho determined that

> the bid documents as a whole show[ed] that the State intended . . . to account for the unit prices for the total number of classroom packages that . . . it could purchase post-bidding. The bid proposal state[d] that the prices proposed were "to cover all expenses incurred in performing the work under the Contract Documents, of which this proposal is a part." The bid documents stated that some classroom packages were "included in the base bid in designated locations, however [the State] wishe[d] to obtain unit prices in order to add them to [other indicated] classrooms. . . ." The bid documents as a whole show that the State wanted to purchase a number of classroom packages concurrent with the other products and services sought in the base bid and alternates.[21]

The Idaho Supreme Court also determined that "An invitation to bid cannot . . . include all terms of the contract that will result from the bidding process.[22] At the least, the price and choice of which bid alternates will be accepted will always be absent.[23] [Instead,] [t]he reference to 'all contractual terms and conditions' unambiguously refers to the general terms of the contract document." As such, the court held that "the lack of specificity regarding how many classroom packages the State would choose to buy should not be considered an omission of a term or condition within the meaning of the statute." Accordingly, the Idaho Supreme Court held that the State did not violate the competition statute in its selection of the lowest bidder.[24]

Other than Full and Open Competition

As mentioned above, while all state procurement codes emphasize competition, many states specifically exempt certain categories of procurement from competitive sealed bidding or competitive sealed proposal requirements. Among the common categories for exemption are human, social, health, and educational services. Maryland, for example, specifically provides for noncompetitive negotiation procedures if the procurement is for "human, social, or educational services to be provided directly to individuals with disabilities, individuals who are aged, indigent, disadvantaged, unemployed, mentally or physically ill, or displaced or minors."[25]

Kentucky also provides for noncompetitive negotiation under certain conditions. According to the state statute, a local public agency may contract or purchase through noncompetitive negotiations when the contract satisfies one of eleven statutory requirements. Among these is the provision that "[t]he contract is for group life insurance, group health and accident insurance, group professional liability insurance, worker's compensation insurance, and unemployment insurance."[26] The statute articulates other areas that are exempt from competitive negotiations, including emergencies that could cause public harm, and if the contract is for the services of a licensed professional (other than an architect or engineer providing construction management services).[27]

Rhode Island statutes also allow for noncompetitive procurement in emergencies. The relevant statute authorizes the purchasing agent to make "emergency procurements when there exists a threat to public health, welfare, or safety under emergency conditions as defined in the regulations."[28] The statute further explains, however, that emergency procurements shall be made "with such competition as is practicable under the circumstances."[29]

Additionally, state codes often have provisions for noncompetitive negotiation if there are only limited services available. Maryland, for example, holds that a procurement officer may award a contract on the basis of noncompetitive negotiation if he or she determines that "at least [two] sources are available for the services; but the absence of effective competition makes it unreasonable to expect bids or proposals from the available sources."[30] Similarly, Rhode Island has a provision allowing noncompetitive contracting when the chief purchasing officer or purchasing agent makes a written determination that there is only one source available for the required item.[31]

What follows is a non-exhaustive list of procurement categories that are exempt from the competition requirement discussed in *The Requirement for Competition*. Even though these procurement categories are exempt from traditional competition requirements, best practices dictate that some level of competition within these categories be applied in order to enhance the perception of integrity within these special processes.

Small Purchases

State codes typically allow for separate procedures for the procurement of small purchases. While the specific amounts as to what constitutes a small purchase vary significantly between states, some general guidelines are common throughout most jurisdictions. Most state codes, for example, contain a provision restricting government agencies from artificially dividing procurement requirements to bypass regular purchasing requirements.

Kentucky's procurement code is indicative of many states. As with most states, Kentucky's code requires that small purchases be made in accordance with the relevant state regulations.[32] The statute limits the amount of small purchases to $10,000 for construction contracts and $1,000 for purchases by any state governmental body.[33] Kentucky's code outlines a list of exceptions and articulates price ceilings for each. The statute states that small purchases may be made up to $40,000 for construction projects or purchases by the state's Finance and Administration Cabinet, state institutions of higher education, and the legislative branch of government.[34]

South Carolina allows a considerably larger ceiling for small purchases, authorizing small purchase procedures for conducting procurements up to $50,000 in actual or potential value.[35] The code explicitly states that the procurement requirements must not be artificially divided in order to constitute small purchases.[36] Such a provision is included in most state procurement codes.[37] Similar to several states with relatively large price ceilings for small purchases, the South Carolina code outlines certain requirements for procurement based on price classification. The state code further provides that purchases less than $2,500 may be made without securing competitive quotations "if the prices are considered reasonable,"[38] but a written endorsement by the purchasing office is required.[39] For purchases over $2,500 and under $10,000, solicitations for written quotes from a minimum of three qualified sources of supply must be made, and the award must be given to the lowest responsive and responsible bidder.[40] For purchases between $10,000 and $50,000, the procurement must be advertised at least once in a South Carolina Business Opportunities publication or by approved electronic advertising means.[41]

Illinois allows state agencies to bypass standard competitive sealed bidding procedures for any individual procurement of supplies or services less than $10,000 or less than $30,000 for construction projects.[42] As with several other states, Illinois outlines the process for modifying these maximum thresholds. The statute states that "[e]ach July 1, the small purchase maximum . . . shall be adjusted for inflation as determined by the Consumer Price Index for All Urban Consumers as determined by the United States Department of Labor and rounded to the nearest $100."[43] Kentucky also has a statutory provision for modification of small purchase price limits. The relevant state statute holds that at least every two years, the secretary of the Finance and Administration Cabinet must review the prevailing costs of labor and materials and may "make recommendations to the next regular session of the General Assembly for the revision of the then current maximum small purchase amount as justified by intervening changes in the cost of labor and materials."[44]

While the monetary threshold for small purchases varies across the country, the danger of abuse, specifically larger purchases being parceled into "small purchases," is constant. In *State Board for Elementary and Secondary Education v. Ball*,[45] the Supreme Court of Kentucky affirmed the removal of members of a county board of education for abusing the state's small purchases procurement procedures. While the primary issue in the case was whether the State Board for Elementary and Secondary Education (SBESE) had the authority to remove members of a county board of education for misconduct in the office, this case provides a detailed example of how small purchase procedures can be manipulated in an attempt to circumvent statutory competitive bidding requirements.

The SBESE case focuses on the removal of three board members from the Harlan County Board of Education that improperly awarded contracts for the construction of a new field house at Cawood High School. While there were multiple allegations of impropriety, of primary significance were the decisions to award contracts in violation of KRS 242.260, which prohibited a district board of education from making a contract expenditure of more than $7,500 without first either publicly advertising for bids or certifying an emergency.[46] The Supreme Court of Kentucky affirmed the removal of members of a county board of education for abusing the state's small purchases procurement procedures because board members were found to have manipulated these procedures in an attempt to circumvent statutory competitive bidding requirements.[47] Specifically, the court determined that the decision to award no-bid contracts to purchase gasoline storage tanks for a total cost of $17,943.30, and the no-bid contracts to purchase furniture from Ball's brother's company at a cost of $12,168.85, were impermissible and in violation of state statutes.[48] While the amounts at issue in *Ball* are not large, the case illuminates the challenges of permitting less than full and open competition in the interest of efficiency and also shows the potential for abuse and fraud.

Emergency Procurement

States vary widely on the issue of emergency procurements. Some state codes define what constitutes an emergency, while others do not. The New Mexico procurement code provides such a definition. The code allows for the state purchasing agent or central purchasing office to make emergency procurements when "there exists a threat to public health, welfare, safety or property requiring procurement under emergency conditions."[49] The statute further holds, "An emergency condition is a situation [that] creates a threat to public health, welfare or safety such as may arise by reason of floods, fires, epidemics, riots, acts of terrorism, equipment failures or similar events and includes the planning and preparing for an emergency response."[50]

Some states leave the definition of what constitutes an emergency intentionally vague. Missouri law, for example, allows the commissioner of administration to waive the competitive bid requirement when the commissioner has determined that there exists "a threat to life, property, public health or public safety or when immediate expenditure is necessary for repairs to state property in order to protect against further loss of, or damage to, state property, to prevent or minimize serious disruption in state services or to ensure the integrity of state records."[51] The statute further requires that such emergency procurements be made with as much competition as is practicable.[52] The Illinois code has a nearly identical provision concerning when emergency procurements are appropriate.[53] However, the Illinois code also requires that the contract file include a written description of the basis of the emergency and the reasons for selecting the particular contractor.[54]

Other states have statutory procedures for emergency procurements that also include notice requirements. Virginia, for example, requires that the public body making an emergency procurement issue a written notice, published on the Department of General Services central electronic procurement website, stating that "the contract is being awarded on an emergency basis, and identifying that which is being procured, the contractor selected, and the date on which the contract was or will be awarded."[55] Illinois also requires that the purchasing agency publish in the Illinois Procurement Bulletin a copy of each written description and the total cost of each emergency procurement.[56]

Some states contain statutory provisions separate from their procurement codes that allow for an emergency override of standard procurement requirements. California, for example, authorizes the governor to "suspend any regulatory statute, or statute prescribing the procedure for conduct of state business, or the orders, rules, or regulations of any state agency . . . where the Governor determines and declares that strict compliance with any statute, order, rule, or regulation would in any way prevent, hinder, or delay the mitigation of the effects of the emergency."[57]

While most emergency situations are obvious (i.e., devastating hurricanes, wildfires, or major earthquakes), sometimes it is not so clear whether a situation calls for the use of emergency procurement procedures. For example, in *Callaway Community Hospital Association v. Missouri Department of Corrections*,[58] it took three years of litigation to ultimately make the determination that a hospital association's services did not fall under the emergency condition exception to the state procurement code.

The primary issue in *Callaway* concerned whether the contractor was entitled to a premium for hospital services provided over a six-month period. For four years prior to the disputed time period, Callaway had furnished hospital services to inmates at the Missouri Department of Corrections (Department) pursuant to written contracts and written extensions. On December 30, 1990, the final extension expired and no written extension was tendered for the period of January 1, 1991 through June 6, 1991. During that time period, Callaway continued to provide services, but demanded to be paid at the same rates it charged the general public instead of the lower rates pursuant to past contracts. For the disputed six-month period, the difference between what the Department paid and what Callaway demanded was over $200,000. Callaway filed a petition with the Circuit Court for payment of the difference and was denied.

On appeal, Callaway's primary argument was premised on the emergency exception to Missouri's competitive bidding requirements. Essentially, Callaway argued that the Department obtained hospital services pursuant to emergency procurement procedures since the Department did not follow any statutory competitive bidding requirements as proscribed by Chapter 34 of the state code, and that not having hospital services for inmates was an emergency condition. In denying Callaway's appeal, the Missouri Court of Appeals noted that to qualify as an emergency procurement, "(1) an emergency condition exists, (2) the element of time is a crucial factor in seeking relief, and (3) the resolution of the condition receives priority over routine operations and duties of the state agency."[59]

The court then noted that while Callaway provided internal Department memoranda indicating "the Department may be in an administrative emergency regarding . . . health care to its inmates" and that "hospital services are necessary and essential for the welfare of incarcerated offenders," those memoranda did not clearly indicate circumstances justifying an emergency procurement.[60] At best, the court concluded that the health care services were "necessary," which did not meet the standards set forth for an emergency procurement.

Special Procurements

Special procurements allow state agencies to bypass the standard competitive bidding requirements when the procurement officer determines that an unusual or unique situation exists that would make the application of standard procurement procedures contrary to the public interest. Given the inherent vagueness of these circumstances, state codes understandably speak about special procurements in generalized terms.

Arkansas state code is indicative of many states' statutes. The relevant code allows for the State Procurement Director or the head of a procurement agency to initiate a contract above the specified bid amount when "the officer determines that an unusual or unique situation exists that makes the application of all requirements of competitive bidding, competitive sealed bidding, or competitive sealed proposals contrary to the public interest."[61] Arkansas code requires a written determination for the basis of the procurement and for the particular contractor. Additionally, the director must file a monthly report with the Legislative Council describing any special procurement decisions.[62]

Some states, such as Oregon, further classify special procurements into different groups. Oregon's state statute breaks down special procurement into "class special procurement" and "contract-specific special procurement."[63] The former relates to contracting procedures that differ from the typical bidding requirements and is for the "purpose of entering into a series of contracts over time for multiple projects."[64] Conversely, contract-specific special procurement refers to contract procedures differing from typical bidding requirements for "the purpose of entering into a single contract or a number of related contracts on a one-time basis or for a single project."[65] Oregon law also requires an application process for special procurements. For a state agency to seek approval of a special procurement, it must first submit a written request to the Director of the Oregon Department of Administrative Services or the local contract review board describing the goods or services and the circumstances justifying the use of special procurement procedures.[66] When the contracting agency is the Office of the Secretary of State or the Office of the State Treasurer, the agency must then submit a written request to the Secretary of State or the State Treasurer describing the special circumstances justifying the procedures.[67]

Sole Source Procurement

Sole source procurement allows for the purchase of materials without competition, as long as it is a condition under which it is impracticable to secure competition. The justification and notice requirements for such procurements vary greatly from state to state. Typically, to avoid the standard process of competitive bidding, a written determination must be made indicating that only a single feasible source exists.

Missouri's code is typical of such statutes. The state code provides that the commissioner may waive the requirement of competitive bids for supplies when he or she has made a written determination that "there is only a single feasible source" for the supplies.[68] If other sources become available, then the commissioner must rescind the waiver and procure the supplies through the standard competitive process.[69] The state code defines that a single feasible source exists when supplies are proprietary, only one distributor services the region in which supplies are needed, or supplies are available at a discount from a single distributor for a limited period of time.[70]

Missouri code also maintains notice requirements for sole-source procurements. The law states that where the estimated expenditure is $5,000 or over, the commissioner of administration must post notice of the proposed purchase. Where the estimated expenditure is $25,000 or over, the commissioner administration "shall also advertise the commissioner's intent to make such purchase in at least two daily newspapers of general circulation in such places as are most likely to reach prospective bidders or offerors and may provide such information through an electronic medium available to the general public at least five days before the contract is to be let."[71] Illinois has similar notice requirements for sole-source procurements. The state code requires the purchasing agency to publish a notice of intent in the Illinois Procurement Bulletin two weeks before entering into a sole-source contract. Some states waive notice requirements under certain circumstances. For example, in Missouri, the notice requirement may be waived if supplies are available at a discount for a limited period of time.[72]

Washington has similar provisions regarding sole-source contracts. Washington law provides that if the managing director determines that it is impracticable to secure competition for the required materials, he or she may authorize the purchase of materials without competition.[73] The statute defines "impracticable" as "[w]hen material, equipment, or supplies can be obtained from only one person or firm . . . or [w]hen specially designed parts or components are being procured as replacement parts in support of equipment specially designed by the manufacturer."[74]

With any sole-source procurement, because there is no competition, the awarding entity faces the perception of possible favoritism. In *McBirney & Associates v. State*,[75] the sole-source award of a lucrative lease contract proved to be rife with favoritism and was ultimately voided *ab initio*. In the mid-1980s, the governor of Alaska instituted a policy of consolidating state offices. One target city for this policy was Fairbanks. Accordingly, the State Department of Administration (DOA) completed a study that identified a bidding zone that ended up being nearly identical to the Fairbanks Development Authority's preferred development zone. Solicitation (RFP) documentation utilizing the "preferred zone boundaries" was then prepared in draft.

While the RFP was still in draft form and prior to its approval, a 48 percent owner of McBirney and a personal friend and fundraiser for the governor asked for a copy of the RFP. Subsequently, the owner met with both the governor and his chief of staff and suggested that the bidding zone be narrowed to the "core" area of downtown Fairbanks. After some consideration, including an additional survey, it was determined by the DOA that if the "core" area of downtown were selected, McBirney would be the only bidder.

Out of concern that the DOA was being pressured to unduly narrow the bidding zone, advice from the Attorney General was solicited. The AG opined that there were three options: (1) not to proceed, (2) to enlarge the zone, or (3) to justify a sole-source procurement. Ultimately, the DOA proceeded on a sole-source basis with McBirney, which included a bid waiver justifying the sole-source award.

Several months after the award, grand jury proceedings commenced on the matter and the contract was voided on the basis that it was "tainted by favoritism." McBirney then filed a claim for specific performance and damages. Ultimately the matter reached the Alaska Supreme Court. In affirming the superior court's judgment that the contract was void due to irregularities in the bidding process, including but not limited to improperly obtaining the draft RFP and then suggesting modifications, the court reiterated two fundamental procurement policies. First, the Alaska Supreme Court reiterated that "the whole matter [was] to be conducted with as much fairness, certainty, publicity and absolute impartiality as any proceeding requiring the exercise of quasi-judicial authority."[76] Second, it stated that "the state cannot be allowed to use the sole-source process to circumvent competitive bidding requirements."[77]

In contrast to the patent anticompetitive conduct in *McBirney*, many procurements that are designated as competitive are actually sole source in disguise. In *E. Amanti & Sons, Incorporated v. R.C. Griffin, Inc.*,[78] a subcontractor was awarded damages for lost profits in a case where the government attempted to let a competitive procurement but actually created a sole-source scenario. In *E. Amanti*, the town of Danvers (the Town) issued specifications for the construction of a new fire station. At issue was the specification for an emergency vehicle exhaust system that had to be specified and manufactured by PlymoVent or be approved by the fire department.[79] The plaintiff, Amanti, was the successful heating, ventilation, and air conditioning

subcontractor of the defendant, R.C. Griffin, the latter being in privity with the Town.

   Shortly after the award, Amanti was informed that its exhaust
system did not meet the procuring agency's requirements. Amanti
sought approval for a proposed emergency vehicle exhaust system
manufactured by Carmon. After approval was denied on the basis
that the proposed Carmon system did not meet performance requirements, Amanti (1) requested it be furnished with the names and
specific model numbers of two additional manufacturers that were
equivalent and (2) reminded Griffin and the Town that the statutes governing their competitively awarded contract "required the
awarding authority to provide three name brands or a description
that could be made by a minimum of three manufacturers," and that
without such provision, the Town would fail to meet its obligation to
follow the steps necessary to "limit the acceptable [v]ehicle [e]xhaust
system to a single supplier."[80] The Town responded that it did not
have the information requested. Amanti then notified the general
contractor that it would furnish the PlymoVent system under protest. Following completion of the project, Amanti filed its claim for
additional costs, based on its assertion that the Town's requirements
created a proprietary, de facto sole-source specification that merely
added the "or equal" language to the designated PlymoVent source.
The superior court agreed with Amanti, holding that the Town "had
a duty to disclose to bidders that PlymoVent requirement was a sole
source specification, and that having failed that duty, the Town was
liable to Amanti for lost profits."[81] Griffin and the Town appealed.

   In affirming the superior court's decision, the Appeals Court
of Massachusetts specifically discussed the proper use of sole-source
specifications in similar procurements involving the town of Lexington. The court noted that although Lexington also required an
emergency vehicle exhaust system "as specified and manufactured by
PlymoVent or an approved equal," it explicitly informed prospective
bidders that "[a] letter discussing PlymoVent as a sole source vendor
pursuant to [G.L. c. 30, § 39M], had been filed with the Awarding
Authority."[82] The court concluded that providing the name of a single vendor and placing the burden on the bidder to discover alternatives did not constitute competitive specifications.[83]

Conclusion

At the heart of the procurement process is the underlying principle of maximizing value by allowing for maximum practicable competition among bidders. There are, however, certain circumstances in which this principle of rigorous competition is sidelined. Emergencies, sole-source procurements, and small purchases are examples of such conditions. Although there are several such exceptions outlined by state laws, it is important to bear in mind that they are limited. Such exceptions should always be considered against the general legislative mandate for maximum practicable competition.

Notes

1. *See* Weed v. Bachner Co. Inc., 230 P.3d 697, 700–01 (Alaska 2010) (agreeing that "an important purpose of the bidding process is to create transparency in the state's procurement system, and to avoid awarding contracts based on improper considerations"); Gostovich v. City of West Richland, 75 Wash. 2d 583, 452 P.2d 737, 740 (1969) ("The purposes of competitive bidding are 'to prevent fraud, collusion, favoritism, and improvidence in the administration of public business, as well as to insure that the [state] receives the best work or supplies at the most reasonable prices practicable.'").
2. *See* Sloan v. Greenville County, 356 S.C. 531, 556, 590 S.E.2d 338, 351–52 (S.C. App. 2003) (recognizing that a written determination of an award decision "must provide the citizens of Greenville County a window into the County's decision-making process—safeguarding the quality and integrity of the contract awards through public accountability.").
3. Steven L. Schooner, *Desiderata: Objectives for a System of Government Contract Law*, 11 Pub. Procurement L. Rev. 103 (2002).
4. N.M. Stat. Ann. § 13-1-164 (West, Westlaw through 2011 Sess.).
5. *Id.*
6. N.M. Stat. Ann. § 13-1-98.1 (West, Westlaw through 2011 Sess.).
7. Colo. Rev. Stat. Ann. § 24-104-205 (West, Westlaw through 2011 Sess.).
8. Ark. Code Ann. § 19-11-241 (West, Westlaw through 2011 Sess.).
9. Del. Code Ann. tit. 29, § 6932 (West, Westlaw through 2011 Sess.).
10. 946 P.2d 1, 4 (Haw. 1997).
11. *Id.* at 4.
12. *Id.*
13. *Id.* at 25.
14. *Id.* at 26 (citing Sen. Stand. Comm. Rep. No. S8-93 (1993)).

15.   167 P.3d 58 (Alaska 2007).

16.   *Id.* at 63.

17.   *Id.* at 64.

18.   140 Idaho 8, 89 P.3d 848 (2004).

19.   IDAHO CODE ANN. § 67-5711C(2) (West, Westlaw through 2011 Sess.).

20.   *See SE/Z Constr.*, 140 Idaho at 11.

21.   *Id.* at 12.

22.   *Id.* at 14.

23.   *Id.*

24.   *Id.*

25.   MD. CODE ANN. § 13-106 (West, Westlaw through 2011 Sess.).

26.   KY. REV. STAT. ANN. § 45A.380 (West, Westlaw through 2011 Sess.).

27.   *Id.*

28.   R.I. GEN. LAWS § 37-2-21 (West, Westlaw through 2011 Sess.).

29.   *Id.*

30.   MD. CODE ANN. § 13-106 (West, Westlaw through 2011 Sess.).

31.   R.I. GEN. LAWS § 37-2-21 (West, Westlaw through 2011 Sess.).

32.   KY. REV. STAT. ANN. § 45A.100 (West, Westlaw through 2011 Sess.).

33.   *Id.*

34.   *Id.*

35.   S.C. CODE ANN. § 11-35-1550 (West, Westlaw through 2011 Sess.).

36.   *Id.*

37.   *See, e.g.*, COLO. REV. STAT. ANN. § 24-103-204 (West, Westlaw through 2011 Sess.); *see also* MONT. CODE ANN. § 18-4-305 (2011).

38.   *Id.*

39.   *Id.*

40.   *Id.*

41.   *Id.*

42.   30 ILL. COMP. STAT. ANN. 500/20-20 (West, Westlaw through 2011 Sess.).

43.   *Id.*

44.   KY. REV. STAT. ANN. § 45A.100(2) (West, Westlaw through 2011 Sess.).

45.   State Bd. for Elementary and Secondary Educ. v. Ball, 847 S.W.2d 743 (1993).

46.   *Id.* at 747.

47.   *See supra* notes 26–28 and accompanying text.

48.   *Ball*, 847 SW2d at 747–48.

49.   N.M. STAT. ANN. § 13-1-127 (West, Westlaw through 2011 Sess.).

50.   *Id.*

51.   MO. REV. STAT. § 34.045. (West, Westlaw through 2011 Sess.).

52.   *Id.*

53.   *See* 30 ILL. COMP. STAT. ANN. 500/20-30 (West, Westlaw through 2011 Sess.).

54.   *Id.*

55.   VA. CODE ANN. § 2.2-4303 (West, Westlaw through 2011 Sess.).

56.   30 ILL. COMP. STAT. ANN. 500/20-30 (West, Westlaw through 2011 Sess.).

57.   CAL. GOV'T CODE § 8571 (West, Westlaw through 2011 Sess.).

58. Callaway Cmty. Hosp. Ass'n v. Missouri Dep't of Corr., 885 S.W.2d 740 (Mo. Ct. App. 1994).
59. *Id.* at 744.
60. *Id.* at 745.
61. ARK. CODE ANN. § 19-11-263 (West, Westlaw through 2011 Sess.).
62. *Id.*
63. OR. REV. STAT. ANN. § 279B.085 (West, Westlaw through 2011 Sess.).
64. *Id.*
65. *Id.*
66. *Id.*
67. *Id.*
68. MO. ANN. STAT. § 34.044 (West, Westlaw through 2011 Sess.).
69. *Id.*
70. *Id.*
71. *Id.*
72. *Id.*
73. WASH. REV. CODE ANN. § 43.52.575 (West, Westlaw through 2011 Sess.).
74. *Id.*
75. McBirney & Associates v. State, 753 P.2d 1132 (Alaska 1988).
76. *Id.* at 1136.
77. *Id.*
78. E. Amanti & Sons, Inc. v. R.C. Griffin, Inc., 53 Mass. App. 245, 758 N.E.2d 153 (2001).
79. *Id.* at 155.
80. *Id.* at 156–57.
81. *Id.* at 157.
82. *Id.*
83. *Id.* at 158.

4

Presolicitation Matters

This chapter discusses two of the most important responsibilities of the chief procurement officer and his or her cadre of government procurement professionals: (1) to anticipate the needs of procuring agencies and (2) to develop acquisition strategies to meet those needs. In performing these vital functions, procurement professionals must always consider the fundamental pillars of government procurement—competition, transparency, and integrity. To respond effectively to meet agency needs, procurement professionals must engage in sound solicitation preparation and acquisition planning, topics for which this chapter provides concrete and comprehensive information for all procurement professionals involved or interested in pre-solicitation matters.

Solicitation Preparation

A quick scan of many state procurement office websites will inevitably unearth publications uniformly called state procurement manuals. These manuals describe the generally uniform procedures that agencies follow when embarking on the preparation of a solicitation. If done correctly, preparing a solicitation takes time, and this time varies depending on the type of solicitation best suited to successfully satisfy the minimum need of the end user. Solicitation preparation encompasses the following: acquisition planning; selecting a solicitation method; and drafting statements of work, specifications, and evaluation criteria.

Acquisition Planning

The significance of acquisition planning to the overall success of state procurements is critical. Acquisition planning can be defined in many ways but generally is considered the "process by which the efforts of all personnel for an acquisition are coordinated and integrated through a comprehensive plan for fulfilling an agency need in a timely manner and at a reasonable cost. It includes developing the overall strategy for managing the acquisition."[1]

Successful acquisition planning for state and local purchasing relies on the early exchange of information. With respect to government personnel, an acquisition plan provides sufficient information so that someone unfamiliar with the program will understand what is being proposed.[2] In addition, all stakeholders must be involved in planning so as to generate commitment and support for the acquisition.

A major aspect of promoting state and local procurement is identifying and resolving concerns of stakeholders, including industry representatives, regarding the acquisition strategy. Government procurement personnel as well as vendors should be provided opportunities to comment on or receive early information about chosen acquisition methods; terms and conditions; the feasibility of the requirement, including performance requirements, statements of work, and data requirements; and the suitability of evaluation criteria.[3] In short, it is a best practice to measure the pulse of vendors during the acquisition planning process.

During acquisition planning, contracting officers have various responsibilities they must meet, depending on the procurement policies and goals implemented within their jurisdictions. Generally, contracting officers must assess the need of the agency for a product or service. Assessing the need requires a combination of market research and an understanding of user requirements. Contracting officers must address the following questions: (1) who will be the ultimate end-user of the product or service; (2) what use will be made of the product or service by the end-user; (3) when will the product be used; (4) where will the product or service be used; (5) why does the end-user need the product or service; and (6) how is the end-user going to use the product? By performing a needs assessment and a cost analysis during acquisition planning, contracting officers are able to better determine the minimum requirements of an agency for a product or service. The needs assessment and cost analysis will assist planners who must identify and document the availability of products and services that satisfy the assessed needs.

Planners must then consult with agency experts when developing procurement plans and preparing statements of work or specifications to ensure incorporation of relevant requirements in procurement planning documents and purchase requests. In developing specifications, planners must prioritize the requirements identified during the needs assessment and include a description of the physical and performance characteristics of the product. When developing performance requirements, planners must identify what standards the product or service must meet. These requirements must be obtainable, measurable, and verifiable. In performing these tasks, planners must address the level of competition available to meet agency requirements. Establishing a set of performance requirements that unreasonably restricts competition among suppliers will violate competition laws and likely result in higher prices being paid by state and local governments. Maintaining an equitable number of suppliers while including specific performance requirements and specifications will result in competitive and fair outcomes.

Selecting a Solicitation Method

The recursive process of acquisition planning helps procurement professionals assess which solicitation method is best suited for a specific acquisition. The section *Project Delivery Methods* in Chapter 5 discusses several source selection methods in detail, but in this section the two most heavily used methods, competitive sealed bidding and competitive sealed proposals, are discussed for the purpose of showing what planners consider when selecting between or among source selection methods.

Competitive Sealed Bidding

Competitive sealed bidding is used when a purchasing agency is capable of specifically defining the scope of work for which a contractual service is required or is capable of developing precise specifications defining the actual commodity or group of commodities required. When competitive sealed bidding is used, the award is made to the responsible bidder having the lowest responsive bid.

With competitive sealed bidding, a solicitation called an invitation for bids is issued. This solicitation describes the procuring agency's needs with precision, informs bidders that competition will be conducted on the basis of lowest price, and provides for the public opening of bids. Because competitive sealed bidding is a formal process, public notice is required to be given sufficiently in advance of bid opening to permit potential bidders the opportunity to prepare and submit their bids in a timely manner.[4] Such public notice is meant to ensure competition by allowing as many bidders as is practicable to compete for the procuring agency's requirements. Formal competitive sealed bidding requires that award be made to the bidder "whose bid conforms to the solicitation."[5] The successful bid is based solely on price.

Competitive Sealed Proposals

Generally, state and local governments will use competitive sealed proposals when the use of competitive sealed bidding is not in the best interest of the procuring agency.[6] The circumstances that may lead to such a determination include the agency's inability to write specifications to define their requirements, the need for more development works, or high performance risk.

In most jurisdictions, use of competitive sealed proposals requires a written determination by a procurement officer. The written determination is a means to balance the need for accountability in the choice of an acquisition method with the need to provide flexibility to the procuring authority to respond to an environment of complex purchasing requirements. The written determination must state, with particularity, that the use of competitive sealed proposals is more advantageous than competitive sealed bidding. Other jurisdictions state that competitive sealed proposals should be used upon advanced written determination when "competitive sealed bidding is either not practicable or not fiscally advantageous to the public."[7]

Reasons for Selecting One Method over Another

Generally, selection of a solicitation method falls within the business judgment of the procuring official. That said, each method offers a guide to the procuring official as to when one method is more suited than another to accomplish a specific acquisition. The generally accepted best practice is to use competitive sealed bidding when it is feasible. The procuring official will assess feasibility by first determining whether a complete, adequate, and realistic description of the good or service to be procured is available. Second, the procuring official will determine whether two or more responsible bidders are willing and able to compete for the work. Third, the procuring official will determine whether the procurement lends itself to a fixed price contract type for which selection of the successful bidder is made primarily on the basis of price.

When competitive sealed bidding is not feasible, procuring officials should use competitive sealed proposals. The latter method is more suited to an acquisition where factors other than price must be evaluated or when the procuring agency does not have reliable, concrete specifications to inform competitors about how to meet government minimum needs. Accordingly, it is a fair statement to make that when the procuring agency does not have the solution to satisfy its minimum needs, it must look to industry to provide the solution at a competitive price or cost, but because the solution originates with the prospective contractor, the procuring agency will have to evaluate the proposed solution, which necessarily encompasses assessing technical and management solutions in addition to price. Where the solution is not known to the procuring agency and a weighing and balancing of factors other than price must occur, the procuring official is best served by selecting the competitive sealed proposal method for such an acquisition.

Drafting Statements of Work

Vendor obligations are often referred to as statements of work (SOW). A SOW is a narrative description of the contract's goals and/ or agenda. The SOW is a key tool of project management; as well, it is the primary means of evaluating proposals and selecting the contractor to perform the contract. Statements of work usually include the following elements:

- *Introduction.* This section identifies the need, the contract's goal, the location of the contract work, and a discussion of how the contract work fits into the agency's missions and goals.

- *Definitions.* This section provides key terms that are not explained in contract boilerplate or applicable regulations.

- *Objectives of the project and the subsequent contract.* This section provides a well-defined statement of the results to be achieved in order for the overall mission of the work to be accomplished. Objectives should be quantifiable criteria that must be met in order for the work to be considered successful.

- *Scope of work.* Not to be confused with statement of work, which serves as a guideline for agreements on performance between the government agency and the contractor, scope of work defines the specific work/tasks that must be accomplished.

- *Task identification.* Tasks are activities and milestones that need to be completed to accomplish the contract objectives and can be structured by milestones, deliverables, or processes.
- *Deliverables.* This section specifically identifies the item or service that must be produced as a result of contract performance. It can be described as the output or end product. The SOW must include clear instructions on exactly what is the deliverable and the method and manner for its acceptable submission.
- *Time frames and deadlines.* Time frames and deadlines establish what items resulting from performance should be delivered and when. Time frames and deadlines apply to scheduled completion of tasks, milestones, and completion of the entire contract.
- *Inspection criteria.* This section identifies specific procedures or criteria for reasonable testing to ensure that the deliverable functions in accordance with established design specifications or technical requirements.
- *Payment and other government responsibilities.* Payment can include instructions for the contractor to receive progress payments or the trigger for receiving complete payment satisfaction. Other government responsibilities include the provision of public resources, such as equipment, data, or information.

Statements of work should include clear, comprehensive, and concise statements of vendors' obligations. They should also delineate performance measures for the vendor. In addition, they should include agency obligations, whether merely payment or some other additional government requirement. A caveat to the discussion in *Solicitation Preparation* above about including stakeholders in acquisition planning is that vendor responses to requests for information, while valuable, should not be adopted as articulations of statements of work for any number of reasons, such as protecting the integrity of the procurement process, protecting competition principles, avoiding risk, and maintaining independence in the exercise of governmental functions.

Statements of work should also be prepared with a view to contract administration. Often, a SOW serves as the roadmap during contract administration. The SOW is the measure by which the government ensures satisfactory performance and proper discharge of the vendor's obligation and responsibilities under the contract. Likewise, the SOW also sets forth the guidelines for timely and effective technical assistance and approval from government staff, who are restrained from imposing additional requirements upon vendors that fall outside the scope of the SOW. In short, the SOW establishes the guidelines for performance by both the vendor and the government.

Drafting Specifications

The 2007 MC PIP dedicates Article 4 to a basic policy supporting objectivity in drafting specifications. Specifically, section 4-101 promotes the policy of maximum practicable competition in the drafting and use of specifications. Section 4-101 provides,

> [a]ll specifications shall seek to promote overall economy for the purposes intended and encourage competition in satisfying the [agency's] needs, and shall not be unduly restrictive.

This means that specifications should be drafted to encourage competition as opposed to restricting competition. A well-drafted specification will invite maximum reasonable competition. Competition in turn promotes overall economy. Careful research and drafting of specifications will invariably result in acquiring a better product, at a lower cost, and with far fewer claims and delays during the life of the project.

In addition, standards for drafting specifications ensure that drafters do not push the state of the art to a new level to acquire the best possible system, regardless of cost. Instead, adhering to basic policies and principles for drafting specifications ensures that the agency's minimum needs are procured in accordance with state and/ or government competition policy.

Specification refers to the description of the characteristics of a commodity or service required or desired. Specifically, it is defined as the explicit requirement furnished with a solicitation upon which a purchase order or contract is to be based.[8] Specifications set forth the characteristics of the property and services to be purchased in order to enable the vendor to understand and determine what is to be supplied. This information may be in the form of a description of the physical, functional, or performance characteristics, a reference brand name, or both.

Drafters do not necessarily have to re-create the wheel when developing specifications. They can rely on a number of sources for information relevant to producing specifications. One of the most reliable sources in the development of specification is the expertise of the end user who can best describe the function and performance of the desired product. Similarly, industry members are a good source of information, as they possess brochures and catalogs for various types of products.[9] Standard setting organizations are also good resources for specification information. The best practice is to gather specification information as a function of market research and to vigilantly maintain objectivity so as not to unwittingly develop a preference for a particular product of one or a few manufacturers.

Just as there are myriad sources to consult in the development of specifications, there are myriad types of specifications. Specifications fall into four main categories:

1. performance specifications;
2. design specifications;
3. brand name "or equal" specifications; and
4. other types of specifications, such as Qualified Product List or Approved Brands

Performance Specifications

Performance specifications are increasingly becoming the most favored type of specification. One reason is that agency use of performance specifications allows the government to shift the risk of appropriate performance to the contractor. Another reason is the agency reliance on performance specifications allows the government to benefit from industry expertise and knowledge about how to most efficiently satisfy agency needs.

Performance specifications state the function that the user desires to achieve. It is not unusual for this type of specification to contain a mix of elements of design and performance. The emphasis is on what the product does, how well it performs, and at what cost in relation to its intended use. Performance specifications encourage innovation, efficiency, and ingenuity. The key to drafting performance specifications is focusing on promoting equal or better performance at lower costs.

Design Specifications

Design specifications used to be the norm in government procurement, but now their use is waning. Design specifications set strict requirements for the good to be purchased by specifically detailing the characteristics that the good must possess. These specifications are used to determine how a product is to be fabricated or constructed and are primarily used where a structure or product has to be specifically made to meet a strict requirement. Design specifications have precise characteristics that can limit competition and generally do not accommodate rapidly changing technology. Moreover, this type of specification places the risk of successful performance on the proponent of the specification, which is usually the government agency.

Brand Name "or Equal" Specifications

The 2007 MC PIP gives special attention to uses of brand name or equal specifications and brand name specifications in article 4. The reason for this extensive treatment is to provide concrete guidance to government agencies and chief procurement officers in the use of these specifications in an effort to further the goal of promoting nonrestrictiveness of specifications and the protection of competition.

Brand names are used to indicate general performance and quality levels. As mentioned earlier in the discussion about drafting specifications, drafters routinely use manufacturers' brands as one method of gathering information about a product's characteristics. There is nothing inherently wrong with this practice so long as efforts are made to use brand name designations that are known throughout the industry or have specifications that are readily available.

When using brand names, the specification should describe the minimum salient characteristics to be used in comparing brands and making awards. This practice allows competitors to propose acceptable models on an equal basis. As well, the 2007 MC PIP instructs the chief procurement officer to provide a written justification for using a brand name or equal specification in solicitations in order to make transparent those circumstances that warrant such use. To illustrate, section 4-106(1), Brand Name or Equal Specification, provides,

> [b]rand name or equal specifications may be used when the Chief Procurement Officer determines in writing that: (a) no other design or performance specification or qualified products list is available; (b) time does not permit the preparation of another form of purchase description, not including a brand name specification; (c) the nature of the product or the nature of the agency's requirements makes use of a brand name or equal specification suitable for the procurement; or (d) use of a brand name or equal specification is in the agency's best interests.

Furthermore, the 2007 MC PIP section 4-106(2) advances the goals of competition by promoting the designation of three or more brands, other than the specified brand name, as equal references. Finally, when only brand name specifications are suitable, the chief procurement officer is required to provide a written justification that only the identified brand name item will satisfy the agency's need.

Qualified Product List or Approved Brands

A qualified product list (QPL) specification specifies a brand name, model number, or identifiable designation of an approved product that has undergone certain relevant testing or other objective criteria that examined products prior to issuing a solicitation. The purpose of a QPL specification is to determine, in advance, those products that are acceptable.

The benefits that accrue from using a QPL specification are simplified evaluation standards, greater emphasis on price as the most significant evaluation factor, and improved efficiency in determination of vendor conformance with specifications. The disadvantages associated with using a QPL specification are the restriction on competition resulting from exclusion of non-approved products, the potential for staleness resulting from products on the list becoming outdated, and the perpetual task of conducting field testing to ensure the acceptability of similar products. It is important to note that state and local governments may have restrictions or limitations on the use of QPLs and, therefore, it is prudent to research specific QPL inclusions or exclusions.

Drafting Evaluation Criteria

Drafting measurable and transparent evaluation criteria is important in all procurements that are not solely price driven. Specifically, well-drafted evaluation criteria for solicitations employing the negotiated procurement contract method are vital to ensuring fairness to and promoting meaningful competition among prospective vendors. As with specifications, the goal for evaluation criteria is that they put prospective vendors on notice of the agency's approach to evaluating proposal submissions. As such, the evaluation criteria must reflect the essential qualities or performance requirements necessary to achieve the objectives of the contract. The criteria should allow evaluators to fairly and comprehensively evaluate proposal submissions. The evaluation criteria may take a variety of sources of information into consideration such as the written response, the oral presentation, and documented contractor past performance.

To ensure fairness in evaluation, the evaluation criteria should reflect only those requirements specified in the solicitation document. The language within the solicitation will determine the scope of the evaluation criteria and the flexibility that evaluators will have when evaluating proposals, so the evaluation criteria should not be unduly restrictive. Prospective vendors must have notice in the solicitation of all requirements. The solicitation should clearly state the consequence of failing to meet these requirements such as reduction in evaluation score or disqualification.

Unlisted factors and sub-factors are not prohibited. The test the agency must meet is to fairly advise vendors that a factor will be considered. Factors and sub-factors that are logically and reasonably related to a stated factor or sub-factor will result in a decision that the government fairly advised vendors. Regardless, government agencies are well advised to consider that evaluation criteria not included in a solicitation generally may not be used in the selection or ranking of a proposal. For example, if evaluators expect vendors to possess national accreditation or want them to meet the unique needs of the end-user, these criteria must be included in the solicitation so that the vendors know they must address these factors in order to obtain credit during the evaluation. Likewise, if this information is not requested in the solicitation, vendors who fail to offer these options should not be penalized. There are several schools of thought on how much information should be provided to the vendors regarding the evaluation criteria. Some agencies prefer to give more detailed information as to how each factor is broken down into sub-factors, or they include a copy of the evaluation scoring sheets with the solicitation.

Factors and significant sub-factors must represent the key areas of importance and emphasis to be considered in the source selection decision. They must support meaningful comparison and discrimination between and among competing proposals. As demonstrated in the table below, the three categories of factors/criteria include

1. quality factors,
2. capability factors, and
3. cost/price factors

Generally, the cost/price factors must be evaluated in all procurements.[10] The capability factors are similar to the responsibility determination, but the two can be distinguished. Agencies generally evaluate experience and past performance at the time of the proposal

evaluation for purposes of scoring. In contrast, responsibility determinations must be made before award.

When determining the evaluation criteria, agencies must also
consider the proposal submission requirements associated with each
factor. In the sample criteria listed below, methodology is a criterion
on which the vendors will be evaluated. What information needs to
be included in the response in order to effectively evaluate a vendor's
methodology? For example, did they copy a project management
technique straight from a training manual, or did they tailor this
technique specifically to meet the needs of the solicitation? Another
example is the experience, skills, and qualifications of company and
staff. What information is required for the evaluation team to score
this criterion—years in business, years of staff experience, certified
or licensed employees, or performing similar size projects? The table
below indicates sample evaluation criteria.

Sample Evaluation Criteria	Sample Weight
Cost	60%
Proposed services, including work plan and methodology	20%
Experience, skills, and qualifications of company and staff	20%

Cost is typically the most significant evaluation factor. However, there are procurements in which the skills and experience of
the contractor or other factors may be more important than cost. For
example, if a trainer has to have a specific set of skills, the agency
may be willing to pay more for these skills. When establishing the
weight of each factor, consider the importance of the factor to the
overall project. The factor deemed most important by the agency
should be weighted higher than the other factors.

After the requirement to state the important or significant sub-
factors, there is a requirement to state the relative importance or
weight of the factors and sub-factors in the cost/price area. Thus,
the relative weight of the factors to one another should be provided
as well as a decisional statement or rule regarding the weight of

non-cost/price factors against the cost/price factor. Relative importance or weight can be achieved by the following:

- listing criteria;
- listing in descending order of importance;
- adjectival descriptions of importance; or
- numerical systems.

Publicizing Solicitations

Publishing notice of state government contract actions is a simple yet critical component of the procurement process. Keeping prospective contractors apprised of current public contract opportunities
is a best practice in promoting meaningful competition. Publicizing
solicitations can be achieved by various methods, including, but not
limited to, publication in newspapers and trade or industry journals;
online solicitation publication systems encompassing all statewide
competitive procurements; and any other established or new media
outlets.

Publication notice requirements will vary from state to state,
but there are some generally applicable standards that permeate each
system. First, most states enforce a synopsis requirement. Specifically,
most states expressly require both legal and public notice of anticipated contract actions.

Second, most states' synopsis requirements are triggered by dollar amount thresholds. The dollar amount may differ from state to
state, but most states will have a publication requirement spectrum
based on this dollar amount. This spectrum will exempt agencies
from publication requirements at the lower dollar threshold levels.
At the center threshold level, agencies may only be required to post
public notices in centrally accessible locations. At the higher end of
the dollar threshold, agencies will be required to give legal notice in
official newspapers as well as through officially established Internet
portals.

Third, the dollar amount of the anticipated procurement will also determine the amount of lead or response time provided to vendors. When an agency is required to synopsize, the agency is required to establish a solicitation response time that will afford prospective vendors a reasonable opportunity to respond to each proposed contract action. The length of time allowed for the solicitation response will be dependent upon the complexity of the procurement; whether the procurement is for the acquisition of commercial items; the size of the business; the availability of the supplies or services; and government urgency.

New Jersey offers a good example of synopsis requirements for advertising contract actions. Under N.J.S.A. section 52:34-6, the general requirement is to advertise for all agency procurements. Advertising is required when the contract amount is expected to exceed the public bidding threshold or is not subject to the exceptions of either N.J.S.A. section 52:34-9 or -10. The notice of bid opportunity is to be placed in newspapers and other media, such as the Division of Purpose and Property's website, so as to give the best notice to prospective bidders. Advertisements must be made at least ten business days in advance of the bid opening to encourage competition. If, during the interim between publication of an advertisement and the deadline for submission of responsive bids, the agency changes any of the terms, conditions, or requirements of the request for proposal, it must advertise such amendments at least five business days in advance of the bid opening. In addition to statutorily mandated public advertising, the DPP also publishes notices of bidding opportunities on its website.

Electronic Procurement Systems and e-Purchasing

Electronic commerce (EC) is an outgrowth of the private sector. It is a paperless process for accomplishing business transactions that relies on electronic mail, electronic bulletin boards, electronic funds transfer, electronic data interchange (EDI), and similar technologies.[11] The federal government began implementing EC in the early 1990s, and state and local governments followed suit but at a much more conservative pace. Even so, those driving e-procurement the hardest have come from the private sector. They see the Internet as the best vehicle for B-2-B and B-2-G (business-to-business and business-to-government) buying-and-selling relationships—more e-purchasing than e-procurement.

The goals and objectives of the private sector in supporting e-purchasing are to increase efficiency, lower administrative costs, and increase profits. Often these private sector goals and objectives are not completely aligned with state and local government goals and objectives of policy development, equity, and competition, which are more suitably described as functions covered by e-procurement. Accordingly, many government agencies have attempted to develop electronic systems that respond to the entire procurement process, not just the means and manner of electronic purchasing.

For example, at the federal level, the U.S. General Service Administration established GSA Advantage!. This federal portal offers an online shopping and ordering system that provides access to thousands of contractors and millions of services and products.[12] One component of GSA Advantage! is e-Buy.[13] e-Buy is an electronic system designed to allow government agencies (federal buyers) to obtain a quotation or proposal directly online for a wide-range of services and products from contractors (schedule contractors). e-Buy allows Requests for Quotes (RFQs) to be exchanged electronically between federal agencies and schedule contractors. For federal buyers, "e-Buy maximizes their buying power by leveraging the power of the Internet to increase schedule contractor participation to obtain quotations that result in best value purchase decisions."[14] For schedule contractors, "e-Buy provides greater opportunities to offer quotations and increase business volume for supplies and services provided under their schedule contracts."

At the state level, eMaryland Marketplace is one of the prominent state government procurement portals.[15] It provides the State of Maryland with a tool to expand the pool of Maryland businesses providing goods and services to the state. It achieves efficient procurement activities via the Internet, including posting procurement opportunities, receiving bids, and making purchases. Government agencies can establish real-time communications and business transactions with vendors in a paperless environment, minimizing administrative costs. The system increases buying power through intergovernmental cooperative procurement and heightens competition across a wider spectrum of suppliers. Sellers achieve more timely communications by accessing one portal to conduct business with participating buyers rather than having to visit thousands of procurement officers throughout the state.

The challenge for state and local governments is to shift from traditional procurement as a paper-based process characterized by fragmented purchasing, off-contract buying, and lack of control over expenditure. Another challenge for state and local governments is to avoid focusing first on the technology needed for e-commerce, as opposed to addressing public policy and organizational issues. State and local governments such as Maryland embrace e-procurement as a mechanism to facilitate, integrate, and streamline the entire supply chain process (from consumer to supplier and back again) in a seamless, real-time, and iterative manner.

Conclusion

There is no substitute for sound solicitation preparation and acquisition planning. Both lead to procurement formation and administration outcomes that are transparent, competitive, and defensible. If properly approached and implemented, acquisition planning yields effective, economical, and timely responses to present and anticipated needs of procuring agencies.

Notes

1. Acquisition Guide: Acquisition Planning Ch. 7.1 (Jan. 2012), *available at* http://energy.gov/sites/prod/files/7.1_Acquisition_Planning_0.pdf (last visited Feb. 1, 2012).
2. *See id.*
3. *See id.*

4. *See* 2007 MC PIP, § 3-102 (3), cmt.
5. *See, e.g.*, K.R.S. § 45A.080; W. Va. Code § 8-27-23(f); and A.R.S. § 41-2533(G) (competitive sealed bidding statutes).
6. *See* W. Va. Code R. § 148-1-7.7 (requests for proposals may be used when such a contract is in the best interest of the state).
7. *See* Va. Code Ann. § 2.2-4303(D); *see also* 2007 MC PIP § 3-103(1).
8. *See* 2000 MPC, § 4-101(1).
9. *Cf.* Sutron Corp. v. Lake County Water Auth., 870 So. 2d 930 (Fla. 5th DCA 2004) (upheld agency's decision to reject all bids where the low bidder was involved in specification development based on Section 287.057(18), even though statutory prohibition not applicable to Water Authority). For analysis of the challenging issues regarding vendor assistance with drafting specifications, *see* Robert C. Marshall et al., *The Private Attorney General Meets Public Contract Law: Procurement Oversight by Protest*, 20 Hofstra L. Rev. 1, 16–19 (1991) and Keith R. Szeliga, *Conflict and Intrigue in Government Contracts: A Guide to Identifying and Mitigating Organizational Conflict of Interest*, 35 Pub. Cont. L.J. 639, 651–661 (2006).
10. Following the Federal American Recovery and Reinvestment Act of 2009, the Arizona State Legislature changed the CMAR statutes to allow the contracting agency to consider price as a factor for awarding the contract if the contract involves federal funds. *See* A.R.S. § 41-2578. This change applies to all requests for qualifications issued on or before December 31, 2014, after which the stimulus monies will expire and Arizona's CM-at-Risk provisions will revert to prior law. Prior to the change, price was not considered a factor in the selection process; rather, qualifications such as past performance, similar project experience, capacity to perform the work, and financial strength were used in the evaluation.
11. Jean-Pierre Swennen & John E. McCarthy, Jr., *Electronic Commerce in Federal Procurement*, 98-08 Briefing Papers 1 (1998).
12. *See* Ichiro Kobayashi, *Private Contracting and Business Models of Electronic Commerce*, 13 U. Miami Bus. L. Rev. 161 (2005).
13. *See* GSA Advantage! eBuy website, at https://www.ebuy.gsa.gov/advantage/ebuy/start_page.do (last visited Feb 1, 2012).
14. *See* GSA iGuide, https://vsc.gsa.gov/iGuide/iGuide/eBuy.html.
15. *See* eMaryland Marketplace website, at https://emaryland.buyspeed.com/bso/ (last visited Feb 1, 2012). The State of Maryland, Department of General Services provides agency professionals and vendors with an online resource, called eMaryland Marketplace, that gives access to procurement-related information and opportunities. eMaryland Marketplace "combines interactive bidding with catalog purchasing in an efficient and effective manner while maintaining strict security, business controls, and fiduciary accountability for our agencies and suppliers. The entire process allows suppliers to more efficiently trade with Maryland agencies, resulting in reduced maintenance costs and lower per-order fulfillment costs. The electronic processing of orders eliminates errors and increases the speed of delivery of your products

and services to our agencies, significantly accelerating payment cycles and improving your cash flow.

"Interactive bidding is a service that allows the State to post solicitations and receive bids online. Registered vendors can search and bid online for State opportunities, potentially saving you thousands of dollars in travel and submission related costs."

5

Contract Formation

This chapter provides an introduction to contract formation principles by reviewing and analyzing well-established general contract doctrines applicable to private contracts and their application to public contracts. With regard to government contracts, this chapter discusses the use of well-worn contract types while also introducing more modern contract types that have grown out of the need to keep pace with procurement innovations. The chapter concludes with a description and analysis of source selection methods and project delivery methods.

Manifestation of Mutual Assent

State and local procurement law generally recognizes the "mirror image" rule.[1] This rule says that the contractor's bid or offer must conform to the requirements of the solicitation to demonstrate mutual assent and agreement of the parties. The bid or offer cannot vary materially from the terms of the solicitation and, similarly, the governments cannot change the terms of the solicitation without issuing an amendment and allowing prospective bidders and offerors the opportunity to respond to the changed requirements. The parties must also have a present intent to be bound. In addition, the terms of the contract must be definite. All terms need not be spelled out, but there should be enough information about the terms of the contract in order to allow for determinations about the existence of a breach of contract.

As with private contracts, state and local governments and their prospective contractors must demonstrate a present intent to be bound. Mutual assent is the cornerstone of common law contracts.[2] It is a well-known requirement of an enforceable contract, and it must be judged objectively based upon the manifestation of intent of the parties. As with private contracts, mutual assent is a requirement for public contracts at state and local government levels. However, private contracts and public contracts are distinguishable. The Supreme Court of Montana explained that "there is a difference between public works contracts and other contracts,"[3] the former usually being governed by a distinct set of public contract formation rules. A unique aspect of public contracts is that their governing competitive bidding and proposal statutes and rules "are primarily intended for the benefit of the public rather than for the benefit or enrichment of bidders [or offerors], and consideration of advantages or disadvantages to bidders [and offerors] must be secondary to the general welfare of the public."[4]

Even making such distinctions, the requirement of mutual assent is ever-present.[5] For example, in Indiana, "the written proposal of a public entity for work to be done, the written bid of a party to do the proposed work, and the written acceptance of such bid by the proper authorities, constitutes a contract to do the proposed work, even though a formal contract to do the work has not been executed."[6] Although there are no statutes on point, Indiana also adopts the 17 *Am. Jur. 2d Contracts* §§ 18–19 (1964) requiring "mutual assent or a meeting of the minds on all essential elements or terms in order to form a binding contract."

Indiana's interpretation of mutual assent in public contracts is also illustrated by *Mid-States General & Mechanical Contracting Corp v. Town of Goodland*[7] and *Board of School Commissioners v. Bender.*[8] In *Mid-States*, the town of Goodland had sought bids to renovate a school building into a town hall and brought a breach of contract action against a construction contractor that refused to perform the work in accordance with its bid price. The court held that the contractor's bid on the project, coupled with the unambiguous language of the bid documents, constituted a manifestation of assent and the formation of a contract between the contractor and the town.[9] In *Bender*, a contractor did not receive subcontractors' bids until 30 minutes before the bid submission deadline. In a rush, the contractor made a mistake as to the price of the contract.[10] In allowing the contractor not to be bound by the low contract price, the court held that in his own mind and judgment Bender "did not agree to enter into a contract to furnish the material and do the work according to the plans and specifications furnished him by the architect in the amount designated by his bid."[11] The court went on to state that "where the mistake is of so fundamental a character that the minds of the parties have never in fact met, or where an unconscionable advantage has been gained by mere mistakes or misapprehension, and there was no gross negligence on the part of the plaintiff, either in falling into the error or in not sooner making redress, and no intervening rights have accrued, and the parties may still be placed *in statu quo*, equity will interfere, in its discretion, in order to prevent intolerable injustice."[12]

Offers

State and local governments rarely go into the contracting market and supply offers for performance. Rather, they issue solicitations that invite bids or request offers from contractors. The replying contractors are called "bidders" or "offerors" and the state and local governments are usually considered "offerees." As offerees, state and local governments are in the best position to control contract formation.

An invitation to bid on a public contract is not an offer to contract but a solicitation for an offer.[13] The contractor's bid is the offer to contract.[14] Likewise, a public entity's advertisement for bids is a solicitation for offers, and the responsive bids are offers that may then be accepted.[15] Thus, an advertisement, being no more than a solicitation of bids or proposals for doing the work or furnishing the materials, does not impose a contractual obligation. In addition, when advertisements specifically reserve the right to reject any and all bids, no bidder may claim any contractual rights until a contract award is made.[16] Accordingly, in *William A. Berbusse, Jr., Inc. v. North Broward Hospital District*,[17] Florida's Second District Court of Appeal held that

> [i]t is the acceptance, and not the tender, of a bid for public work which constitutes the contract, and it follows, therefore, that the mere submission of the lowest bid in answer to an advertisement for bids for public work cannot be the foundation of an action for damages based upon the refusal or failure of public authorities to accept such bid, and this is true although a statute requires the contract to be let to the lowest bidder, where the advertisement reserves the right to reject any and all bids.[18]

Other states have also held that a bid made pursuant to an invitation to bid does not form a contract.[19]

Solicitations for offers come in five basic forms: invitation for bids (competitive sealed bidding), request for proposals (competitive sealed proposals), request for quotations, invitations to negotiate, and requests for qualifications. In competitive sealed bidding, state and local governments receive contractor bids in response to issuance of invitations for bids (IFB).[20] Contractor bids are the offer, and state and local governments' awards are acceptance. The process of competitive sealed proposals is sufficiently more complex in that there are opportunities for discussion and modification of proposals. Thus, state and local governments have the potential to make offers under this method of procurement. State and local governments will rely upon requests for quotations in small purchase situations where it is inefficient to receive bids or offers from contractors. There are a variety of procedures that can follow a request for quotations— including negotiations, quotes by the contractor, or the forwarding of a contract by a public entity to the contractor. If the public entity sends a contract, say in the form of a purchase order, then it becomes the offeror.

Invitations to negotiate are used when procuring agencies deem it in the best interest of the state or local government to negotiate with offerors to achieve the best value. Generally, there are two negotiation methods permitted by invitations to negotiate:

single negotiations and concurrent negotiations. Both methods rely on the compilation of a short list of acceptable offerors. With single negotiations, the technical and price proposals are evaluated and offerors are ranked. The top rated offeror has the opportunity to negotiate with the procuring agency. If an agreement cannot be reached with the top-ranked offeror, the procuring agency moves down to negotiate with the next highest-rated offeror. This process continues until an agreement is reached. With concurrent negotiations, after evaluating technical and price proposals, the procuring agency can revise the scope of services, hear oral presentations, and then negotiate concurrently to receive best and final offers or move directly to negotiating best and final offers without revision or oral presentations.

Requests for qualifications are official government notices of a need for professional services. Requests for qualifications solicit statements of interest from consultants qualified to perform architectural and engineering work on projects identified by procuring agencies.[21] The purpose of the request for qualifications is to identify qualified respondents from which a short list, between three and five firms, will be created, and those on the short list will be invited to participate in further competition under a designated source selection method. The shortlisted firms are interviewed. Generally, the interview entails making a presentation, discussing suggested solutions, responding to the expectations and goals of the procuring agency, and agency assessment of the qualifications and project teams of shortlisted firms. Additionally, shortlisted firms are usually directed to bring a sealed fee proposal to the interview. They are then ranked. Generally, selection is based on qualification, not fee proposal, so long as the proposed fee comes within procuring agencies' budgeted amounts.

Revocation of Offers

State and local governments recognize revocation of bids or offers. Revocation may occur because of withdrawal of a bid or an offer or modification of an offer. The method of procurement determines the form for revocation. Conventional wisdom provides that in competitive sealed bidding the contractor may revoke a bid before the date and time established for bid opening. Bids cannot be modified or revoked after bid opening because to do so would disadvantage other bidders in the field. In competitive sealed proposals, there are times when all offerors will be allowed to either modify or revoke their offers. These rules typically do not disadvantage other competing contractors because all offerors are provided an equal opportunity to engage in clarifications, communications, or discussions with a view toward modifying their respective proposals.

In addition to the method of procurement determining whether revocation is permissible, some jurisdictions have specific statutes governing the revocation of bids and offers, while other jurisdictions rely on regulations or actual bid specifications. While public entities may have a strong interest in ensuring that a low bidder does not withdraw its bid between the time the bid is opened and the time it is accepted, there are equally strong interests grounded in equity and fairness that support allowing bidders or offerors to withdraw bids or proposals. Statutes, rules, regulations, and/or specifications may also require the forfeiture of bid bonds if bids or offers are withdrawn during certain phases of the contract formation process. For example, Arkansas statutorily provides for withdrawal in accordance with A.C.A. section 19-11-229 (g)(1), which states "[c]orrection of patent or provable errors in bids that do not prejudice other bidders or withdrawal of bids may be allowed only to the extent permitted under regulations promulgated by the director and upon written approval of the Attorney General or a designee of such officer."

Similarly, Colorado's Procurement Code[22] provides in section 24-105-201(4) that "[a]fter the bids are opened, they shall be irrevocable for the period specified in the invitation for bids, except as provided in section 24-103-202(6). If a bidder is permitted to withdraw his bid before award, no action shall be had against the bidder or the bid security."[23] Section 24-103-202(6) provides that "[w]ithdrawal of inadvertently erroneous bids before the award may be permitted pursuant to rules if the bidder submits proof of evidentiary value which clearly and convincingly demonstrates that an error was made. Except as otherwise provided by rules, all decisions to permit the withdrawal of bids based on such bid mistakes shall be supported by a written determination made by the executive director or the head of a purchasing agency."

California,[24] like many other jurisdictions, establishes clear-cut procedures that allow bidders to assert mistakes in bids without the necessity of filing an action in rescission, although failure to comply with the procedure could be deemed a waiver of the right to relief.[25] The bidder must establish that a mistake was made; that the bidder gave notice to the public entity within five days after the bid opening, specifying in detail how the mistake occurred; and that the mistake was material and not due to an error in judgment or to carelessness in inspecting the site or in reading the plans and specifications.

As discussed above, the most typical scenario in which revocation or withdrawal is at issue is in the case of mistakes in bid. For example, in *Elsinore Union Elementary School District v. Kastorff*,[26] the prime contractor listed the names and bids of various subcontractors on its worksheets. In order to reach the ultimate bid, the prime carried the lowest sub-bid in each category to the right-hand column of the sheet. A plumbing bid of $9,285 had been received. Later, another bid of $6,500 was received. Because the second bid was lower, the prime deducted $3,000 from the bid total, arriving at a final bid price of $89,994. But the prime failed to enter the original $9,285 figure in the right-hand column; therefore, the total bid contained a negative allowance for plumbing.

After bid submission, the prime discovered the error and requested by letter that the school board allow it to withdraw the bid. Although the school board accepted the prime's bid, the prime refused to sign the tendered contract, and the school board filed suit against the prime for the difference between the prime's bid and the amount of the cost to build the job. The court of appeal, reversing the trial court, said the bid was the result of an excusable and honest material mistake, and that, in justice, the school board should not be allowed to take advantage of the prime's mistake. The court said, "Under the circumstances, the 'bargain' for which the board presses . . . appears too sharp for law and equity to sustain."

In a similar case, *M. F. Kemper Construction Co. v. City of Los Angeles*,[27] Kemper, by clerical error, submitted a bid that unintentionally omitted an item of $301,796. The public agency, though it was informed of the error, tried to hold Kemper to the bid. The invitation for bids provided that bidders would not be released on account of errors. But the California Supreme Court drew a distinction between clerical errors and errors of judgment. The court opined that if the bidder makes an error of judgment (for example, failing to allow for possible labor and material price increases or failure to recognize the cost of disposing of surplus dirt), it cannot be released from the bid. That would permit a contractor to get out of a contract at any point when it might decide it was not going to make a profit. However, to hold a contractor to a bid made only because of a clerical error of computation would be manifestly unfair, since it would hold the contractor to a bargain it never actually intended to make.[28] Therefore, the court construed the language in the invitation for bids—bidders will not be released on account of errors—to mean bidders will not be released on account of errors *in judgment.*[29]

Acceptance of Offers

The time, manner, form, and any other conditions associated with the method of acceptance of a bid or offer are generally within the control of the bidder or offeror. But bidders and offerors in the government contracts context do not have this amount of control because government solicitations have very specific requirements and, depending on the method of procurement, the contractor who deviates from the solicitation may not be chosen as the responsive and responsible bidder in the case of competitive sealed bidding or the most advantageous offeror in competitive sealed proposals.

Government acceptance of a bidder's bid or an offeror's proposal generally results after the public entity executes the standard form contract. The acceptance manifests the government's assent to the terms specified by the bidder or offeror. Thus, "[t]he general rule . . . is that '[t]he acceptance of a valid bid by the proper government authorities, where all legal requirements are observed, constitutes a binding contract.'"[30] But "the mere acceptance of a bid does not necessarily constitute a contract."[31] When a bid requires "certain formalities . . . , such as a written contract, or the furnishing of a bond," such language "often indicates that even after acceptance of the bid no contract is formed until the requisite formality has been complied with."[32]

Contract Types

State and local governments can choose from a number of contract types that best suit their interests by providing the flexibility for acquiring the large variety and volume of supplies, services, and construction to satisfy their minimum needs. In prescribed cases, contract types may be dictated by statutes, rules, or policies. They vary according to the degree and timing of the responsibility assumed by the contractor for the costs of performance. Contract types also depend upon the amount and nature of the profit incentive offered to the contractor for achieving or exceeding specified standards or goals. Selection of a contract type requires an understanding of the purpose of and circumstances surrounding an acquisition. The 2007 MC PIP provides,

> Subject to the limitation of this Section, any type of contract which will promote the best interests of the [Purchasing Agency] may be used; provided that the use of cost-plus-a-percentage-of-cost contract is prohibited. A cost-reimbursement contract may be used only when a determination is made in writing that such contract is likely to be less costly to the [Purchasing Agency] than any other type or that it is impracticable to obtain the supplies, services, or construction required except under such contract.[33]

Section 3-401 gives the purchasing agency discretion in choosing a contract type, but it also establishes a clear prohibition on cost plus percentage of cost contract types as well as places conditions on the use of cost-reimbursement contracts in general. The commentary to the section explains that the contract types permissible are firm fixed-price, fixed-price with economic price adjustments, fixed-price incentive, cost-reimbursement, and time and materials contracts. The commentary explains further that

> Other types of cost reimbursement contracts may be used when uncertainties involved in the work to be performed are of such magnitude that the cost of performance is too difficult to estimate with reasonable certainty, and use of a fixed-price contract could seriously affect a contractor's financial stability or result in payments by the [Purchasing Agency] for contingencies that never occur. Use of cost-type contracts is also authorized when it is impracticable to contract on any other basis.[34]

Fixed-Price Contracts

In a fixed-price contract, the contractor must complete the work to receive payment. Thus, under this type of contract, the risk of performance is allocated to the contractor. The contractor may receive progress payments, but the payments are subject to finance costs. A fixed-price contract is required in competitive sealed bidding.[35] This contract uses the basic profit motive of business enterprise by placing the risk on the contractor to perform at a specified price.[36] A fixed-price contract is distinguishable from a firm fixed-price contract in that the latter is not subject to adjustment, for example, in the case of economic contingencies.

The purpose of the fixed-price contract is to place the risk of performance on the contractor without unduly subjecting the contractor to unreasonable risk under which he or she has no control or in which unpredictable circumstances occur. Under a fixed-price contract, there is no compensation for unforeseen contingencies. A fixed-price contract carries risks for both the purchasing agency and the contractor. The contractor's risk stems from a possible failure to perform when the cost of performance exceeds the price quoted in the bid or offer. The purchasing agency is at risk when the contractor is financially unable or unwilling to complete the work required under the contract.

When using a fixed-price contract, the purchasing agency should ensure that (1) specifications are detailed and definitive;

(2) prices can be established fairly and reasonably; (3) adequate price competition exists; (4) there are reasonable price comparisons with prior purchases of the same or similar supplies or services made on a competitive basis; (5) available cost or pricing information permits realistic estimates of the cost; and (6) performance uncertainties can be identified and reasonably estimated regarding their impact on cost.

A fixed-price contract with economic price adjustment provides for upward and downward revision of the stated contract price upon the occurrence of specified contingencies. A fixed-price contract with economic price adjustment may be used when there is serious doubt concerning the stability of market or labor conditions that will exist during an extended period of contract performance, and when contingencies that would otherwise be included in the contract price can be identified and covered separately in the contract. Generally, fixed-price contracts with economic price adjustments are ties to a specific price index agreed upon ahead of time.

As mentioned previously, a firm fixed-price contract provides for a price that is not subject to any adjustment on the basis of the contractor's cost experience in performing the contract. This type of contract is suitable for acquiring commercial items or for acquiring other supplies or services on the basis of reasonably definite functional or detailed specifications when the purchasing agency can establish fair and reasonable prices at the outset. This contract type places maximum risk and full responsibility for all costs and resulting profit or loss on the contractor.

Most states expressly address the use of fixed-price contracts in statutes or regulations. For example, Maryland addresses this contract type in the Code of Maryland Regulations (COMAR) 21.06.03.02. This rule states that a "fixed-price contract is appropriate for use when the extent and type of work necessary to meet State requirements can be reasonably specified and the cost can be reasonably estimated, as is generally the case for construction or standard commercial products. A fixed-price type of contract is the only type of contract that can be used in competitive sealed bidding."

An example of a statutory requirement to use fixed-price contracts in competitive sealed bidding and competitive sealed proposals is the Kentucky Model Procurement Code, which states,

No contract providing for the reimbursement of the contractor's cost plus a fixed fee, hereinafter referred to as a cost reimbursement contract, may be made under KRS 45A.085, 45A.090, or 45A.095, unless it is determined in writing by the secretary of the Finance and Administration Cabinet that such contract is likely to be less costly to the Commonwealth than any other type of contract, or that it is impracticable to obtain supplies or services of the kind or quality required except under such a contract.[37]

In *Kentucky Utilities Co. v. South East Coal Co.*,[38] the Kentucky Supreme Court stated,

The normal risk of a fixed-price contract is that the market price will change. If it rises, the buyer gains at the expense of the seller (except insofar as escalator provisions give the seller some protection); if it falls, as here, the seller gains at the expense of the buyer. The whole purpose of a fixed-price contract is to allocate risk in this way. A *force majeure* clause interpreted to excuse the buyer from the consequences of the risk he expressly assumed would nullify a central term of the contract.[39]

The Kentucky Supreme Court ultimately determined that "risk of price fluctuations was held to be inherent and a central term of the contract" and that fixed-price contracts will be upheld since the parties are assumed to have agreed to this risk.

An innovative type of contracting vehicle sharing the risk of cost overruns and the reward of cost underruns is a fixed-price incentive fee contract. A fixed-price incentive contract includes a target cost and target profit, a ceiling price, and a profit adjustment formula. Unlike cost-plus-incentive-fee contracts, there is no ceiling or floor on profit. At the end of the contract, using the formula, target profit is either increased for a cost underrun or decreased for an overrun up to a ceiling price. The contractor assumes full responsibility for all costs incurred beyond the ceiling. The contractor must successfully perform to the contract requirements within the ceiling price. Fixed-price incentive contracts are appropriate when a realistic firm target cost and profit and a profit formula can be established at the outset of the contract that will provide a fair and reasonable incentive for the contractor. Technical and cost uncertainties must be reasonably identified, and the parties should be confident that performance can be achieved. A more detailed explanation of target and successive targets for fixed-price incentive fee contracts is found in Federal Acquisition Regulation Part 16.4.

Another innovative contract vehicle is the fixed-price award fee contract, which provides a fixed price consisting of all estimated costs and profits established at contract award along with an additional, separate award fee amount. The fixed price is paid for satisfactory performance; the award fee, if any, is earned for performance beyond that required. Generally, this combination is used when the procuring agency, although wanting to incentivize the contractor to deliver at an excellent or outstanding technical level, is unable to define that level in quantitative terms, or when metrics are unavailable or their use is not practical. Again, a more detailed explanation is found in Federal Acquisition Regulation Part 16.4.

Cost-Reimbursement Contracts

In the great majority of states, cost-reimbursement contracts are approved contract types. Cost-reimbursement contracts provide for payment of allowable incurred costs in accordance with contract terms and code provisions.[40] Cost-reimbursement contracts establish an estimate of total costs for the purpose of obligating funds and establish a ceiling that the contractor may not exceed (except at its own risk) without the approval of the purchasing agency. These types of contracts are suitable for use only when uncertainties involving contract performance do not permit cost to be estimated with sufficient accuracy to use any type of fixed-price contract.

The cost-reimbursement contract contains a standard limitation of cost clause. This clause provides that the contractor is under no further obligation to continue performance or incur costs if all of the funds that were contemplated by the contract have been expended fully. If the government provides additional funds, then the contractor must continue performance as long as funds are available until completion of the specified work. The purchasing agency will pay the contractor's costs during contract performance up to a certain dollar level. The purchasing agency pays the contractor's allowable costs plus a fee as prescribed in the contract.

Cost-reimbursement contracts can take various forms and range on a spectrum from cost contracts with no fee to cost contracts with fees. Common cost-reimbursement contracts include the following: cost contracts, cost-sharing contracts, cost-plus-incentive-fee contracts, cost-plus-award-fee contracts, and cost-plus-fixed-fee contracts. In a cost contract, the contractor receives no fee. This type of contract may be appropriate for research and development work, particularly with nonprofits or facilities operations. In a cost-sharing contract, the contractor receives no fee and is reimbursed only for an agreed-upon portion of its allowable costs. In the cost-plus-fixed-fee contract, the parties negotiate separately the estimated cost of performance and the pre-established fee resulting from performance. The fixed fee is stated as a set amount of dollars that will vary only if the contractor is required to perform additional work not included in the original contract. The estimated cost will ideally reflect the best estimate of the amount that will be spent in accomplishing the work called for by the contract, except estimated cost can be underestimated for two reasons: (1) to fall within the government's available funding and (2) to increase or enhance competition. The fixed fee can be determined in one of two ways. In the first method, the fee is a source-selection criterion where one contractor's fee is compared to another contractor's fee. In the second method, the fee is established using agency profit formulas, thereby taking the fee out of the competitive evaluation process.

A cost-plus-incentive-fee contract is a cost-reimbursement contract that provides for an initially negotiated fee to be adjusted later by a formula based on the relationship of total allowable costs to total target costs. A cost-plus-award-fee contract is a cost-reimbursement contract that provides for a fee consisting of a base amount (which may be zero) fixed at inception of the contract and an award amount, based upon a judgmental evaluation by the purchasing agency, sufficient to provide motivation for excellence in contract performance.

One type of cost-reimbursement contract that is prohibited by regulation in most jurisdictions is the cost-plus-percentage-of-cost contract. This type of contract is prohibited because it has the potential to motivate contractors to increase costs regardless of the need for incurring the cost in hopes of recovering a greater fee at the end of contract performance. For example, Maryland has a blanket prohibition on the use of these contract types in contracts and subcontracts.[41] But a handful of jurisdictions allow for limited use of these types of contracts in certain defined circumstances. For example, one such jurisdiction, Arkansas, provides that

> unless the context otherwise requires, the cost-plus-a-percentage-of-cost and cost-plus-a-fixed-fee system may be used under the authority of the State Procurement Director when:
>
>   (1) There exists no other economically practicable price arrangement to secure the commodity;
>
>   (2) A cost saving may be proved over the least expensive alternative; or
>
>   (3) The pricing schedule involved is tied to an industry standard or other reliable system of cost prediction.[42]

Multiple-Award Contracts

Traditionally, purchasing agencies procured good and services through agency-specific single contract awards.[43] But single contract awards and the concept of full and open competition open to all sources appear to be the exception rather than the rule in the modern procurement environment. Contracting methods have had to keep pace with the substantial increase in state and local government procurement of supplies and services. Most state and local governments procuring goods and services in this new environment have incorporated the use of the multiple-award contract, implemented through the issuance of task and delivery orders[44] or through federal- or state-sponsored supply schedules.

Multiple-award contracts are open-ended contracts.[45] Instead of creating a contract for a definite amount of goods or services, the government announces that it will have certain needs in the future. Contractors respond with information regarding their ability to meet those needs. Thereafter, the government awards several contractors the opportunity to sell those goods and services to the government in the future. When the contract is created, the government agency does not have to order any goods or services immediately.[46] Rather, the agency can place orders as the need arises.

Indefinite Delivery/Indefinite Quantity Contracts

Single- and multiple-award indefinite delivery/indefinite quantity (ID/IQ) contracts are contract forms through which purchasing agencies create preferred provider relationships with contractors. These umbrella contracts outline the basic terms and conditions under which the government may order goods or services. An umbrella contract typically is managed by one agency, the sponsoring agency, and is available for use by other agencies. The umbrella contracts are competed within the industry, and one or more contractors are awarded contracts to be qualified to perform the work. The competitive process for procurement of work to be performed under the contract, called delivery orders with respect to goods and task orders with respect to services, is limited to the preselected contractor when a single ID/IQ is awarded or the group of contractors each receiving one of multiple awarded ID/IQ contracts.

If the ID/IQ contract has a single prime contractor, the award of delivery orders or task orders is limited to that single party. If the contract has multiple prime contractors, the award of delivery orders or task orders is competitively determined. Some contracts are limited to specific agencies and purposes; others are government-wide, available to all agencies. Multiple-contractor ID/IQ contracts that are open for any government agency to use for the procurement of goods and services are commonly referred to as government-wide acquisition contracts (GWACs).

The current trend in multiple-award contracting is for an agency to bundle its requirements under a master agreement and then issue task or delivery orders under such a contract. The primary concern with bundling is promoting policies regarding full and open competition. Critics argue that this bundling results in an unreasonable restriction on competition. Similar to the counterarguments developed in the antitrust context relating to pro-competitive effects of restrictions on competition, proponents of bundling assert that the practice is a positive, efficient contracting method. In particular, small business concerns argue that bundling requirements restrict small business participation because small businesses cannot compete for the complete packaged procurement.[47]

Multiyear Contracts

The multiyear contract method allows procuring agencies to contract for more than one fiscal year when certain requirements are met. The 2007 MC PIP provides model language for use of multiyear contracts. Specifically, section 3-403 states,

> Unless otherwise provided by law, a contract for supplies or services may be entered into for any period of time deemed to be in the best interests of the [Purchasing Agency] provided the term of the contract and conditions of renewal or extension, if any, are included in the solicitation and funds are available for the first fiscal period at the time of contracting. Payment and performance obligations for succeeding fiscal periods shall be subject to the availability and appropriation of funds therefor.

The objective of the multiyear contract method is to encourage effective competition and to promote economies in state procurement. The 2007 MC PIP commentary explains that "[m]ultiyear procurements should attract more competitors to submit bids or offers for the larger contract awards and thereby provide the jurisdiction with the benefits of increased competition." The 2007 MC PIP also incorporates the principles of the bona fide needs rule by requiring that future payment and performance obligations be contingent upon the proper appropriation and availability of funds. The 2007 MC PIP states that multiyear contracts are authorized for use where

> (a) estimated requirements cover the period of the contract and are reasonably firm and continuing; and
> (b) such a contract will serve the best interests of the [Purchasing Agency] by encouraging effective competition or otherwise promoting economies in [Purchasing Agency] procurement.[48]

This model language has been adopted by several jurisdictions, including Louisiana,[49] Georgia,[50] and Utah.[51] In addition, a multiyear contract adopting similar language was deemed enforceable and constitutionally valid in *Greene County School District v. Circle Y Construction, Inc.*[52]

Letter Contracts and Definitization

Letter contracts are instruments that allow a contractor to start work immediately, without waiting for the details of the final contract to be negotiated. Definitization is the process of specifying the contract terms once performance has started. The Virginia Administrative Code defines a letter contract as "a written preliminary contractual instrument that authorizes a contractor to begin immediately to produce goods or perform services."[53] Undefinitized contract actions are rare in state and local government procurement. One reason for this may be the availability of emergency procurement procedures that facilitate expeditious execution of contracts coupled with the absence of circumstances, such as combat operations, that would justify the need for a state agency to authorize a contractor's performance prior to the execution of a final contract.

Methods of Source Selection

Methods of source selection include competitive sealed bidding, competitive sealed proposals, reverse auctions, public-private partnerships, and qualification-based selection.[54]

Competitive Sealed Bidding

Competitive sealed bidding is used when a purchasing agency is capable of specifically defining the scope of work for which a contractual service is required or is capable of developing precise specifications defining the actual commodity or group of commodities required. When competitive sealed bidding is used, the award is made to the responsible bidder having the lowest responsive bid.

Competitive sealed bidding thresholds vary among jurisdictions, but the objective is to use this method when it is most efficient and appropriate. Accordingly, each jurisdiction will determine the threshold at which small purchase procedures or purchases from approved vendor lists will prove more efficient than competitive sealed proposals. These thresholds can range from $25,000–$100,000 for small purchases or purchases from vendor lists, with competitive sealed bidding being used once the respective uppermost thresholds are reached. Small purchase procedures are typically less formal competitive procedures that are used when the dollar amounts do not warrant the time and expense involved in conducting a formal process.[55]

Competitive sealed bidding is a formal process that requires the issuance of an invitation for bids that includes specifications or a purchase description and all contractual terms and conditions applicable to the procurement. The agency must give adequate public notice. Bids are opened publicly at a designated time and place. Criteria for evaluations are threefold: The successful bid is based upon (1) lowest price, (2) whether a bid as submitted meets all material contract requirements, without qualification or condition, and (3) whether the bidder is responsible. Some jurisdictions require prospective contractors to go through a prequalification process. The prequalification process might entail proof of required licenses and/or meeting minimum responsibility thresholds to include financial capacity, experience, and training.

Jurisdictions may create alternative procedures such as multistep bidding, where unpriced bids are first submitted to narrow the purchase description and acceptable bidders are then invited to submit prices at the second step. Additionally, jurisdictions may use a reverse auction process in certain circumstances.

Invitation for Bids

When competitive sealed bidding is used, a solicitation called an invitation for bids is issued. This solicitation describes the procuring agency's needs with precision, informs bidders that competition will be conducted on the basis of lowest price, and provides for the public opening of bids. Because competitive sealed bidding is a formal process, public notice is required to be given sufficiently in advance of bid opening to permit potential bidders the opportunity to prepare and submit their bids in a timely manner.[56] Such public notice is meant to ensure competition by allowing as many bidders as is practicable to compete for the procuring agency's requirements.

Submission of Bids

Procurement agencies must give bidders sufficient time to prepare and submit bids. The complexity of the procurement and the number of amendments issued drive the time given for bid preparation and submission. The procuring agency must instruct bidders about acceptable mechanisms for submission, such as hard copy submission in sealed envelopes, telegraphic or facsimile submission, or e-mail submission. Generally, sealed bids are subject to the firm bid rule, which prohibits modification or withdrawal of bids after bid opening.

Responsiveness and Responsibility

Formal competitive sealed bidding requires that the award be made to the bidder "whose bid conforms to the solicitation." The successful bid is based solely on price. All nonconforming bids are not nonresponsive. The materiality of the nonconformance will determine if a bid is nonresponsive. If the nonconformity is immaterial, the bid will be considered responsive. Minor informalities that can be waived include the wrong number of copies of the bid, information on the number of employees, failure to acknowledge nonsubstantive amendments, or failure to follow form rather than substance of the IFB. A jurisdiction may even decide to accept a materially nonconforming bid if acceptance does not prejudice other bidders.

A responsiveness determination is based upon the evaluation of the bid, specifically its price and the promise to meet all material requirements of the solicitation. In contrast, a responsibility determination is based on the evaluation of the actual bidder, separate and distinct from the bid submitted. Responsiveness is measured by the bidder's promise to do or provide exactly what the procuring agency has requested.[57] Responsibility measures the contractor's ability and willingness to perform as promised. The purchasing agency has little discretion in the former, yet broader discretion in the latter. For additional discussion of responsibility, refer to *Contractor Responsibility* in Chapter 6.

Competitive Sealed Proposals

Generally, state and local governments will use competitive sealed proposals when the use of competitive sealed bidding is not in the best interest of the procuring agency.[58] The circumstances that may lead to such a determination include the agency's inability to write specifications to define their requirements, the need for more development works, or high performance risk.

In most jurisdictions, use of competitive sealed proposals requires a written determination by a procurement officer. The written justification is a means to balance the need for accountability in the choice of an acquisition method with the need to provide flexibility to the procuring authority to respond to an environment of complex purchasing requirements. The written determination must state, with particularity, that the use of competitive sealed proposals is more advantageous than the use of competitive sealed bidding. Other jurisdictions state that competitive sealed proposals should be used upon advanced written determination when "competitive sealed bidding is either not practicable or not fiscally advantageous to the public."[59]

Request for Proposals

Procuring agencies provide the information about their needs, the evaluation factors and sub-factors, and the relative importance of those sub-factors in a solicitation called a request for proposals (RFP).[60] In Virginia, for example, the competitive sealed proposals process begins with the government agency issuing a written RFP "indicating in general terms that which is sought to be procured, specifying the factors that will be used in evaluating the proposal and containing or incorporating by reference the other applicable contractual terms and conditions, including any unique capabilities or qualifications that will be required of the contractor."[61] The agency must provide public notice of the RFP.

Receipt of Proposals

In submitting a proposal in response to an RFP, the offeror generally writes three sections: the technical proposal, the management proposal, and the cost proposal. The contractor may make modifications before the date and time that proposals are due. One purpose for allowing modifications is to ensure that the government has the best offer prior to evaluation. The procuring official may also allow or require the revision of a proposal after the solicitation closing date. In most cases, the opportunity to revise proposals will be afforded to all offerors, especially depending on the respective deficiencies identified in each proposal by the contracting officer. In many jurisdictions, to promote fairness, proposals may be withdrawn by an offeror any time before award.

Competitive Pool

After assessing proposals, procuring agencies can award the contract without conducting negotiations or establish a competitive pool and conduct negotiations with all the offerors who are deemed competitive. Selection for inclusion in the competitive pool is based on those offerors who are deemed to be fully qualified and best suited among those submitting proposals, on the basis of the factors and sub-factors in the solicitation, including price.[62] Selection of offerors for the pool is followed by discussions. Discussions are conducted with offerors in the competitive pool to assure full understanding of and conformance with solicitation requirements. During discussions, offerors must be treated fairly and equally with respect to the deficiencies in their proposals by being given the opportunity for revision and by maintaining the confidentiality of their submissions.[63] After receipt and evaluation of final revised proposals, award is made to the responsible offeror whose proposal conforms to the solicitation and is deemed, in writing by the procurement official, to be most advantageous to the procuring agency, taking into consideration price as well as the other solicitation factors.[64] Accordingly, award can be made to an offeror that does not propose the lowest price.

Reverse Auctions

State and local governments have only recently begun to take advantage of reverse auction procedures in the procurement arena. In a reverse auction, also referred to as a procurement auction, a single buyer solicits bids from multiple suppliers of a product or service, then the suppliers bid the price down. Sellers drive reverse auctions, determining how low the market can go while still making a profit, allowing buyers to sit back and watch prices fall. And to the benefit of some local governments, they sometimes fall very low.

Reverse auctioning is an online procurement method wherein bidders bid on specified goods and nonprofessional services through real-time electronic competitive bidding, with the award being made to the lowest responsive and responsible bidder. During the bidding process, bidders' prices are public and are revealed electronically, and bidders have the opportunity to modify their bid prices for the duration of the time period established for the auction. A sample bid of requirements and documents for reverse auctions from the University of Texas at Austin appears in the chapter appendix at page 114; see also www.utexas.edu/admin/purchasing/tcrevauc.html (last visited Mar. 11, 2012).

Reverse auctions generally are used for commodities and some services in the federal market or at other levels of government. Orbis Online, Inc., the San Antonio–based online auction firm, was selected as a contractor for the General Services Administration to conduct online reverse auctions for government agencies. Under the five-year contract agreement, Orbis facilitates self-service (desktop) and full-service (hosted) auctions. In an online reverse auction, vendors' identities are concealed but their bids are not. Unlike the sealed-bid process, the online auction allows vendors to make multiple bids in real time. Once the auction is completed, the government agency can evaluate the bids and award the contract.

Many states use the method for high-volume buys of such things as highway maintenance supplies; however, some states limit the use of reverse auction procedures. For example, the Alabama procurement code provides that the reverse auction process shall not be used to procure professional services of architects, landscape architects, engineers, land surveyors, geoscientists, and others, as described in section 41-16-51(a)(3), or for contracts for construction, repairs, renovation, or maintenance of public works.[65] One reason for cautious use of reverse auctions is the avoidance of over-relying on procurement at the lowest cost at the expense of obtaining the best value for state government.

Public-Private Partnerships

Public-private partnerships (PPPs) qualify as one of several modern acquisition methods that govern the relationship between the public and private sectors to produce an asset or deliver a service for the benefit of public sector infrastructure.[66] PPPs are modern contractual methods that respond to complex public infrastructure requirements that involve long-term obligations and the sharing of risks and rewards between the public and private sectors. PPPs are recognized acquisition methods that are best suited for complex public infrastructure requirements that involve long-term obligations.

PPPs are used throughout the United States at both the federal and state levels. For example, at the federal level, the Department of Transportation Federal Highway Administration (U.S. DOT) uses and encourages PPPs in the development of transportation improvements.[67] The U.S. DOT has a solid PPP or P3 program that provides legislative and contract drafting templates conducive for use in other public sectors. The U.S. DOT guidance in this area provides that early involvement of the private sector in public infrastructure projects can bring creativity, efficiency, and capital to address complex transportation problems facing state and local governments. In collecting and disseminating information on P3 programs and projects, the U.S. DOT has developed a web resource that identifies 23 states and one

U.S. territory that have authorized enabling legislation for highway projects.

Similarly, as of 2008, 31 states and two territories have enacted legislation addressing one or a number of forms of PPP transactions.[68] In fact, several of these states have robust PPP legislation allowing for private delivery and maintenance of infrastructure across various public sectors.[69] These states are California, Virginia, and Texas, and the various sectors include water and wastewater, education, health care, corrections, building construction power, parks and recreation, and technology.

Specific state legislation can minimize the risks of litigation and delay overuse of PPPs. Authorizing and implementing PPPs in the appropriate circumstances can achieve one or a combination of the goals referenced in the previous paragraph. At the heart of concern with PPPs is the question of limited competition and transparency. In response to these concerns, agencies implement various safeguards, such as written justification, compliance with specific aspects of the Procurement Code, and sound acquisition planning.[70] Specifically, acquisition planning is the key task for agencies embarking on complex public infrastructure projects. Effective use of PPPs or any other progressive procurement method will require use of adequate acquisition planning tools, processes, and in-house management.

There are many reliable and credible sources of information and legislative models and templates available to policymakers and procurement professionals who are planning for the use of a PPP as one procurement method to assist in building public infrastructure. Most notable, the U.S. DOT manages a robust website with detailed information on public-private partnerships, project finance, and the Transportation Infrastructure Finance and Innovation Act (TIFIA) program.[71] With respect to PPPs, the U.S. DOT website offers state legislative resources that report on and offer guidance about drafting and enacting legislation authorizing PPPs. Specifically, the website provides model legislation that is based on a survey of existing state statutes that authorize public-private initiatives. The model PPP legislation gives an example of the basic elements to consider and address in PPP authorizing legislation. This model legislation is meant to serve as a representation of the core provisions dealing with issues to consider when pursuing greater private sector involvement in the delivery of transportation services. The website also provides case studies and sample PPP agreements.

The 2007 MC PIP includes new materials to guide state and local jurisdictions in the use of new methods of public and private collaboration in infrastructure development. The drafters of the 2007 MC PIP intend for state and local governments to "benefit from use of the Code's best practices for risk allocation, competition, public oversight, disputes, and other basic principles of good public procurement, without limiting their ability to use the best of innovative new methods for infrastructure design, finance, construction, and maintenance."[72]

A final resource is the National Council for Public-Private Partnerships (NCPPP), which maintains a website composed of valuable literature and presentations meant to educate stakeholders about the importance of the role of PPPs in meeting state and local infrastructure needs.[73] The NCPPP's mission is "to advocate and facilitate the formation of public-private partnerships at the federal, state and local levels, where appropriate, and to raise the awareness of governments and businesses of the means by which their cooperation can cost effectively provide the public with quality goods, services and facilities."

Qualification-Based Selection of Professional Services

Qualification-based selection (QBS) is an objective and fair process used by several state and local governments to select architects, engineers, and land surveyors based on design professionals' qualifications in relation to public projects. QBS is required by federal law[74] for procurement of architectural, engineering, and related services,[75] and is also included in the 2007 MC PIP, as well as enacted in over 40 states, including Arizona,[76] Colorado,[77] Nevada,[78] Utah,[79] Michigan,[80] and Wyoming.[81] QBS is the preferred method for procuring professional services because of the emphasis on quality over low price. Selection of firms to perform architectural, engineering, and related services is made on the basis of competence, qualification, and past performance. The 2007 MC PIP specifically incorporates QBS at section 5-104 and requires that this section be read in conjunction with section 5-202, which deals with source selection methods assigned to project delivery methods.[82]

The QBS process is competitive.[83] It begins with the procuring agency preparing and issuing project descriptions. The agency then requests statements of qualifications from professional services firms. Next, it evaluates submitted statements of qualifications against previously established and publicly available criteria. The agency then makes a determination as to those firms that have made the short list of preferred service providers and conducts interviews with these preferred providers. Following the interviews, the agency ranks the preferred service providers against previously established interview criteria. Finally, the agency and the highest ranked preferred service provider negotiate the scope of work and the design fee before awarding contract.

QBS statutes express that procuring professionals' services be done competitively through evaluations based on competence and not price. For example, Arizona Revised Statute section 34-603 provides that an agency shall provide notice of the procurement of professional services and shall award a single contract on the basis of demonstrated competence and qualifications for the type of professional services required. In procuring professional services in accordance with QBS, the Arizona statute prohibits the selection committee from requesting or considering fees, price, man hours, or any other cost information at any point in the selection process, including the selection of persons or firms to be interviewed, the selection of persons or firms to be on the final list, and determining the order of preference of persons or firms on the final list, or for any other purpose in the selection process. Furthermore, in determining the persons or firms to participate in any interviews and in determining the persons and firms to be on the final list and their order on the final list, the selection committee shall use and shall consider only the criteria and weighting of criteria specified by the agency for that purpose. No other factors or criteria may be used in the evaluations, determinations, and other actions.

In *Professional Engineers in California Government v. Kempton*,[84] the Supreme Court of California held that Proposition 35, a measure authorizing the California Department of Transportation and other state and local agencies to contract with private engineering and design firms for design and engineering services, was consistent with the Little Brooks Act, found at California Government Code section 4525 *et seq.*[85] The Little Brooks Act permits selection of professionals such as architects and engineers on the grounds of qualifications, not just low cost.[86] In concluding that Proposition 35 did not override the procedures of the Little Brooks Act, the court noted that it was a competitive process, albeit with costs of less importance than in other types of bidding.[87]

The 2007 MC PIP promotes QBS for professional services because of the special relationship between the procuring agency and the professional, in which the latter is engaged to represent the interests of the agency as opposed to the relationship that normally exists in a buyer-seller scenario. Thus, the 2007 MC PIP deems it more desirable to make the qualification selection first and then discuss price because both parties need to review in detail the scope of the work. Once the scope of work has been fully discussed and understood, then the professional firm proposes a fee that is independently evaluated for reasonableness by the procuring agency. According to this preferred process, price is clearly an important factor in the award of a professional services contract. The critical difference between the QBS procedure and those for garden-variety competitive source selections is the point in time at which price is considered.

Project Delivery Methods

According to the 2007 MC PIP, competitive sealed bidding and competitive sealed proposals are authorized for use in the following project delivery methods: design-bid-build, design-build, operations and maintenance, design-build-operate-maintain, and design-build-finance-operate-maintain.[88] The purpose of these delivery methods is to provide procurement officials with increased flexibility in the procurement of public infrastructure facilities and services.[89] There are two primary components of all project delivery methods. The first is that the delivery methods are integrated into a single decision-making process allowing the procurement official to assign different project delivery methods to a number of infrastructure facilities based upon the jurisdiction's overall capital development program in order to best allocate scarce resources across all infrastructure holdings. The second is related to integrated delivery methods in that it requires procurement officials to deploy project delivery methods pursuant to a centrally coordinated management plan.

Design-Bid-Build

Design-bid-build (DBB) is the most common form of project delivery method for construction projects. Conceptually, it provides for a linear sequence of work that occurs over three phases and involves three players: the government, the architect, and the construction contractor. Specifically, the government hires an architect to design and prepare construction documents, which include detailed plans and specifications for an impending construction project. The government then uses the construction documents to support the formal bidding process from which the construction contractor is selected based upon a determination of being the responsible bidder with the lowest responsive bid.

The advantages associated with the DBB delivery method stem from its wide applicability, familiarity, and universality throughout the general procurement community. DBB is accepted because it is consistent with formal competitive acquisition processes. At each phase in this delivery method, the source for producing the design or the construction is selected after a process of formal competitive procedures, whether by competitive sealed proposals in the case of architect and engineer services or by competitive sealed bidding in the case of construction services.

A disadvantage associated with DBB is its susceptibility to longer procurement processes, change orders, delay claims, and protest disputes. Another disadvantage of DBB is that the design services provider does not capitalize on the cumulative knowledge and experience of the construction contractor, the latter having more experience in new construction methods and life-cycle costs, which in turn may not yield the most advantageous cost and price outcomes for state and local governments. Thus, DBB is best suited for "improvement projects that do not demand advanced knowledge of construction practices, projects in which the time frame is not of great importance, and projects that require the involvement of only one or a few building trades."[90]

Design-Build

In the design-build (DB) delivery method, the government contracts with a single entity to provide both design and construction services. This comports with the definition of design-build as a "team-based system organized to provide efficient design and construction processes."[91] The public agency, the architect/engineer (A/E), and the general contractor are teamed shortly after the need for the project is identified. The A/E and the contractor joint venture with each other to form one entity to balance the competing priorities of initial cost to construct, ongoing maintenance costs, operating costs, life-cycle costs, aesthetic design, and user functionality in order to design and construct a project to meet the procuring agency's need.[92] Although widely used in the private sector, this delivery method is not authorized in some state and local jurisdictions.

A significant advantage of DB over DBB is that the government has a single contract and point of contact for the design and construction of the project, which means that accountability and liability for the project are clear. The contract is fully inclusive of all services and products to be delivered by the team. The relationship between the design services provider and the construction contractor is irrelevant for purposes of project accountability. The single line of accountability reduces litigation and contract changes because the contractor and designer are both responsible for working collaboratively through the design process. An added benefit of DB is that the contractor gains a thorough and detailed knowledge of the design intent and the architect designs according to the details and systems that the contractor can provide most efficiently. Another benefit is that the government enters into an enforceable contract that establishes the price of construction early in the life of the project.

The 2007 MC PIP provides that "contracts for design-build shall be procured by competitive sealed proposal . . . [except that the regulations . . . may describe the circumstances under which particular design-build procurements will not require the submission of proposal development documents]. . . ."[93] The general rule in this section would require the design-construction team to submit proposal development documents that would then be evaluated by the procuring agency against performance specifications and evaluation factors and sub-factors. The conditional language of the provision allows design-build procurement to be exempted from the requirement to solicit proposal development documents and instead base award of a DB contract primarily on the team's qualifications.[94] This basis for award invokes QBS, which promotes competence of the architect/engineer over cost. QBS focuses on a professional architect/engineer firm's qualification and competence in relation to the scope and particular needs of a project.

Operations and Maintenance

In the operations and maintenance (O&M) delivery method, state and local governments contract with private partners to provide and/or maintain a specific service. Under the private operation and maintenance option, state and local governments retain ownership and overall management of the public facility or system. The O&M delivery method focuses on providing service levels over a facility's life cycle, thus lowering overall project delivery costs and fully funding the proper maintenance of public assets.[95] As part of life-cycle delivery, the project's ability to produce a return—be it through user fees, availability payments, rents, or some other means—is assessed.[96] These revenue returns also have the capacity to attract either direct or indirect funding through government financing or private sector financing, respectively.[97] This delivery method normally follows after completion of a DBB or DB procurement.[98] According to the 2007 MC PIP, this delivery method can be procured by any method of source selection, ranging from small purchase procedures to QBS.[99] This delivery method is also considered a type of PPP.[100]

Design-Build-Operate-Maintain

The design–build–operate–maintain (DBOM) delivery method is an integrated partnership that combines the design and construction responsibilities of design-build procurements with operations and maintenance. These project components are procured from the private sector in a single contract with financing secured by the public sector. The public agency maintains ownership and retains a significant level of oversight of the operations through terms defined in the contract.

The DBOM delivery method represents a combined approach to providing public infrastructure. This approach allows governments to combine design, construction, and long-term operations and maintenance in a single contract with a single entity.[101] That single entity performs one or more of these functions itself and subcontracts to construction contractors to deliver the completed project over a life cycle.[102] Projects delivered through a combined or life-cycle strategy are a type of PPP.[103]

DBOM envisions that the contract team is responsible for design, construction, operation, and maintenance of the facility for a specified period of time, whereby payment beyond project completion is predicated on meeting certain prescribed performance standards. This is an extension of DB that provides an inherent incentive for the design-builder to provide a better quality plan and project by creating a life-cycle responsibility and accountability for the performance of the facility by the design-builder. According to the 2007 MC PIP, this delivery method shall be procured by competitive sealed proposals.[104]

Design-Build-Finance-Operate-Maintain

The design-build-finance-operate-maintain (DBFOM) delivery method bundles the responsibilities for designing, building, financing, operating, and maintaining the public facility and then transfers the facility to private sector partners.[105] There is a great deal of variety in DBFOM arrangements, especially the degree to which financial responsibilities are actually transferred to the private sector.[106] One commonality that cuts across all DBFOM projects is that they are either partly or wholly financed by debt-leveraging revenue streams dedicated to the project.[107] Direct user fees (tolls) are the most common revenue source.[108] Other sources range from lease payments to shadow tolls[109] and vehicle registration fees.[110] Future revenues are leveraged to issue bonds or other debt to provide funds for capital and project development costs.[111] They are also often supplemented by public sector grants in the form of money or contributions in kind, such as right-of-way.[112] In certain cases, private partners may be required to make equity investments as well.[113] According to the 2007 MC PIP, this delivery method shall be procured by competitive sealed proposals.[114] DBFOM is also considered a type of PPP.[115]

Conclusion

The formation phase of government contracting is one of the first opportunities for state and local governments to demonstrate to prospective contractors and to the public at large that their contracting mechanisms are competitive, transparent, and fair. When procurement professionals understand and apply established and new mechanisms of contract formation that respond to agency needs while considering performance risk and reward, they build confidence and certainty into a system that is often perceived as tainted. The information in this chapter, while not comprehensive, is meant to assist procurement professionals in understanding the nuances of contract formation with a view toward enhancing competition, transparency, integrity, and efficiency.

Appendix

Sample of Reverse Auction Bid Requirements and Documents

REVERSE AUCTION TERMS AND CONDITIONS OF BID

THE [STATE AGENCY] HAS DETERMINED THAT THIS
PROCUREMENT WILL UTILIZE THE REVERSE AUCTION
METHOD AS DEFINED IN THE [STATE] GOVERNMENT CODE
§ XX-XXX.XX AS A MEANS OF PROCUREMENT.

1.   BID REQUIREMENTS:

1.1   Vendors must comply with the following four requirements in order
       to be eligible to participate in the reverse auction event.

1.1.1 Vendor must **register** with Orbis Online, Inc., at www.orbisonline.
       com/ut and establish a company profile.

1.1.2 Once registered, vendor must select "view" for the specific reverse
       auction event by IFB number (or corresponding "RFQ number"
       provided by Orbis Online for that specific event) and click "partici-
       pate" on the bottom of the screen. Note: Vendor is only required to
       register once, but registered vendors must click "participate" for each
       reverse auction event vendor intends to participate in.

1.1.3 Vendor must **train** on the Orbis Online reverse auction platform
       for bidding instructions and to ensure vendor meets system require-
       ments. Deadline for registering, "Clicking to Participate" and train-
       ing is at least one hour prior to the event. Vendors are responsible for
       contacting Orbis Online directly for training.

1.1.4 Vendor must **Return Completed Invitation to Bid (ITB) Pack-
       ages**. All vendors participating in the reverse auction event must
       submit invitation to bid to the [State] by IFB due date. Submit
       completed IFB with all appropriate supplements and/or samples to
       [State]'s Purchasing Office by the IFB due date. Each completed IFB
       Package is to be placed in a separate envelope and properly identi-
       fied with Bid No., Reverse Auction event date and IFB due date.
       All vendors must return completed signed bid packages by the time
       and date specified in the IFB. HUB Subcontracting Plans (HSP), if
       required, MUST be included in the bid package or bid will be dis-
       qualified. Pricing on IFB must match final pricing submitted during
       reverse auction event. **In all cases, unit prices shall govern in
       the event of extension errors. Late IFB packages will be con-
       sidered non-responsive**. Notice to Vendors: Failure to submit the

completed bid package after participating in online auction event will result in an unsatisfactory vendor performance report. The bid evaluation is not complete until the contract is awarded.

Documents can be faxed or mailed to:

1.2 Early Proxy Bidding—Early bids submitted via proxy should be submitted using this Invitation to Bid document to Orbis Online. Bids must be time stamped a minimum of one hour prior to the scheduled auction start time specified in the Invitation to Bid document. Reverse Auction Early Proxy Bidding requires that the vendors be registered at least one hour before the start of the event. Early proxy bids will be entered online by Orbis Online, Inc. during the auction event. If submitting a proxy bid, Bidder is still responsible for complying with requirements of Section 1.1.

Assisted Bidding by Proxy—In the event of technical issue(s) when bidding online, bids may be submitted by proxy using this Invitation to Bid document. Proxy bids are to be faxed or delivered to the address below prior to the end of the auction event, in accordance with the auction rules:

Address
FAX number for proxy bidding only is:

1.3 Quote F.O.B. Destination. Bid pricing must include all cost for item, delivery and installation (if requested). In case of errors, unit prices shall govern. Bid prices entered online will be considered firm for acceptance within 30 days unless otherwise specified. Cash discounts will not be considered in determining award; all cash discounts offered will be taken if earned. List and deduct trade, educational or other discounts, not based on early payment, from prices quoted.

1.4 [State] is exempt from State Sales Tax and Federal Excise Tax. Do not include in bid. Tax Exemption Certificate furnished on request.

1.5 Bids must give full name and address of bidder.

1.6 [State] reserves the right to accept or reject all or part of any bid, waive any formalities or technical inconsistencies, delete any requirement or specification from this Invitation, or terminate this solicitation when deemed to be in University's best interest.

1.7 Telegraphic/facsimile response to any bid invitation must be on the bid invitation form. Telephone bids are not acceptable in response to this invitation to bid. CAUTION: The [State] and Orbis Online, Inc. offer facsimile service as a convenience only. The [State] and Orbis Online, Inc. shall not be responsible for bids received late, illegible, incomplete, or otherwise non-responsive due to failure of electronic equipment or operator error. Confirmation of facsimile bids is not required.

1.8   Vendor hereby assigns to purchaser any and all claims for overcharges associated with this contract which arise under the antitrust laws of the United States, 15 U.S.C.A. § 1 et seq. (1973) and the State antitrust laws.

1.9   The Vendor ID Number is the taxpayer number assigned and used by the Comptroller of Public Accounts of [The State]. If the Vendor ID number is not known, enter your Federal Employers Identification Number or Social Security Number if a sole owner.

1.10   In the case of tie bids, the award will be made in accordance with the [State] Building and Procurement Commission Rule on (preferences).

1.11   Vendor shall not assign any purchase order resulting from reverse auction event without prior written approval of the [State] Purchasing Office.

2.   SPECIFICATIONS:

2.1   Unless specifically stated, any catalogue, brand name or manufacturer's reference used is descriptive (not restrictive), and is used to indicate type and quality desired. Bids on brands of like nature and quality will be considered. If bidding on other than referenced specifications, bid MUST show manufacturer brand or trade name and description of product offered. Illustrations and complete descriptions of product offered should be made part of the bid. If no exception is taken to the specifications shown, bidder will be required to furnish brand names, numbers, etc., as shown in the invitation.

2.2   All items bid shall be new, in first class condition, including containers suitable for shipment and storage, unless otherwise indicated in bid invitation. Verbal agreements to the contrary will not be recognized.

3.   DELIVERY:

3.1   Bid should show number of days required to place material in designated location under normal conditions. Unrealistically short or long delivery promises may cause bid to be disregarded. Failure to state delivery time obligates the bidder to complete delivery in 14 calendar days

3.2   The [State] Hazard Communication Act requires chemical manufacturers and distributors to provide Material Safety Data Sheets

(MSDS) for hazardous materials sold. Products covered by The Act must be accompanied by a Material Safety Data Sheet and such product labeled in compliance with the law. If the product is not covered under the Act, a statement of exemption must be provided.

4.   VENDOR AFFIRMATION: BY SIGNATURE HEREON,

4.1   Bidder affirms that he has not given, offered to give, nor intends to give at any time hereafter any economic opportunity, future employment, gift, loan, gratuity, special discount, trip, favor, or service to a public servant in connection with the submitted bid. Failure to sign the bid may, or signing it with a false statement shall, void the submitted bid or any resulting contracts, and the bidder will be removed from all bid lists.

4.2   Bidder affirms that no affiliation exists between owners, officers, administrators and employees of the bidder and the [State] which could be construed as a conflict of interest.

4.3   Bidder certifies that he is not currently delinquent in the payment of any franchise tax owed the State under Chapter XXX, Tax Code. Making a false statement as to corporate tax status is a material breach of contract.

4.4   Bidder hereby certifies that neither the bidder nor the firm, corporation, partnership or institution represented by the bidder, or anyone acting for such firm, corporation, or institution has violated the antitrust laws of this State, nor communicated directly or indirectly the bid made to any competitor or any other person engaged in such line of business.

4.5   Bidder has not received compensation for participation in the preparation of the specifications for this Invitation to Bid.

4.6   Under Section X Government Code (relating to collection of state and local sales and use taxes) the bidder certifies that the individual or business entity named in this bid is not ineligible to receive the specified contract and acknowledges that this contract may be terminated and/or payment withheld if this certification is inaccurate.

4.7   Bidder agrees that any payments due under this contract will be applied towards any debt, including but not limited to delinquent taxes and child support owed to the State.

4.8   The contractor shall defend, indemnify, and hold harmless the State, all of its officers, agents and employees from and against all claims, actions, suits, demands, proceedings, costs, damages, and liabilities, arising out of, connected with, or resulting from any acts or omissions of contractor or any agent, employee, subcontractor, or supplier of contractor in the execution for performance of this contract.

4.9   Bidder certifies that they are in compliance with section Y of the Government Code, relating to contracting with executive head of State agency. If section Z applies, bidder will complete the following information in order for bid to be evaluated.
Name of Former Executive: _____

Name of State Agency: _____

Date of Separation
from State Agency: _____

Position with Bidder: _____

Date of Employment
with Bidder: _____

4.10   Bidder agrees to comply with Government Code XX, pertaining to service contract use of products produced in the State.

5.   [STATE] RESIDENT AFFIRMATION CLAUSE:
[State] Resident Affirmation Clause:

By signing this bid, bidder certifies that if a [State] address is shown as the address of the bidder, bidder qualifies as a [State] Resident Bidder as defined in Rule YY.

6.   GENERAL:

6.1   Inquiries pertaining to bid invitations must give Bid Invitation No. and Opening Date.

6.2   This bid invitation and any order issued as a result shall be governed by the laws of the State. Under Section ZZ, Family Code, the vendor or applicant certifies that the individual or business entity named in this contract, bid, or application is not ineligible to receive the specified grant, loan, or payment and acknowledges that this contract may be terminated and payment may be withheld if this certification is inaccurate. If the paragraph above is applicable, provide names and social security numbers of each person with at least 25% ownership in space provided below. Bidders that have pre-registered this information on the [State] Building and Procurement Commission's Centralized Master Bidders List have satisfied this requirement.

Percentage of Ownership	*Full Name*	*Social Security Number*
_____	_____	_____
_____	_____	_____

———————   ———————————————   ———————————
———————   ———————————————   ———————————
———————   ———————————————   ———————————
———————   ———————————————   ———————————

(Attach any additional documentation as necessary)

FAILURE TO MANUALLY SIGN MAY DISQUALIFY BID.

Notes

1. The mirror image rule may be modified, when applicable, by the UCC for contracts involving the sale of goods.
2. *See* Restatement (Second) of Contracts § 18 (1981).
3. E.H. Oftedal & Sons, Inc. v. State, 2002 MT 1, ¶ 17, 308 Mont. 50, 40 P.3d 349 (explaining further that although the public bidding statutes were established for the benefit of the public rather than to establish the rights of bidders, this does not necessarily exempt public contracts from fundamental contract analysis or remedies at law or in equity provided by other statutes).
4. *Id.*
5. *See* Swanson v. Holmquist, 539 P.2d 104, 106 (Wash. Ct. App. 1975) (holding that "[t]o form a contract, the parties must mutually assent to the agreement"); *see also* Barry v. Pacific West Construction, Inc., 103 P.3d 440, 444 (Idaho 2004) (Idaho courts will treat public contracts similar to private contracts. In fact, Idaho courts have stated in a matter dealing with public contracts that "in order for a contract to be formed, there must be a meeting of the minds on all material terms to the contract.").
6. Jackson v. Union-North United Sch. Corp., 582 N.E.2d 854, 857 (Ind. Ct. App. 1991).
7. 811 N.E.2d 425 (Ind. Ct. App. 2004).
8. 72 N.E. 154 (Ind. Ct. App. 1904).
9. 811 N.E.2d at 435; *cf.* Cal Wadsworth Constr. v. City of St. George, 898 P.2d 1372, 1376 (Utah 1995) (noting that "[a]n acceptance is a manifestation of assent to an offer, such that an objective, reasonable person is justified in understanding that a fully enforceable contract has been made").
10. *Bender*, 72 N.E. at 155–56.
11. *Id.* at 157.
12. *Id.* (citing 1 J. STORY, COMMENTARIES ON EQUITY JURISPRUDENCE § 138i (10th ed. 1870); *see also* Boise Junior Coll. Dist. v. Mattefs Constr. Co., 450 P.2d 604 (Idaho 1969) (Idaho courts have recognized that a mathematical or clerical error yields an unintended bid, while an error in judgment, such as an error in estimating the number of hours of work necessary to complete a project,

yields precisely the bid intended and is not deemed a mistaken bid. This means that if there is a clerical or mathematical error, there is no assent and therefore no contract. However, if the error is in judgment, there is assent and the contract remains intact.).

13.   Hadaller v. Port of Chehalis, 986 P.2d 836, 839 (Wash. Ct. App. 1999); *see* Peerless Food Prods., Inc. v. State, 119 Wash. 2d 584, 595, 835 P.2d 1012 (1992) *and* Mottner v. Town of Mercer Island, 75 Wash. 2d 575, 578, 452 P.2d 750 (1969).

14.   *See* J.J. Welcome & Sons Constr. Co. v. State, 497 P.2d 953, 956 (Wash. Ct. App. 1972).

15.   Rapp v. Salt Lake City, 527 P.2d 651, 654 (Utah 1974).

16.   John J. Brennan Constr. Corp. v. City of Shelton, 448 A.2d 180, 184 (Conn. 1982).

17.   117 So. 2d 550 (Fla. Dist. Ct. App. 1960).

18.   *Id.* at 552.

19.   *See* North Cent. Utils., Inc. v. Walker Cmty. Water Sys., Inc., 506 So. 2d 1325, 1328–29 (La. Ct. App. 1987) (holding that there could be no recovery even where the invitation to bid did not reserve the right to reject any and all bids); King v. Alaska State Hous. Auth., 633 P.2d 256 (Alaska 1981) ("It is established that in Alaska, as elsewhere, an agency's solicitation of bids is not an offer, but rather a request for offers; no contractual rights based on the content of a bid arise prior to its acceptance by the agency." (citing Beirne v. State Housing Authority, 454 P.2d 262, 264 (Alaska 1969).) *See also* Heyer Prods. Co. v. United States, 140 F. Supp. 409, 412 (Ct. Cl. 1956), *superseded by statute as stated in* B.K. Instrument, Inc. v. United States, 715 F.2d 713, 717 (2d Cir. 1983); Nat'l Const. Servs., Inc. v. Philadelphia Reg'l Port Auth., 789 A.2d 306, 309 (Pa. Commw. Ct. 2001) (explaining that a solicitation for bid proposals is not an offer but only an invitation for parties to submit bids in response to this request. The submission of the bid is, in fact, the offer which the contracting agency is free to accept or reject. . . . [W]hen someone advertises for bids [it] is the same as that pertaining to auctions. The advertisement is not an offer. It is a request for offers. This is so even if the common practice is to accept the best bid made. Occasionally, and especially in public bid-letting procedures, the best bidder will have a statutory right to be awarded the contract. This statutory right does not create a contract. (internal citation omitted)).

20.   These documents are also known by the following names: invitations to bid, requests for bids, and requests to bid.

21.   For more detailed information about quality-based selection of professional services, refer to Chapter 7.

22.   COLO. REV. STAT. §§ 24-101 through 112 (2010).

23.   *Id.* § 24-105-201(4) (2010).

24.   CAL. PUB. CONTRACT CODE §§ 5100–5107 (West 2011).

25.   *See* A & A Electric, Inc. v. City of King, 126 Cal. Rptr. 585 (Ct. App. 1976).

26. 276 P.2d 112 (Cal. Ct. App. 1954).

27. 235 P.2d 7 (Cal. 1951).

28. *Id.* at 11–12.

29. *See also* Powder Horn Constructors, Inc. v. City of Florence, 754 P.2d 356, 363 (Colo. 1988) (holding that prior to public entity's acceptance of bid for public construction project, bidder may in some circumstances obtain equitable relief from consequences of bid containing mathematical or clerical error).

30. City of Lonsdale v. NewMech Companies, Inc., 2008 WL 186251, *7 (Minn. App. 2008) (citing Johnson v. City of Jordan, 352 N.W.2d 500, 503 (Minn. Ct. App. 1984)).

31. 10 E. McQUILLIN, THE LAW OF MUNICIPAL CORPORATIONS § 29.80 (3d ed. 1999).

32. 1 SAMUEL WILLISTON, WILLISTON ON CONTRACTS § 4:10, 343–44 (Richard A. Lord ed., 4th ed. 1990).

33. 2007 MODEL CODE FOR PUB. INFRASTRUCTURE PROCUREMENT § 3-104 (2007 MC PIP).

34. *Id.* § 3-104, cmt.

35. *See* MD. CODE REGS. (COMAR) 21.06.03.01, .02 (2011), *available at* http://www.dsd.state.md.us/comar/comarhtml/21/21.06.03.01.htm *and*http://www.dsd.state.md.us/comar/comarhtml/21/21.06.03.02.htm (last visited Feb. 3, 2012).

36. *See id.*; *see also* Tri-State Asphalt Corp. v. Ohio Dep't of Transp., 62 Ohio Misc. 2d 319, 322–34 (Ct. Cl. 1991).

37. KY. REV. STAT. ANN. § 45A.130 (West 2011).

38. 836 S.W.2d 392 (Ky. 1992).

39. *Id.* at 406 (citing Northern Indiana Pub. Serv. Co. v. Carbon Cnty. Coal Co., 799 F.2d 265, 275 (7th Cir. 1986) (Lambert, J., dissenting).

40. To be allowable, a cost must be reasonable, allocable, properly accounted for, and not specifically disallowed.

41. WEST'S ANN. CODE OF MARYLAND § 13-214(b)(1)–(2) (2011).

42. ARK. CODE ANN. § 19-11-237 (2011) (LexisNexis).

43. Traditional single award contracts specify the scope of goods or services that will be delivered and the contractor that will provide the specified goods or services.

44. Also referred to as indefinite delivery/indefinite quantity contracts.

45. *See* Michael C. Wong, *Current Problems with Multiple Award Indefinite Delivery/Indefinite Quantity Contracts: A Primer*, 2006-SEP ARMY LAW. 17.

46. *See, e.g.,* LA. REV. STAT. ANN. § 39:1613 (2011).

47. *See generally* Cheryl Lee Sandner & Mary Ita Snyder, *Multiple Award Task and Delivery Order Contracting: A Contracting Primer*, 30 PUB. CONT. L.J. 461 (2001).

48. 2007 MC PIP § 3-403(2).

49. LA. REV. STAT. ANN. § 39:1615 (2011).

50. GA. CODE ANN. § 50-5-64 (2011).

51. UTAH CODE ANN. §63G-6-417 (LexisNexis 2011).

52. 708 S.E.2d 692 (Ga. Ct. App. 2011) (holding that the limitation in the multi-year contract did not override the school district's proprietary function and, thus, the contract was not void even when contract did not include the required termination date as required in governmental function multi-contracts).

53. 11 VA. ADMIN. CODE § 5-20-10 (2011).

54. Alternative procurement methods are discussed in Chapter 7 because of their relation to other collateral policy topics discussed within that chapter. Specifically, IT procurement is covered in Chapter 7, *Information Technology*, and cooperative purchasing is covered in its own section in Chapter 7.

55. *See* 2007 MC PIP, § 3-101, cmt. (3); *see also* Chapter 3, *Conclusion*.

56. *See* 2007 MC PIP, § 3-102(3), cmt.

57. *Id.* § 3-102(7).

58. *See* W. VA. CODE R. § 148-1-7.7 (requests for proposals may be used when such a contract is in the best interest of the state).

59. *See* VA. CODE ANN. § 2.2-4303(D); *see also* 2007 MC PIP § 3-103(1).

60. *See* 2007 MC PIP § 3-103(5)(a).

61. VA. CODE ANN. § 2.2-4301 (West, Westlaw through 2011 Sess.).

62. *Id.* § 2.2-4301.3b.

63. *Id.* § 3-103(6).

64. *Id.* § 3-103(7).

65. *See* ALA. CODE 41-16-4 (2006).

66. A public-private partnership means a contractual relationship between a public agency and a private partner, in which the private partner provides a public benefit, such as building transportation infrastructure improvements, in return for receiving a business opportunity or other benefit from the public agency. *See* U.S. DEP'T OF TRANSP. FED. HIGHWAY ADMIN. INNOVATIVE PROGRAM DELIVERY FAQS, *available at* http://www.fhwa.dot.gov/ipd/p3/faqs/index.htm#10 (last visited July 24, 2011).

67. *Id.*

68. Michael E. Pikiel, Jr. & Lillian Plata, *A Survey of PPP Legislation Across the United States*, 1 GLOBAL INFRASTRUCTURE 52 (2008), *available at* http://www.ncppp.org/resources/State%20PPP%20Legislation%20Survey_2008.pdf (citing 31 states and two territories as having some form of PPP authorizing legislation) (last visited Feb. 3, 2012).

69. Leslie Sluger & Stephanie Satterfield, *How Do You Like Your Infrastructure: Public or Private?*, SOC'Y FOR MARKETING PROFS. FOUND. (2010), *available at* http://ncppp.org/resources/papers/How_Do_You_Like_Your_Infrastructure.pdf (last visited Feb. 3, 2012).

70. These concerns and requisite safeguards are similar to cooperative purchasing, discussed in Chapter 7.

71. *See* U.S. Dep't of Transp. Fed. Highway Admin. Public-Private Partnerships, *available at* http://www.fhwa.dot.gov/ipd/p3/index.htm (last visited Feb. 3, 2012).

72. 2007 MC PIP, p. ii.

73. The Nat'l Council for Public-Private Partnerships, http://www.ncppp.org/index.shtml (last visited July 24, 2011).
74. Brooks Act, 40 U.S.C. § 1101 (The Brooks Act 2010).
75. The types of contracts typically covered by this law include program management, construction management, feasibility studies, preliminary engineering, design engineering, surveying, mapping, or architectural-related services. Some jurisdictions may use QBS to procure professional services, such as services provided by lawyers, accountants, etc.
76. Ariz. Rev. Stat. Ann. § 34-603 (2011).
77. Colo. Rev. Stat. §§ 24-30-1401 to -1408 (2010).
78. Nev. Rev. Stat. § 625.530 (2010).
79. Utah Code Ann. §§ 63G-6-701 to -705 (LexisNexis 2011).
80. Mich. Comp. Laws § 18.1237(b) (2011).
81. Wyo. Stat. Ann. § 9-2-1031 (2011).
82. 2007 MC PIP, § 5-104, commentary.
83. See supra note 13 and accompanying text.
84. 40 Cal. 4th 1016 [155 P.3d 226, 56 Cal. Rptr. 3d 814 (Cal. 2007)].
85. Id. at 1026–232.
86. Id. at 1031–235.
87. Id.
88. See 2007 MC PIP § 3-101, comment (5).
89. See id.; see also § 5-101(1).
90. Timothy D. Hovet, Allowing the Design/Build Project Delivery Method in the Procurement of Public Construction Contracts, Cascade Policy Inst., available at http://cascadepolicy.org/bgc/build.htm (last visited July 24, 2011).
91. Id. (citing Kevin J. Potter & Victor Sanvido, Design/Build Prequalification System, 10 J. of Mgmt. in Engineering 48 (March/April 1994).
92. Id.
93. 2007 MC PIP § 5-102(5).
94. See id., cmt.
95. See Dr. John B. Miller, Life-Cycle Delivery of Public Infrastructure: Precedents and Opportunities for the Commonwealth, 44 Pioneer Institute White Paper 1 (Dec. 2008), available at http://www.pioneerinstitute.org/pdf/wp44.pdf (last visited July 24, 2011).
96. Id. at 2.
97. Id.
98. See 2007 MC PIP, § 5-102(3), commentary.
99. See id. §§ 5-102(3) and 3-101(a)-(g).
100. See Design-Build-Operate-Maintain.
101. See supra note 60.
102. Id.
103. See supra notes 60 and 66.
104. 2007 MC PIP § 5-102(5).
105. See The Nat'l Council for Pub.-Private P'ships, Types of Public-Private Partnerships, available at http://www.ncppp.org/howpart/ppptypes.shtml (last

visited June 12, 2011) (citing U.S. Gov't Accountability Office, GAO/GGD-99-71, *Public-Private Partnerships: Terms Related to Building and Facility Partnerships* (April 1999), *available at* http://www.gao.gov/archive/1999/gg99071.pdf (last visited July 24, 2011)).

106.   *Id.*
107.   *Id.*
108.   *Id.*
109.   A shadow toll is when the government pays the private sector a toll directly, rather than from the actual driver. This shadow toll is often based upon the number of vehicles that use the road.
110.   *See supra* notes 64 and 105.
111.   *Id.*
112.   The Nat'l Council for Pub.-Private P'ships, *Types of Public-Private Parnerships*, *available at* http://www.ncppp.org/howpart/ppptypes.shtml (last visited June 12, 2011).
113.   *Id.*
114.   2007 MC PIP § 5-102(6).
115.   *See supra* note 60.

6

Contractors' Obligations and Requirements

State and local governments are in the best position to exercise oversight early in the procurement process by requiring procuring agencies to render affirmative declarations of responsibility before awarding contracts. When procuring agencies take the duty to assess responsibility seriously, they promote integrity in their respective procurement systems and signal to the contractor community that they will be treated fairly and impartially during contract formation as well, throughout all phases of the procurement process.

Contractor Responsibility

Without exception, in all state and local government procurements, an agency, prior to award, must make a determination that a bidder or offeror is qualified to serve as a contractor. A qualified contractor is one who is deemed responsible by the procuring agency. Procuring officers are vested with significant business judgment when rendering responsibility determinations.[1] Even with such broad discretion, procuring agencies base responsibility determinations on two factors: ability to perform (can the contractor perform the work);

and tenacity, perseverance, and integrity (does the contractor have the will to perform). Agencies rely on responsibility determinations to avoid awarding contracts to unqualified contractors. Responsibility determinations are not meant to penalize contractors; instead, these determinations protect the agency and taxpayers from undue risks associated with contractor nonperformance. For example, the 2007 MC PIP, section 3-301, Comment 1 provides,

> To obtain true economy, the [agency] must minimize the possibility of a subsequent default by the contractor, late deliveries, or other unsatisfactory performance [that] would result in additional administrative costs.

A procuring officer awards a contract to a responsible bidder (competitive sealed bidding) or a responsible source (competitive sealed proposal). Thus, the procuring officer has a duty to render two types of determinations: an affirmative determination of responsibility and a negative determination of nonresponsibility. Generally, the responsibility of a contractor is determined at the time of award as opposed to at the time a contractor submits a bid or proposal, but innovations in responsibility determinations are changing this approach, as is discussed in the section *Prequalification of Contractors*.

Ability to Perform

Several general standards are used for measuring a contractor's ability to perform. One standard is the degree of financial resources such as the ratio of assets to liabilities, working capital, and credit ratings. Another standard is a contractor's history of compliance with delivery schedules. For example, when a significant number of current contracts are delinquent, a nonresponsibility determination is reasonable. A third standard is facilities and equipment. Under this standard, a nonresponsibility determination is reasonable, for example, when a contractor does not have a plant in the United States or Europe, the two locations for performance of a contract. But the contractor may demonstrate responsibility by submitting acceptable evidence of the ability to obtain the required facilities or equipment.

Another standard used to measure a contractor's ability to perform is management and technical capability. The procuring officer must evaluate the contractor's present organization. The experience requirements in the solicitation must be the minimum needs of the government. The last standard, the ability to obtain licenses and permits or to pay taxes, is discussed in the section *Tax Clearances, Licenses, and Permits.*

Willingness to Perform

There are two general standards for measuring a contractor's will to perform. The first is tenacity and perseverance. The contractor must demonstrate that it has the will to complete the required work on time and satisfactorily. State agencies look to past performance on private and public contracts to assess a contractor's willingness to perform. A poor performance record yields a presumption that the contractor's current performance will be poor and unsatisfactory. The procuring officer must inquire about the reason for poor past performance. Poor past performance must be related to serious deficiencies, current information, and current or recent contracts.

Integrity, the second general standard in this area, says that contractors must be honest, upright, and free from criminal involvement or affiliations. The concern with evaluating integrity is the need for due process because a negative evaluation in this category could infringe upon a constitutional protection of a liberty interest.

Special Responsibility Determinations

There are also special standards that are used for measuring the responsibility of a contractor. Procuring officers have the discretion to more specifically define the responsibility criteria. The specific or special standards are called definitive responsibility criteria (DRC). Special standards may be desirable when experience demonstrates that unusual expertise or specialized facilities are required for adequate contract performance.

Imposing special standards limits competition. Therefore, DRC should be limited to matters deemed necessary to satisfy the minimum needs of state agencies and should be thoughtfully constructed. DRC must be specific, objective, and mandatory. If the DRC are not required, the agency can be deemed to have unduly restricted competition. The most typical DRC are experience with certain types of work. For example, a contractor must have a certain number of years of experience with marble restoration for the repair of headstones at a national cemetery.

Collateral Responsibility Requirements

Contractors who appear otherwise responsible may be deemed nonresponsible for failure to meet collateral requirements of contracting with state and local agencies. Some of the collateral requirements include the requirement that contractors have affirmative action plans or a detailed small business subcontracting plan, and a prohibition against contractors who are employees of the state or local government. The contractor has until the time for award to prepare and submit evidence to confirm responsibility as to collateral matters.

Subcontractor Responsibility

Generally, the prime contractor is required to determine the responsibility of its subcontractors. The procuring officer may be called upon to evaluate the responsibility of a prime contractor's proposed subcontractors. In some instances, the responsibility of the subcontractor may form the basis of the responsibility of the prime contractor.

Responsibility Determination Procedures

Most states require that an affirmative responsibility determination be made before awarding a contract. The agency must obtain sufficient information to be satisfied that the contractor meets all applicable responsibility standards. The agency should consider the following information: past performance; suspension and disbarment; records and work experience data; pre-award survey reports and the contractor's replies to questionnaires contained in the solicitation; financial data; personnel information; and equipment information. Consistent with this best practice, the 2007 MC PIP, section 3-301, comment 2 provides.

> The extent to which a review or investigation [into non-responsibility] should be conducted will depend on the value and size of the procurement and the bidder's or offeror's past record of contract performance in the public and private sectors.

Prequalification of Contractors

State and local governments have sought to improve the quality of their contractor pools over the past decade by instituting more rigorous screening of prospective vendors.[2] Prequalification serves a gatekeeping function that disqualifies companies with histories of violating workplace laws and other important regulatory protections. Those state and local governments that have implemented prequalification or responsible bidder programs have found that such programs result in higher quality and more reliable services; increased competition among responsible contractors; reduced project delays and cost overruns; reduced monitoring, compliance, and litigation costs; and stronger incentives for compliance.

Best practices incorporate a front-end prescreening process before selection of a winning bid—a more reliable approach than a responsibility review conducted only for the lowest cost or presumed winning bidder. The prescreening should involve a review of offerors' compliance and financial records and proof of insurance and licensing. Prequalification of contractors can restrict competition; in an effort to achieve due process, agencies should provide clear criteria on what constitutes disqualifying nonresponsible behavior so that procuring officers have adequate guidance in evaluating potential bidders and offerors. The 2007 MC PIP, section 3–302 provides,

> Prospective suppliers may be prequalified for particular types of supplies, services, and construction. The method of submitting prequalification information and the information required in order to be prequalified shall be determined by the [Chief Procurement Officer].

Prequalification does not ensure a determination of responsibility when contract award is being contemplated, as prequalified contractors can later be rejected as nonresponsible. The objective, however, with prequalification or prescreening is to build efficiency into the formation process by reducing the risk of wasted administrative resources that could be incurred if responsibility determination was left until the time of contract award.

California's Department of Industrial Relations has developed a model prequalification questionnaire that is used by several state agencies for public works contracts. The questionnaire inquires into prospective bidders' past legal violations, histories of suspensions and debarments, past contract performance, and financial history. The department provides agencies with a model scoring system for evaluating a firm's answers to these questions and recommends a minimum passing score. Firms that pass then become eligible to bid on public works projects.[3]

Indiana offers a good illustration of a comprehensively applied prequalification requirement. According to Indiana Code section 8–23–10, all bidders must be prequalified before they may submit a bid. Generally, this prequalification requires an application verified by the contractor. Unqualified bidders' bids must be disqualified or rejected, even if not discovered until after bids are opened.[4] Part of prequalification is the requirement for bidders or offerors to provide financial statements that demonstrate sufficient assets to execute contracts and meet obligations.[5] Indiana's prequalification requirements extend to subcontractors engaged in subcontracts valued at over $300,000.[6]

The State of Ohio has prequalification requirements for both nonconstruction and construction projects. For example, Ohio Rev. Code Ann. section 5525.02 requires prequalification of bidders for road and highway projects. In the process of prequalification, the department of transportation may consider equipment, past records, experience, personnel, and other matters deemed necessary to a determination of a bidder's qualifications.[7] As well, bidders must possess sufficient assets or working capital to assure satisfactory completion of the contract.[8] Furthermore, successful contract awardees may not enter into subcontracts with nonqualified companies.[9]

Bonding, Insurance, and Guarantees

The purpose of bonding, insurance, and guarantee requirements is to appropriately manage contractual risk. State and local governments are routinely exposed to risk because of the very nature of their required contracting functions. Recognizing the risks associated with numerous contract actions and addressing them properly are the reasons for establishing bonding, insurance, and guarantee requirements that transfer risk from state and local governments to contractors.

Bonding

Many state legislatures have enacted statutes regarding the form of conditions and provisions for bonds that contractors should follow when submitting bids or offers. The purpose of bonds is to manage risk incurred by state and local governments as a result of contractor failure to execute contracts, deliver performance, or pay subcontractors or suppliers.[10] Most bonding requirements are associated with construction contracts or infrastructure facilities contracts. Generally, there are three categories of bonds: bid security payments or bonds, performance bonds, and payment bonds.

Bid Security Payments or Bonds

Bid security, which is provided either in the form of cash or by a bond, secures the contractor's promise to enter into the contract after award has been made. The purpose of the bid security is to protect state and local government interests. In the case of public works projects, it protects the public interest and permits public entities to gain the benefits of competitive bidding while discouraging gamesmanship by bidders.[11]

In Arizona, bid security is required for all construction procured under sections 41-2533 and 41-2578 of the Arizona Revised Statutes.[12] Bid security requirements typically allow the bidder the choice of posting a bid bond, certified check, or cashier's check. The bid security amount is ten percent of the amount of the bid.

In New Jersey, bid security is determined on the basis of the discretion of the agency director. Specifically, section 17:12-2.4 of the New Jersey Administrative Code[13] provides that the director of the DPP may require bid security when appropriate, based upon a review of market conditions and an evaluation of potential risk to the state. Bid security, if required, must consist of one of the following: a certified or cashier's check drawn to the order of "Treasurer, State of New Jersey," an individual or annual bid bond issued by an insurance or security company authorized to do business in the State of New Jersey, or an irrevocable letter of credit issued by a federally insured financial institution and naming "Treasurer, State of New Jersey" as beneficiary. A bidder's failure to submit the required bid security with its proposal is a cause for automatic rejection.

A successful bidder who fails or refuses to execute a contract when the contract is awarded by the public agency forfeits its bid security payment or bond. For example, in Ohio, if the bidder fails to execute the contract and the public owner awards the contract to the next lowest bidder, the former bidder and its surety are liable. Liability is the lesser of the contracting authority's increased cost or a ten percent penalty.[14] If the contracting authority re-advertises the bid, then liability is a ten percent penalty or the costs associated with re-soliciting the procurement, whichever is less.[15]

Performance Bonds

The performance bond guarantees the faithful performance of the contract by the contractor in accordance with the plans, specifications, and conditions of the contract. Generally, agencies have the discretion to determine that performance security is warranted for a particular contract and, if so, to set the amount of security necessary to protect state and local government interests. In New Jersey, for example, a requirement to provide performance security can be satisfied by the same formal mechanisms as those used for bid security.[16] Some state and local governments require that the performance bond amount equal 100 percent of the price specified in the contract.[17] Other states require similar bond amounts only when the cost of a project will exceed a certain amount.[18] A contractor's failure to submit the required performance security is sufficient cause for the agency to cancel the contract and assess the contractor for any costs incurred by the state.[19]

Payment Bonds

Payment bonds shift the risk of payment to contractors and their sureties while also providing a means to secure the claims of laborers, mechanics, or material suppliers employed on the work under contract. Similar to the thresholds for performance bonds, payment bonds are typically executed and furnished in an amount equal to 100 percent of the price specified in the contract for the protection of all persons supplying labor or materials to the contractor or its subcontractors.[20] Some states will only require a payment bond if the estimated cost of a project exceeds a certain threshold.[21]

Bond Withdrawal

In some jurisdictions, contractors may withdraw construction contract bid bonds without penalty under certain circumstances. In the case of substantial and unintentional error, contractors may withdraw bids.[22] This rule applies only to good faith bids that are significantly lower than the other bids. The contractor's error must have been caused by a substantial arithmetic error or an unintentional omission of a substantial quantity of work, labor, or material in the compilation of the bid. Contractors may not withdraw bids if withdrawal would result in an award to the same bidder on a different bid or if the error was based on poor judgment.[23]

Insurance

State and local governments face the risk of their contractors being insolvent, underinsured, uninsured, or otherwise unable to pay claims. Therefore, many state and local governments require all contractors, with certain limited exceptions, to maintain reasonable insurance coverage and provide written proof of this protection. Written proof consists of certificates of insurance and endorsements to policies.

Specific coverage and limits required will vary depending on the nature of the contract. The insurance required in the contract varies, depending on the nature of the work being performed. The question often arises of whether or not professional liability coverage (errors and omissions) should be required when drafting a service agreement. The general rule is if special intellectual ability (rather than physical activity) is required to perform the contracted services, then professional errors and omissions coverage is required.

In the case of professional liability insurance, it is usually not possible or desirable for the state to be an additional insured on the policy, nor will the policy cover liability assumed in a contract. However, commercial general liability and automobile liability coverage should be required in most contracts involving professional services and, when appropriate, the terms should include a requirement for the state to be named an additional insured under the commercial general liability coverage.

Guarantees

Bid guarantees are pledges of security normally issued by commercial institutions, whereas insurance companies issue bid bonds. Thus, bid guarantees can cover security backed by letters of credit or equity lines established at banking institutions. The difference for the contractor is that risk of liability for losses charged against the guarantee cannot be spread out over other holders of lines of credit.

Bid guarantees can be used in place of bonds when goods or nonprofessional services over a certain dollar threshold are desired.

Bid guarantees must be conditioned on the execution of a contract conforming to the invitation to bid. In Ohio, when the bid guarantee is a check or letter of credit, the winning bidder must submit performance and payment bonds for the amount of the contract.[24]

Tax Clearances, Licenses, and Permits

Some state and local governments may condition a responsibility determination on a contractor's ability to obtain tax clearances, licenses, and/or permits. The purpose for imposing a tax-clearing requirement is to be able to collect tax debts from contractors who are paid for goods or services delivered to the state. As such, a tax clearance requirement imposed against vendors and contracts would allow state departments and agencies to "garnish" contract payments to satisfy overdue tax liabilities.

Along the same lines of protecting state interests, licensing and permit requirements are risk avoidance measures. In *Martinez v. Goddard*,[25] the district court upheld an Arizona licensing scheme that sought to "protect the public from unscrupulous, unqualified, and financially irresponsible contractors."[26] The district court found that the scheme's requirements were constitutional in that it required contractors to meet numerous qualifications, including a written examination, relevant experience, posting a bond based on business volume, submitting a detailed financial statement, demonstrating good character, and paying an application/renewal fee each year.[27]

Conclusion

Responsibility determinations and prequalification serve a preventative function by avoiding bid awards to unqualified contractors. Bonding and insurance requirements minimize the risk of contract breaches. Tax clearances protect the public against unscrupulous contractors. And licenses and permits assure the public that a contractor is operating at an acceptable threshold of competency. Where state and local governments have implemented one or all of these mechanisms, their goal is to protect the public purse and guard the public trust through oversight during the formation phase of public contracting.

Notes

1. *See generally* Ind. Code § 4-13.6-6-2 (2011) ("the division shall award the contract to the lowest responsible and responsive" bidder); *see also* Bowen Engineering Corp. v. W.P.M. Inc., 557 N.E.2d 1358, 1364–66 (Ind. Ct. App. 1990) (award to the lowest responsible and responsive bidder gives the division "wide discretion." "[A] reviewing court must not substitute its judgment for that of the awarding body, but will reverse only when the challenged determination is clearly arbitrary, illegal, corrupt or fraudulent." "In the determination of whether a bidder is 'responsible,' the awarding body may properly consider a variety of factors, such as: ability and capacity, capital, character and reputation, competency and efficiency, energy, experience, facilities, faithfulness, fraud or unfairness in previous dealings, honesty, judgment, promptness, quality of previous work, and suitability to the particular task." "[T]he determination of 'responsibleness' is to be made *independently* for each bidder. The Board may not make comparisons of bidders to determine responsibleness. Responsibleness is a minimal requirement of bidders, not a competitive standard among bidders. A bidder can be unresponsive only if the awarding body would not award the contract to the bidder *even if* that bidder had submitted the sole bid." (emphasis in original)).
2. *See* David Madland, Karla Walter, Paul K. Sonn, & Tsedeye Gebreselassie, *Contracting that Works: A Toolkit for State and Local Government*, Ctr. for Am. Progress Action Fund (Mar. 2010), http://www.americanprogressaction.org/issues/2010/03/pdf/contracting_that_works.pdf (last visited Oct. 8, 2011).
3. *Id.*
4. Ind. Code § 8-23-10-6 (2011).
5. *Id.* § 8-23-10-3.
6. *Id.* § 8-23-10-4.
7. Ohio Rev. Code Ann. § 5525.05 (LexisNexis 2011).
8. *Id.* § 5525.04.
9. *Id.* § 5525.06.
10. *See* Edward Etcheverry, Rights and Liabilities of Sureties in Florida Construction Law and Practice Ch. 8 (2006), stating,

> Federal, state, and local government agencies, as well as an increasing number of private project owners, require general contractors to obtain surety bonds before they commence work on construction projects. Additionally, to shift risk, general contractors may require their

subcontractors to obtain surety bonds. There are three types of surety bonds used on construction projects: (1) bid bonds, (2) payment bonds, and (3) performance bonds. The bid bond surety guarantees that the bidder has submitted its bid in good faith and, if awarded the contract, will execute the contract at the bid price and provide the required payment and performance bonds. The payment bond surety guarantees that the principal will pay certain subcontractors, suppliers, and materialmen associated with the project. The performance bond surety guarantees that the principal will complete the work required under the bonded contract (internal citations omitted).

11. *See* STEVEN J. FOWLER, CONSTRUCTION LAW AND CONTRACTING IN MILLER AND STARR CALIFORNIA REAL ESTATE Ch. 27 (3d ed. 2010) (citing Palo & Dodini v. City of Oakland, 79 Cal. App. 2d 739, 750, 180 P.2d 764, 769 (1947) and A & A Electric, Inc. v. City of King, 54 Cal. App. 3d 457, 126 Cal. Rptr. 585 (1976)).

12. ARIZ. REV. STAT. ANN. §§ 41-2533, 2578 (2011).

13. N.J. ADMIN. CODE § 17:12-2.4 (2011) (Bid Security).

14. OHIO REV. CODE ANN. § 153.54(D) (Lexis 2011).

15. *Id.* § 153.54(E); *see also* City of Crockett v. Murdock, 440 S.W.2d 864 (Tex. Civ. App. 1969) (forfeiture of $1,500 cashier check upheld where contractor complaining of but failing to prove that material changes in the contract submitted for his signature were materially different than what had been agreed to. The city had required a cashier's check or a certified check as "bid security" in the amount of not less than five percent of the contract).

16. N.J. ADMIN. CODE § 17:12-2.4 (2011) (Bid security).

17. *See* ARIZ. REV. STAT. § 41-2574 (2011).

18. *See* IND. CODE § 4-13.6-7-7(a) (2011) (entitled "Performance Bonds." The section states, "If the estimated cost of the project is at least $200,000, the division shall require a performance bond equal to 100% of the total contract price.").

19. N.J. ADMIN. CODE § 17:12-2.5 (2011) (Performance security).

20. ARIZ. REV. STAT. § 41- 2574 (2011).

21. *See* IND. CODE § 4-13.6-7-6(a) (2011) (if the estimated cost of the project is more than $200,000, the division shall require a payment bond equal to 100 percent of the total contract price).

22. For a more detailed discussion of withdrawal of bids, refer to *Revocation of Offers* in Chapter 5.

23. *See* OHIO REV. CODE ANN. §§ 9.31, 153.54(B) (LexisNexis 2011).

24. *Id.* §§ 153.54(B)(2), 153.54(C)(1).

25. 521 F. Supp. 2d 1002 (D. Ariz. 2007).

26. *Id.* at 1008–09 (citing Aesthetic Property Maintenance Inc. v. Capitol Indemnity Corp., 900 P.2d 1210, 1213 (Ariz. 1995)).

27. *Id.* at 1009.

7

Special Policies and Provisions

State and local governments can address special policies through the use of their purchasing power. Special policies can include a government's willingness to implement procurement mechanisms that promote efficiency and uniformity over competition, such as implementing or instituting cooperative purchasing programs. Special policies might also encompass implementing collateral policies that achieve social, economic, and political goals and objectives within state borders, such as establishing rules for geographic preference or set-asides based on race, gender, or veteran status. With all of these examples, it is clear that state and local governments are making trade-offs between fundamental principles of competition and transparency on the one hand and special policies on the other. There will always be arguments for and against special policies, but it is vital to know what special policies and provisions are and how they impact state and local procurement. This chapter addresses special policies, which include those that promote efficiency and accountability as well as collateral policies that often target wealth redistribution by implementing legislation, such as buy American legislation.

Geographic Preferences

Most states have geographic preference laws that are implemented in several ways (see the chapter appendix). These geographic preference laws, in whatever type or form, place restrictions on the evaluation of bids or offers. A geographical preference provides an advantage (usually implemented by providing for a percentage on price preference) to in-state or local bidders over out-of-state bidders.[1] States will protect their processes from preemption by only imposing geographic preferences when they do not offend federal law. Geographic preferences can take the form of (1) a percentage preference for in-state or local bidders as compared to out-of-state or nonresident bidders; (2) a tie-bid preference in which a local bidder receives a specific advantage over a nonresident bidder when the bids are essentially equal; (3) an absolute preference for products or services within a designated geographical area; or (4) a reciprocal preference to residents who hail from a state that does not impose preference laws. Proponents of these policies suggest that state funds are prevented from leaving state boundaries, which means that state taxpayer dollars are spent within state borders.

Minnesota provides a general geographic preference that mirrors the restriction in other jurisdictions. Its geographic preference requires that the "acquisition of goods and services must be awarded according to the provisions of this chapter except that a resident vendor shall be allowed a preference over a nonresident vendor from a state that gives or requires a preference to vendors from that state. The preference shall be equal to the preference given or required by the state of the nonresident vendor."[2] In other words, if another state imposes a percentage preference on out-of-state bids or offers, then Minnesota will exact the same imposition on nonresident bids or offers submitted within its jurisdiction. However, Minnesota's geographic preference is limited in that it does not apply to procurements where federal funds are expended.

Michigan offers an example of a tie-bid geographic preference that advantages in-state bidders. Section 261(1) requires preference to be given to products manufactured or services offered by

Michigan-based firms if all other things are equal and if not inconsistent with federal statute.[3]

Mississippi provides two types of geographic preferences. The first is similar to that of Minnesota in that a nonresident bidder domiciled in a state having laws granting preference to local contractors shall be awarded Mississippi public contracts only on the same basis as the nonresident bidder's state awards contracts. Several Attorney General Opinions have addressed this particular statute. In 2007, the City of Pass Christian received bids for a construction project, and the lowest apparent bidder was a nonresident contractor. The next lowest bidder was a Mississippi contractor. The foreign state statute favors resident bidders under similar circumstances. The City inquired if it would be required to reject the bid of the foreign bidder if the nonresident contractor fails to include a copy of the foreign statute regarding preference of bidders with his bid package as required by § 31-3-21. The Attorney General opined that the failure to provide a copy prior to the time of award should result in rejection of the bid, as it is not in compliance with the statutory requirement and such requirement is not waivable.[4]

In another Mississippi case, *Billy E. Burnett, Inc. v. Pontotoc County Board of Supervisors*,[5] the Pontotoc County Board of Supervisors solicited and received four bids for a contract for the exterior repair and renovation of the Pontotoc County courthouse. The low bidder for the contract, with a bid of $914,000, was a nonresident contractor domiciled in Alabama. A resident contractor submitted the second-lowest bid at $936,000. The board awarded the contract to the resident on the basis that it submitted the best, though not the lowest, bid. First, the board stated its belief that the two bids were "substantially equal," and that under Mississippi Code 1972 Annotated section 31-7-47, the resident should be given preference over the nonresident.[6] The order also stated that the board had directed the project architect to contact references for both contractors, that responses from the nonresident's references were "mixed," and that the mixture of the responses evaluating the nonresident contractor's work "was mediocre."[7] The order also stated that resident had previously been awarded public construction contracts in Pontotoc County, and that its reputation for construction work was excellent.[8]

The board further found that resident was likely to take "great pride" in its work because its owners and many of its workers lived in Pontotoc County.[9]

The State Court of Appeals affirmed the circuit court's and the board's award to the resident. The court noted that the circuit court's ruling was not based solely upon its determination that the resident was entitled to a preference pursuant to section 31-3-21.[10] The circuit court found an independent basis for the award to the resident, namely, that the board rightly considered the relative experience and reputation of the two firms, and made the award to the resident after taking these factors into consideration.

The second geographic preference under Mississippi law provides for absolute preferences for products and services in a designated area. This particular provision requires a preference for purchases of commodities grown, processed, or manufactured within Mississippi.[11] Hawai'i's procurement code contains similar local preferences.[12] The general definition for local Hawai'i products is "products that are mined, excavated, produced, manufactured, raised, or grown in the state . . . where the cost of the Hawai'i input towards the product exceeds fifty per cent of the total cost of the product . . ."[13] Goods are then divided into three categories based on the percent of Hawai'i materials in the product. In category one, the value of the input constitutes 25 percent or more, but less than 50 percent, of the manufactured cost; category two is between 50 and 75 percent; and category three is 75 percent or more.[14]

The local preference applies to competitive sealed bidding and competitive sealed proposals.[15] The purchasing agency reviews the specifications and creates a list of Hawai'i products that meet the minimum specification and selling price of the jobsite and do not exceed the lowest delivered price of a similar non-Hawai'i product by three percent for class one products, five percent for class two products, or ten percent for class three products.[16] The Hawai'i products list is included with solicitations, and prospective contractors use this list to designate the individual products in their bids or proposals that qualify as Hawai'i products.[17] If a contractor's bid or proposal contains Hawai'i and non-Hawai'i products, the price of the former will be reduced by three, five, or ten percent, depending on the category of the good. This reduction is only for valuation of the offer, not for payment of the contract.[18]

In addition to general products, Hawai'i has local preferences for software development[19] and printing, binding, and stationary work.[20] A Hawai'i "software development business" is defined as "any person, agency, corporation, or other business entity with its principal place of business or ancillary headquarters located in the State and that proposes to obtain eighty per cent of the labor for software development from persons domiciled in Hawai'i."[21] Local printing, binding, and stationary work requires that "all work will be performed in-state, including all preparatory work, presswork, bindery work," and "any other production-related work, to include storage and shipping costs, shall receive a fifteen per cent preference for purposes of bid evaluation."[22] The primary case on local preferences is *Southern Food Group, L.P. v. Department of Education*,[23] in which the Supreme Court of Hawai'i upheld the disqualification of a bidder who submitted two bids, one with Hawai'i products and one with non-Hawai'i products, as nonresponsive.[24]

State Adoption of the Buy American Act

State and local government procurement is significant to both domestic and global markets. Among the 50 states, 6 territories, and 87,525 local governments comprising the United States,[25] state and local procurement spending may be roughly valued at approximately $1.5 trillion[26] annually for the purchase of goods, supplies, equipment, services, and construction. The unprecedented growth of U.S. state and local procurement markets can be attributed largely to the federal government's policies shifting program responsibility more and more to the states, a trend that seems to be accelerating rather than stabilizing. The upward trend in procurement spending by state and local governments has major implications for international trade as well as for domestic economic development.

State and local "buy American" legislation and policies, until recently, have had an ameliorative impact on local markets, especially during times of economic downturn. The basic principle of the buy American preference requires state and local government to purchase goods and services domestically. Proponents of domestic preference policies argue that directing government expenditures to American produced materials is a major macroeconomic instrument that boosts the domestic economy.[27]

Some opponents, however, view state- and local-level domestic preferences as the principal barrier to international trade as well as domestic economic development. Generally, buy American policies and laws restrict or prohibit nondomestic sales to state and local governments. Imposing domestic buying preferences arguably invokes the regulatory power of state and local governments. As such, domestic preference provisions invite constitutional challenges, especially in the context of international trade. Beyond the complex constitutional questions raised by buy American preferences, a discussion of which is outside the scope of this book, even the most well-intended domestic policies may harm the same segment of society that the preference was intended to benefit when the greatest opportunity for growth exists outside state and local borders.[28]

Various state and local governments have incorporated the federal Buy American Act into state laws, the latter often referred to as Little or State Buy American Acts.[29] Buy American statutes and provisions at the state level may prohibit purchasing foreign products, but most states only either partially restrict such purchases or provide for percentage differential preferences in favor of a supplier of American-made goods and equipment. For example, Oklahoma requires all state agencies and governmental bodies and all individuals making purchases on their behalf to purchase goods and equipment manufactured or produced in the United States.[30] This law, however, is subject to exceptions. These exceptions exempt application of the state's buy American provision when a foreign-made product is cheaper and of equal quality, the foreign-made product is of substantially superior quality to the American products and is comparably priced, or a reciprocal trade agreement or treaty has been negotiated by the State of Oklahoma or by the U.S. government to further nondiscriminatory governmental procurement practices or policies with a foreign nation or government.[31] The state has the discretion to give a two and one-half percent differential preference to the cost of goods and equipment manufactured or produced in the United States that are not of inferior quality over foreign-made products.[32]

The Attorney General of Oklahoma has opined that the Oklahoma Buy American Act is valid and legal and its use in the state's purchasing program falls within state law.[33] The opinion recognizes the applicability of the Act to those purchases where the foreign product is not substantially cheaper or is not substantially superior in quality at a competitive price to American-made products.[34] In applying the preference law, the Attorney General opined that the Oklahoma Buy American Act would not justify the State Board of Public Affairs granting a preference to a domestic producer whose bid was ten percent higher than a supplier who submitted a bid for a foreign product identical in quality.[35]

Socioeconomic or Collateral Policies

State and local government procurement and the policies related to it are vital to achieving economic, social, and political goals and objectives within state borders. These economic, social, and political objectives are often referred to as collateral policies. State and local governments are fervent about addressing collateral policies through use of their purchasing powers. Various methods, including preferences, set-asides, and mandatory purchasing programs, implement state and local collateral policies.

There are myriad preferences found in state and local government procurement, as discussed previously in this chapter. In addition to geographic and buy American preferences, state and local governments have socioeconomic policies that are implemented through set-aside programs and mandatory purchase programs.[36]

State and local governments are unique in that they implement collateral policies consistent with social and economic objectives found within their respective borders. Collateral policies advance important and unique social and economic goals pursued by state and local governments that view their role in the procurement process as true market actors (as opposed to acting as a monopsonist).[37]

Many of the social and economic goals relevant to state and local governments result because of the uniquely American experience. In this regard, state and local governments use their purchasing power to correct past injustices visited upon certain groups within state borders. Collateral policies are not meant to impose harmful discrimination against contractors; instead they are meant to remedy harms visited upon identifiable segments of society.[38]

No doubt tension results from implementing collateral policies through the acquisition process that can conflict with the primary policy objective of achieving full and open competition. Specifically, proponents of collateral policies urge that aiding the various categories of small businesses reduces unemployment, pollution, and energy loss while also broadening the base of government suppliers, which ultimately increases competition on state and local government contracts. Opponents of collateral policies argue that aiding the various categories of small businesses increases prices by excluding competitors; increases administrative costs; increases the potential for contractor defaults; sours relations with potential contractors; and slows the formation phase of the procurement process.

Despite these tensions, state and local governments are committed to balancing competition with collateral policies.[39] For example, Connecticut enacted a supplier diversity statute that requires the head of each state agency to set aside in each fiscal year contracts or portions of contracts for the construction, reconstruction, or rehabilitation of public buildings, the construction and maintenance of highways, and the purchase of goods and services. These contracts are set aside for small contractors, minority business enterprises, nonprofit organizations, and individuals with disabilities, on the basis of competitive bidding procedures.[40] In lieu of setting aside prime contracts for small business competition, the head of any state agency may require general or trade contractors to set aside portions of any contract for subcontractors who are eligible for set-aside contracts. In support of its supplier diversity statute, the Connecticut legislature found and determined that there is a serious need and a public necessity and interest to help small contractors, minority business enterprises, nonprofit organizations, and individuals with disabilities to be considered for and awarded state contracts.[41]

Collateral policies in Arizona are governed by statute.[42] According to Arizona law, any procurement that does not exceed the aggregate dollar amount of less than $50,000 shall be restricted, if practicable, to small businesses as defined in rules adopted by the director. The procurement officer shall rotate the small business solicited to compete for any procurement of less than $50,000. If it is impracticable to restrict a particular procurement to small businesses, the procurement officer shall provide a written determination setting forth the reasons for not setting aside the procurement for small business participation.

Similarly, the State of New Jersey established a set-aside program to assist small business owners. The goal of this program is to award approximately 25 percent of state contracts and purchase order dollars to registered small businesses.[43]

Intellectual Property

There is little uniformity with regard to state approaches to intellectual property rights, and few states have articulated specific standard terms and conditions on this matter. Further, only a handful of states have addressed the issue of rights in preexisting intellectual property used during performance of the contract, as would be used under a "limited rights" or "restricted rights" license. Among these states are Georgia, Idaho, Illinois, and Ohio. By contrast, some states such as Kentucky and Montana have confiscatory approaches to intellectual property rights by which the state claims the right to use and disclose all data contained in proposals it receives.[44]

While Georgia uses standard terms and conditions that do not specifically address intellectual property rights, the State Vendor Manual includes a noteworthy "State Property" provision that states,

> All tools, dies, jigs, patterns, equipment, plates, cuts, negatives, artwork, or other items purchased, furnished, charged to or paid for by the State and produced in conjunction with or in order to fulfill any state contract, and any replacement thereof, shall

become and remain the property of the State. The contractor
shall hold such property for the benefit of the State, and upon
the State's written request deliver the property to the State.[45]

The Georgia Technology Authority (GTA) has issued its Procurement Rules containing further detail. In a provision on confidentiality, the manual states that the offeror may designate documents or
records as proprietary or trade secret, "however this may not prevent
disclosure under the Georgia Open Records Act (O.C.G.A. 50-18-
70 *et seq.*)"[46] The manual further maintains that only documents or
records that meet the criteria under the Act can be kept from disclosure by the GTA pursuant to an Open Records Request.[47] To ensure
the integrity of the public purchasing process, this same rule also
grants state agencies considerable discretion to "maintain the confidentiality of trade secrets, and other procurement materials, and
like information as the CIO or his designee or the agency's executive
officer or his designee may determine necessary."[48]

The Idaho state contracting statutes are silent with regard to
intellectual property rights, the state's Division of Purchasing contains
"Special Terms and Conditions for Customized Software and Related
Services" under which, unless specifically provided otherwise, the
state "shall own and retain all rights to hardware and other goods purchased by the State under the Agreement and to information, materials, procedures, processes and data developed, derived, documented,
stored, or furnished by the Contractor under the Agreement."[49]

The Idaho Vendor's Guide also contains a "public records" policy by which "all records of purchase and of the Division of Purchasing are open and accessible to the public" pursuant to the Idaho Public
Records Act. If an offeror believes that its proposal contains a trade
secret, it should mark each relevant portion of its proposal accordingly
and submit a statement articulating the reasons for nondisclosure.[50]

Information Technology

Most states have specific statutory language addressing information technology (IT) in government contracts, and several states

have created separate departments that work exclusively with IT. While the definitions of what constitutes information technology vary from state to state, the general definition tends to cover a wide range of technologies. For example, Florida defines IT as "equipment, hardware, software, firmware, programs, systems, networks, infrastructure, media, and related material used to automatically, electronically, and wirelessly collect, receive, access, transmit, display, store, record, retrieve, analyze, evaluate, process, classify, manipulate, manage, assimilate, control, communicate, exchange, convert, converge, interface, switch, or disseminate information of any kind or form."[51] Further, several states have clear definitions of an "information technology policy." Florida statute contains the following definition:

> "Information technology policy" means statements that describe clear choices for how information technology will deliver effective and efficient government services to residents and improve state agency operations. A policy may relate to investments, business applications, architecture, or infrastructure. A policy describes its rationale, implications of compliance or noncompliance, the timeline for implementation, metrics for determining compliance, and the accountable structure responsible for its implementation.[52]

Maryland has a more concise definition of what constitutes IT, stating, "'Information technology' means all electronic information processing hardware and software, including: (1) maintenance; (2) telecommunications; and (3) associated consulting services."[53] Maryland has an additional classification for "major" technology development projects. To qualify as a major information technology project, the project must fulfill one of three criteria: (1) its estimated total cost of development must equal or exceed $1,000,000; (2) it must support a critical business function associated with public health, education, safety, or the financial well-being of the citizens of the state;[54] or (3) the Secretary can determine that the project requires special attention.[55]

Maryland has also adopted a streamlined procurement process specifically for information technology services. This process includes

(1) the categories of information technology services in which an offeror may submit a proposal for qualification;

(2) a procedure for the consideration and approval of proposals for qualification of an unlimited number of offerors in each category of information technology services;

(3) the execution of a standard contract for a specified period of time between the State and an offeror approved for qualification in a category of information technology services;

(4) the policies and procedures to be followed by a unit of the Executive Branch in the issuance of a solicitation for a task order for information technology services to a qualified offeror that has executed a contract with the Secretary; and

(5) a performance evaluation procedure to be used by a unit of the Executive Branch to evaluate the performance of a qualified offeror that has completed work on a task order.[56]

California also has a procurement process for information technology. The state has devised a six-step process, requiring the state to

Identify the legislative mandate, state business, or operational reason for the information technology procurement. Identify the existing business processes currently used to accomplish the legislative mandate, state business, or operational reason. Identify the most important priorities for the information technology project to accomplish. Identify what current technology is being used and how it is being used. If the data used in a proposed information technology system comes from multiple sources, identify the existing business processes or technical systems that produce and maintain the source data to ensure interoperability. Identify how the new information technology project leverages existing technology investments while accomplishing its business objectives.[57]

State Labor Standards

There are various fair labor standards laws applicable to public contracts. The most common of these laws relate to prevailing wages, labor, health, and worker's compensation. For example, Nebraska requires all contractors bidding on public works to file a statement that they comply with fair labor standards. Every contract for public works must also contain a specific provision that "in the execution of such contract fair labor standards shall be maintained."[58] These fair labor standards are defined as "such a scale of wages and conditions of employment as are paid and maintained by at least fifty percent of the contractors in the same business or field of endeavor as the contractor filing such statement."[59]

Similarly, Virginia requires that contractors meet a variety of employer requirements. Specifically, all contractors must have workman's compensation insurance.[60] Also, every public contract must have a written provision declaring that "the contractor does not, and shall not during the performance of the contract for goods and services in the Commonwealth, knowingly employ an unauthorized alien as defined in the federal Immigration Reform and Control Act of 1986."[61] As well, for contracts over $10,000, a contractor must provide a drug-free workplace for its employees.[62] While treatment of all fair labor standards laws is beyond the scope of this book, labor standards for prevailing wages for construction, services, and suppliers of materials are addressed.

Little Davis-Bacon Acts (Prevailing Wages on Construction Projects)

The Davis–Bacon Act, at both the federal and state levels, is designed to prohibit wage exploitation in public construction contracts by preventing the undercutting of local standards. Kansas was the first state to adopt a prevailing wage law, in 1891, followed by New York, Oklahoma, Idaho, Massachusetts, and New Jersey. The first and most significant of the federal laws establishing the prevailing wage rule was the 1931 Davis-Bacon Act, which requires payment of wages "prevailing" in a local area to workers on federally financed construction projects worth at least $2,000.[63]

Under Davis-Bacon, the prevailing rate is the rate paid to at least 50 percent of workers in a construction occupation for a local area. If there is no single rate for at least 50 percent of workers in that occupation, then the prevailing wage is the average rate paid in the area for that occupation.[64] States, counties, and cities have adopted their own prevailing wage legislation, and policies vary widely. Prevailing wages in states and localities might be set as the local union wage rate, the average wage for construction occupations in the area, or a combination of the two. Thirty-two states and the District of Columbia currently have prevailing wage laws. Nine states, including Florida and Alabama, had laws but repealed them.[65]

Most states refer to their prevailing wage law as "little Davis-Bacon Acts." For example, Arkansas has adopted this designation and places responsibility for its enforcement in the state's Labor Standards Division. Arkansas law requires the division to issue a wage determination for each public works project where the cost of all labor and materials exceeds $75,000.[66] There are exemptions from the requirement, including public school construction and maintenance work performed by or on behalf of the public body.[67]

The wage determinations issued by the division establish the minimum wages for laborers and mechanics employed on public works projects, thus assuring fairer bidding among contractors, fair wages for skilled craftsmen, and quality construction for the public. Annual wage surveys are conducted in order to keep these determinations current. These surveys conducted by the Labor Standards Division determine the hourly prevailing wage rates paid to building and construction tradesmen performing work on public works projects within the state.[68]

Service Contract Wage Determinations

The federal McNamara-O'Hara Service Contract Act requires contractors and subcontractors performing services on prime contracts with federal agencies and the District of Columbia in excess of $2,500 to pay service employees in various classes no less than the wage rates and fringe benefits found prevailing in the locality or the rates (including prospective increases) contained in a predecessor contractor's collective bargaining agreement. The Department of Labor issues wage determinations on a contract-by-contract basis in response to specific requests from contracting agencies. These determinations are incorporated into the contract. For contracts equal to or less than $2,500, contractors are required to pay the federal minimum wage as provided in Section 6(a)(1) of the Fair Labor Standards Act. For prime contracts in excess of $100,000, under the provisions of the Contract Work Hours and Safety Standards Act, as amended, contractors and subcontractors must also pay laborers and mechanics, including guards and watchmen, at least one and one-half times their regular rate of pay for all hours worked over 40 in a workweek. The overtime provisions of the Fair Labor Standards Act may also apply to SCA-covered contracts.[69]

States set minimum wage rate requirements by statute. Federal minimum wage law supersedes state minimum wage law where the federal minimum wage is greater than the state minimum wage. In those states where the state minimum wage is greater than the federal minimum wage, the state minimum wage prevails. Arkansas, Georgia, Minnesota, and Wyoming have a minimum wage set lower than the federal minimum wage. There are 18 states (plus Washington, D.C.) with minimum wage rates set higher than the federal minimum wage. There are 23 states that have a minimum wage requirement that is the same as the federal minimum wage requirement. Alabama, Louisiana, Mississippi, South Carolina, and Tennessee do not have an established minimum wage requirement.[70]

The living wage law in Maryland, for example, requires contractors and subcontractors to pay a living wage to employees performing work on certain state service contracts in excess of $100,000.[71] Maryland's Commission of Labor and Industry administers and enforces the living wage law. The living wage law defines the employer as a contractor who has a state contract for services valued at $500,000 or more or a contractor who employs more than ten employees and has a state contract for services valued at greater than $100,000 but less than $500,000.[72]

Wage Determinations for Suppliers of Materials

The federal Walsh–Healey Public Contracts Act (PCA) requires contractors engaged in the manufacturing or furnishing of materials, supplies, articles, or equipment to the U.S. government or the District of Columbia to pay employees who produce, assemble, handle, or ship goods under contracts exceeding $10,000 the federal minimum wage for all hours worked and time and one-half their regular rate of pay for all hours worked, over 40 in a workweek.[73] The PCA covers employees who produce, assemble, handle, or ship goods under these contracts. The PCA does not apply to executive, administrative, and professional employees, or to outside salespersons exempt from the minimum wage and overtime provisions of the Fair Labor Standards Act, nor does it apply to certain office and custodial workers.

State and local laws regulating wages and hours of work may also apply to employment subject to the PCA. When this happens, the employer must observe the law setting the stricter standard. For example, Maine has a State Purchasing Code of Conduct that requires a bidder to "sign an affidavit affirming, to the best of its knowledge, that suppliers at the point of assembly comply with workplace laws of the vendor's or supplier's site of assembly and with treaty obligations that are shared by the United States and the country in which the goods are assembled."[74] The code also requires that any contracting party must comply with applicable "wage, health, labor, environmental and safety laws, legal guarantees of freedom of association, building and fire codes and laws relating to discrimination in hiring, promotion or compensation on the basis of race, disability, national origin, gender, sexual orientation or affiliation with any political, nongovernmental or civic group except when federal law precludes the State from attaching the procurement conditions."[75]

Cost and Pricing Principles

The overriding objective in support of requiring the use of cost and pricing principles in state and local government procurements is the allocation of risk between governments and their contractors. Using cost and pricing principles assures contractors fair compensation for costs they have incurred while protecting taxpayers from shouldering the burden of excessive costs and wasted funds. Cost or price analysis can be used whenever there is a risk that the contractor's price or the cost to the government may be either unfairly high or unfairly low. Cost analysis is a routine requirement for contracts not awarded based on "adequate price competition;"[76] pricing change orders or modifications; pricing settlement payments in the case of terminations for the convenience of the government; and whenever it is deemed necessary to fairly allocate cost risks. Several states have enacted statutory language as well as regulations adopting these cost principles.[77]

The basic formula used to determine the amount to be paid to a contractor measures the total allowable costs. Depending on the amount claimed by the contractor as total allowable costs, the contractor is required to submit cost and pricing data certified to be accurate, complete, and current. To obtain total allowable costs payable to the contractor, procuring agencies will rely on the following formula:

$$TAC = (\text{allowable direct costs} + \text{allocable portion} \\ \text{of indirect costs}) - \text{credits}$$

Allowable costs are those that the government can reasonably be expected to pay for the contract work. To be deemed allowable, the cost must be appropriate, allocable, lawful, and not unallowable.

An appropriate cost must be the kind of cost that an "ordinarily prudent person" would incur. Some factors that are helpful in this determination include an interpretation of the contract terms; the type of business involved; restraints imposed by sound business practices, arm's-length bargaining, and federal and state rules and laws; general public policies and responsibility of business owners and the state; any deviation from the contractor's established policies that unjustifiably increases costs; and government guidelines, such as travel compensation rules. The bottom line for assessing appropriateness is whether the cost is reasonable in light of all the circumstances.

After assessing that costs are appropriate, a contractor must specifically segregate direct costs and indirect costs. All direct costs are allowable. Direct costs are determined by whether the cost is identified as contributing to the final contract cost objective as opposed to the cost benefiting other work independent of the cost objective.

Allocable indirect costs are those costs that can be distributed in a reasonable proportion to the benefits received by the government. This means that contractors must show a rational percentage of value provided to the governments.

Finally, credits must be deducted from the sum of direct costs and allocable indirect costs. One purpose for contractors being required to submit cost and pricing data certified as accurate, complete, and correct is to ensure disclosure by the contractor of any funds received as a result of contract operations. These funds or credits must be deducted from the costs claimed by the contractor. Credits can come in the form of rebates the contractor received from a materials supplier, discounts on invoice prices received from vendors, or revenues realized from sales of materials not used for the government contract.

State statutes also prohibit claims for certain costs. These are considered unallowable costs. Unallowable costs can include interest expenses, taxes, losses from other contracts, entertainment expenditures, bad debts, depreciation and use allowances, fines and penalties, gifts and donations, and certain contingencies.

State procuring officials may decide to use federal cost principles instead of those found in state statutes and regulations. In such cases, procuring officials should notify contractors in advance in order for contractors to comply with federal cost principles as well as ensure that their cost accounting procedures are in line with federal standards.

Privatization

Generally, privatization in the procurement context encompasses contracting out government services to private sector firms based on the theory that private firms are better able to perform certain services more economically and more efficiently than government personnel providing direct services.[78] States are increasingly exploring the use of private contractors to improve efficiency in the operation of traditional government functions.[79] Accordingly, several state statutes contain specific language regarding privatization contracts, among them Iowa,[80] Kansas,[81] Kentucky,[82] Utah,[83] New Jersey,[84] and Connecticut.[85]

Kentucky's laws, although more specific than most, present a clear picture of the rigorous approval process by which a state agency may enter into a privatization contract. First, the state agency must provide three factors in writing: (1) the necessity for the service and its intended goals; (2) the problems with the existing governmental operation of the service; and (3) a determination of whether the service can efficiently be provided by the agency.[86] If the state agency finds that the service cannot be efficiently provided, they can continue the normal contracting process for the service.[87]

If the service can be efficiently provided by the agency but the agency still chooses to proceed with privatization, it must complete a much more rigorous application to the Finance and Administration Cabinet. The requirements for this process are numerous; the agency must set forth in writing the tangible benefits of privatizing the service, all applicable state and federal restraints that may conflict with privatization, the availability of competitive private vendors, an extensive cost-benefit analysis, and an assistance plan for all state employees who will be adversely affected.[88]

Additionally, Kentucky specifically addresses the privatization of contracts for drinking water projects and wastewater projects.[89] Before entering into a privatization contract, the governing authority must create a notice of its intent pursuant to relevant statutory code regarding legal notices.[90] This notice must include "a brief summary of the privatization contract provisions, and set a time and place for a public hearing to be conducted by the executive authority of the political subdivision."[91]

Though less specific than Kentucky, Utah's rules are designed to increase cooperation between the state agency and the private contractor during the bidding process. Utah's statutes state that the affected department "shall provide each private entity with access to all information, records, documents, and reports related to the proposal and the project that are designated public records under Title 63G, Chapter 2, Government Records Access and Management Act" in order to assist each private entity in preparing its proposal.[92] State statutes further require that the affected department cooperate with each private entity to assist in the development of a proposal that is practical, efficient, and economically beneficial to the state and the affected department.[93]

Kansas also has extensive law surrounding the privatization of contracts. Article 55 of Chapter 12 of the statutory code is dedicated chiefly to the privatization of public services.[94] Though there are eleven sections in Article 55, the first five sections represent the majority of the relevant law and delineate the general terms and processes by which state agencies may privatize government contracts. The first section, 12-5501, lays out the key definitions of the statute.[95] The second section, 12-5502, gives the powers to municipalities to seek a private contractor to perform public services.[96] The third section, 12-5503,[97] sets out the terms for service agreements, terms, service fees, and limitations, while section 12-5504 provides for proposals, public hearings, feasibility analyses, and protest petitions.[98] Finally, the fifth section, 12-5505, allows the municipality to levy taxes, fees, charges, and special assessments in the same manner it would if the municipality had performed the public service itself.[99]

Other areas of the Kansas statutory code also address privatization issues. Section 46, for example, addresses oversight issues, requiring "[t]he oversight committee [to] monitor, review and make recommendations relating to privatization efforts at the state hospitals. . . ."[100] Additionally, Kansas statutes require the committee to provide oversight, review, and make recommendations relating to "(A) privatization of children service programs of the department of social and rehabilitation services including family preservation, foster care and adoption programs, (B) privatization of child support collection programs and any other programs of the department of social and rehabilitation services, and (C) privatization of any programs of the department on aging."[101]

Finally, Kansas statutes contain specific guidelines for privatization of contracts in the area of corrections and juvenile justice. The statutes empower the committee to draw from a master plan that addresses "private expansion with specific recommendations on criteria to guide the determination of any program appropriate for privatization, to assist in determining the placement of any such facility and to guide in the selection of any private provider."[102]

There are several opinions by the state's Attorney General (AG) that are relevant to privatization. In one opinion, the AG held that because the power of a state agency to contract with private industry must be conferred by statute, the Employment Security Systems Institute "lack[ed] authority to contract with and provide training to persons in private industry in data processing and related areas."[103] Conversely, in an opinion regarding a correctional facility, the AG held that there was "no statutory or constitutional impediment which would prevent a city, county or the state from contracting with a private entity for the construction or operation of a jail or correctional facility for placement or confinement of persons held pursuant to Kansas law."[104]

More recently, the AG decided that the Military Housing Privatization Initiative, which facilitates the construction of military housing by private developers, does not address the subject of taxation of property leased to participating private parties, thereby precluding possible questions of preemption of taxation.[105] Under Kansas law, taxation is the rule and exemptions are the exception, with the burden of establishing an exemption on the party requesting it.[106] Here, the AG followed the opinion of *Clyde Graeber Donald Navinsky Gerald D. Oroke*, which was issued in 2005. In this opinion, under P.L. 104-106, 110 Sat. 544, Title XXVIII, Subtitle A, section 2801, the Army was considering privatizing approximately 1,583 housing units that were located on a federal enclave situated within the corporate limits of the city of Leavenworth. The AG held that real or personal property owned by a private corporation within the Fort Leavenworth enclave should be valued and taxed at the rates applicable to such property generally.[107]

In some states, there are additional agencies beyond the AG's office that contain relevant material on issues of privatization. In Iowa, for example, the Public Employment Relations Board has issued three decisions concerning issues of privatization. In one case, the United Electrical, Radio and Machine Workers of America filed a complaint against Western Iowa Tech Community College for violating Iowa Code when it terminated custodians after the union rejected modification to the collective bargaining agreement. The Board found the college could have laid off the employees unilaterally, but instead it attempted to negotiate with the union to save money and jobs. Consequently, the Board concluded that after the union rejected the college's furlough offer, the college was free to terminate the custodians and sub-contract out the work.[108] Significantly, the Board was careful to distinguish its decision from a similar case where the central issue was the lack of research into the relative cost of privatization. In this case, the Board articulated that "meaningful" studies are necessary in collective bargaining agreements to avoid the appearance of union animus.[109] The other two decisions also continued to address these same issues of how privatization can be used or viewed as being a retaliative budget-cut measure, and thus how "meaningful" studies into cost-saving measures are necessary to avoid union animus.[110]

Grants and Cooperative Agreements

Grants and cooperative agreements are funds-out mechanisms in which the government pays funds for research and seeks, when practicable, cost-sharing agreements with grantees.[111] Because grants and cooperative agreements are not procurement instruments, they typically cannot be used to acquire goods and services for the direct benefit of the government.[112] However, if the government's primary purpose is to provide technical assistance, or provide assistance relationships for a public good, then grants or cooperative agreements may be available to the state or its agencies. Grants are used when government involvement in an activity conducted for a public purpose is less than substantial. Cooperative agreements are used when the government intends to be substantially involved in a project.[113]

Ohio code has two notable areas that contain specific provisions for cooperative agreements. Under one provision, the state must adhere to the terms and conditions of any federal grant or cooperative agreement when accepting federal funds for roads, highways, and bridges.[114] In another statutory provision, the state adjutant general may enter into cooperative agreements with any agency or department of the United States, but the general must abide by the terms and conditions of the agreement and expend any federal funding in accordance with relevant laws.[115]

Other states have statutes that are considerably more vague with regards to cooperative agreements. Oklahoma, for example, addresses cooperative agreements peripherally as opposed to addressing them in a single chapter. Oklahoma law states that for mines, mining, mine reclamation, and small operator assistance programs, the department may enter into a cooperative agreement with the Secretary of the Interior.[116] Other statutes state that, in the area of water and water rights, the board may accept funds by grant, contract, "or other cooperative means."[117] Additionally, in the School Code of 1971, statutes hold that "grants, contracts, and cooperative agreements" can be a source of funding for teachers' salaries.[118]

By contrast, some states specifically forbid cooperative agreements in certain areas. Missouri, for example, prohibits such agreements for construction projects, stating that "the state, any agency of the state, or any instrumentality thereof shall not issue grants or enter into cooperative agreements for construction projects, a condition of which requires that bid specifications, project agreements, or other controlling documents pertaining to the grant or cooperative agreement contain any of the elements specified in section 34.209."[119] The statute further holds that the state, or any state agency, must exercise its authority in order to preclude "a grant recipient or party to a cooperative agreement from imposing any of the elements specified in section 34.209 in connection with any grant or cooperative agreement awarded or entered into."[120]

Cooperative agreements have found their way into case law across the country. In Ohio, the Court of Appeals held that under a cooperative agreement with the Ohio Water Development Authority, a local water district had an unqualified obligation to repay funds borrowed to investigate a water project.[121] Further, the court found that the district could be compelled to impose new special assessment measures on property owners to repay funds.[122]

In a North Dakota case, the state supreme court found that cooperative agreements between the state Department of Transportation and the city did not vest sufficient control in the city to support a plaintiff's claim that the city was liable for failing to establish a pedestrian crossway near a state highway.[123] Here, a major factor the court considered was that the cooperative agreement expressly reserved to the Department the right to approve traffic signals, signs, markings, and all control measures necessary to establish crosswalks.[124]

In addition to cases, there are also several Attorney General opinions on cooperative agreements. In Oregon, the AG held that the Department of Human Resources (DHR) was contractually required to pay participating counties the full amount agreed to under a cooperative agreement.[125] The DHR, therefore, did not have the authority to decrease the amount paid under a cooperative agreement.[126] In another opinion, the Attorney General held that the Department of Fish and Wildlife was eligible to enter into an agreement for the management of estuarine sanctuaries, and that such an agreement was not incompatible with the criteria of Coastal Zone Management Act of 1972.[127]

Ohio's Attorney General, by contrast, held that members of a regional council could not lawfully enter into a cooperative agreement under which their respective police departments participated in joint activities throughout the entire territory encompassed by the council.[128] In another opinion, the AG held that a city and county could enter into a cooperative agreement concerning repairs on a bridge on a road within the municipal limit, whereby the city authorized the county to perform repairs on behalf of the city, and the city agreed to reimburse the county for a portion of the cost.[129]

Cooperative Purchasing

According to the American Bar Association's 2000 MPC and 2007 MC PIP, "cooperative purchasing" is the sharing of procurement contracts between governments or, more precisely, procurement conducted by or on behalf of one or more units. Cooperative purchasing generally occurs when two or more governmental units have a common need for the same type of commodity. Common items for cooperative purchasing include office supplies, furniture, copiers, laboratory supplies, and fleet vehicles.

An overwhelming majority of states have statutes regarding intergovernmental relations or joint powers agreements that address cooperative purchasing by public agencies or governmental units.[130] Generally, these statutes authorize public entities to participate in, sponsor, conduct, or administer a cooperative purchasing agreement. The establishment of these programs allows for joint purchasing actions between qualified agencies and organizations within the state or by other states pursuant to reciprocal interstate agreements. Cooperative purchasing is a collaborative effort to obtain benefits in pricing, product quality, and contract process efficiencies for public purchasing entities. A central requirement for cooperative purchasing is that it be conducted pursuant to contracts awarded through full and open competition.

The National Association of State Procurement Officials recognizes three types of cooperative purchasing: true cooperatives, piggyback contracts, and third-party aggregators. In a true cooperative, two or more governmental units pool their resources and work together to develop specifications for commodity items that meet their needs. Under piggybacking arrangements, a governmental unit may make use of a commodities contract negotiated by another governmental unit. In using third-party aggregators, several governmental units join together to procure commodities using their buying power to obtain the best prices.

Broadly drafted cooperative purchasing statutes provide authorization for states to engage in partnerships to share contracts and pricing.[131] For example, the Illinois intergovernmental cooperation statute states,

> Any power or powers, privileges, functions, or authority exercised or which may be exercised by a public agency of this State may be exercised, combined, transferred, and enjoyed jointly with any other public agency of this State and jointly with any public agency of any other state or of the United States to the extent that laws of such other state or of the United States do not prohibit joint exercise or enjoyment and except where specifically and expressly prohibited by law.[132]

Similarly, the Delaware statute entitled Authorization for cooperative purchasing states, "[t]he Division may, with written approval of the Secretary, participate in, sponsor, conduct or administer a cooperative purchasing agreement for the procurement of materiel or non-professional services with 1 or more public procurement units either within the State or with another state in accordance with an agreement entered into between the participants."[133]

Other state statutes are more comprehensive and provide specific requirements for establishing intra- or interstate cooperative procurement procedures. For example, Oregon authorizes interstate cooperative procurement if

> (a) the administering contracting agency's solicitation and award process for the original contract is an open and impartial competitive process and uses source selection methods substantially equivalent to competitive sealed bidding and competitive sealed proposals; (b) the administering contracting agency's solicitation and the original contract allows other governmental bodies to establish contracts or price agreements under the terms, conditions and prices of the original contract; and (c) the administering contracting agency permits the contractor to extend the use of the terms, conditions and prices of the original contract to the purchasing contracting agency.[134]

In addition to these competition, contract, and price requirements, the Oregon interstate cooperative procurement statute requires the contracting agency or the procurement group to provide specific public notice of the proposed cooperative action as well as an opportunity for prospective bidders or offerors to comment on the action.

State Purchasing under U.S. General Services Administration Supply Schedules

Two major federal regulations, the Federal Acquisition Regulation (FAR) and the General Services Administration (GSA) Acquisition Manual (GSAM), determine policy for the GSA Schedules program. The Schedules program provides eligible federal agencies and state and local government entities with a simplified process for obtaining services and supplies. A Schedule is a listing of companies that supply comparable commercial services and supplies through contracts awarded by GSA.

Schedule contracts are indefinite delivery/indefinite quantity (IDIQ) contracts awarded to responsible companies that offer commercial services or supplies at fair and reasonable prices for a fixed period of time. Under the GSA Schedules program, GSA establishes long-term government-wide multiple award schedule (MAS) contracts with commercial firms to provide access to millions of commercial supplies (products) and services at volume discount pricing. After GSA awards the contracts, ordering activities order from Schedule contractors, and deliveries are made directly to the customer. These can be ordered directly from GSA Schedule contractors or through the GSA Advantage!®[135] online shopping and ordering system. Each GSA Schedule is segmented into Special Item Numbers (SINs). The tens of thousands of supplies and services offered through GSA Schedules are all associated with a Schedule and SIN. Multiple companies are awarded contracts for every Schedule and SIN.

Multiple authorized programs allow state and local governments the eligibility to use GSA Schedules for select purchases.[136] These programs include the Cooperative Purchasing Program; the Disaster Recovery Purchasing Program; the Public Health Emergency Program; and the Section 1122 Program.

Under the Cooperative Purchasing Program, state and local government entities may purchase a variety of IT products, software, and services from contracts awarded under GSA Federal Supply Schedule 70, Information Technology, as well as from contracts under the Consolidated Schedule containing IT SINs.

Under the Disaster Recovery Purchasing Program, state and local government entities may purchase a variety of products and services from contracts awarded under GSA Federal Supply Schedules to facilitate recovery from a major disaster, terrorism, or nuclear, biological, chemical, or radiological attack. This Disaster Recovery Purchasing authority is limited to GSA Schedule contracts and does not include any other GSA programs.

When a Public Health Emergency (PHE) is declared, state, local, tribal, and territorial governments can use Federal Supply Schedules. These eligible ordering entities are authorized to access all Federal Supply Schedules for the purchase of supplies and services when expending federal grant funds in response to PHEs declared by the Secretary of Health and Human Services.[137] Access to the Federal Supply Schedules under this program is limited to state, local, tribal, and territorial governments receiving grant funds in direct response to a PHE. When purchasing from Schedules, state, local, tribal, and territorial governments should follow ordering and competitive procedures that meet their own procurement regulations and any requirements stipulated in the grant funding.

Section 1122 of the fiscal year 1994 National Defense Authorization Act established the authority for states and units of local government to purchase law enforcement equipment through federal procurement channels. This authority is limited and requires that such equipment be used in the performance of counter-drug activities.

State Supply Schedules

In addition to GSA Supply Schedules, states also have their own supply schedules made possible by negotiation and award of MAS contracts. Similar to GSA MAS contracts, state MAS contracts are procurement vehicles offered by states to simplify purchasing for state agencies, university systems, local governments, municipalities, school districts, and other public entities. State MAS contracts are based on existing commodity or service contracts, such as the GSA's Federal Supply Schedule. The majority of state MAS contracts are created from already existing GSA contracts.[138] Generally, states use GSA MAS pricing but then incorporate state terms and conditions with suppliers.[139] California,[140] Texas,[141] Ohio,[142] and Louisiana[143] have state supply schedules that incorporate GSA schedule pricing.

Conclusion

State and local government procurement has become quite complex and dynamic. Acquisition innovations coupled with state and local government collateral policy objectives have transformed what was once plain old garden-variety purchasing. Now state and local governments are using their purchasing power to build and sustain industries within their respective borders by implementing some or all of the special and collateral policies discussed within this chapter. Accordingly, it is vital to have a working knowledge of these policies and provisions as well as a general understanding as to why state and local governments will promote these policies over and above fundamental principles of competition and transparency.

Appendix

Reciprocal Preference Information

State	Reciprocal Law/Statute	Tie-Bid Preference	Reciprocal Preference	Date of Verification
Alabama (AL)	Yes	Yes	Yes	October 2011
Alaska (AK)	Yes	No	Yes	September 2011
Arizona (AZ)	No	Yes	Yes	September 2011
Arkansas (AR)	No	No	Yes	December 2011
California (CA)	No	Yes	Yes	October 2011
Colorado (CO)	Yes	Yes	Yes	October 2011
Connecticut (CT)	Yes	Yes	Yes	September 2011
Delaware (DE)	No	No	Yes	November 2011
Florida (FL)	Yes	Yes	Yes	December 2011
Georgia (GA)	Yes	Yes	Yes	December 2011
Hawai'i (HA)	Yes	Yes	Yes	October 2011
Idaho (ID)	Yes	Yes	Yes	September 2011
Illinois (IL)	Yes	Yes	Yes	May 2002
Indiana (IN)	Yes	No	Yes	October 2011
Iowa (IA)	Yes	No	Yes	December 2011
Kansas (KS)	No	Yes	None	October 2011
Kentucky (KY)	No	Yes	Yes	December 2010
Louisiana (LA)	Yes	Yes	Yes	October 2011
Maine (ME)	Yes	Yes	Yes	October 2011
Maryland (MD)	Yes	Yes	Yes	January 2001
Massachusetts (MA)	Yes	Yes	Yes	January 2001
Michigan (MI)	Yes	No	Yes	October 2011
Minnesota (MN)	Yes	No	Yes	September 2011

Note: Content for this appendix was retrieved from State of Oregon, State Procurement Office Reciprocal Preference Information website, http://www.oregon.gov/DAS/SSD/SPO/reciprocal_detail.shtml (last visited Oct. 8, 2011). The information in this appendix provides a relatively current status update of state geographic and reciprocal preferences.

Mississippi (MS)	Yes	Yes	None	October 2011
Missouri (MO)	Yes	Yes	Yes	October 2011
Montana (MT)	Yes	Yes	Yes	December 2011
Nebraska (NE)	Yes	Yes	Yes	December 2010
Nevada (NV)	Yes	Yes	Yes	December 2011
New Hampshire (NH)	No	No	None	December 2011
New Jersey (NJ)	Yes	No	Yes	December 2011
New Mexico (NM)	No	Yes	Yes	May 2002
New York (NY)	Yes	Yes	Yes	November 2011
North Carolina (NC)	Yes	Yes	Yes	November 2011
North Dakota (ND)	Yes	Yes	Yes	August 2011
Ohio (OH)	Yes	No	Yes	December 2011
Oklahoma (OK)	Yes	No	None	September 2011
Oregon (OR)	Yes	Yes	Yes	December 2011
Pennsylvania (PA)	Yes	Yes	Yes	September 2011
Rhode Island (RI)	No	No	None	March 2009
South Carolina (SC)	No	Yes	Yes	May 2002
South Dakota (SD)	Yes	Yes	Yes	October 2011
Tennessee (TN)	Yes	Yes	Yes	October 2011
Texas (TX)	Yes	Yes	Yes	September 2011
Utah (UT)	No	Yes	Yes	October 2011
Vermont (VT)	No	Yes	None	December 2011
Virginia (VA)	Yes	Yes	Yes	October 2011
Washington (WA)	Yes	No	Yes	October 2011
Washington, D.C. (District of Columbia)	Yes	No	Yes	December 2011
West Virginia (WV)	Yes	No	Yes	October 2011
Wisconsin (WI)	Yes	No	Yes	December 2011
Wyoming (WY)	No	Yes	Yes	October 2011

Notes

1. GLEN CUMMINGS, ROBERT E. LLOYD, YUHUA QIAO, & KHI V. THAI, STATE AND LOCAL PROCUREMENT PREFERENCES: A SURVEY (on file with the author), *available at* http://unpcdc.org/media/5268/us%20local%20procurement.pdf (last visited Feb. 3, 2012).
2. MINN. STAT. § 16C.06 (2010).
3. *See* MICH. COMP. LAWS § 18.1261 (2011).
4. *See Non-resident Bidder Preference*, Miss. Op. Att'y Gen. No. 2007-00452 (2007), 2007 WL 3356834 (citing *Contractor Certificates of Responsibility*, Miss. Op. Att'y Gen. No. 2001-0480 (2001), 2001 WL 1082606; *Zebert*, Miss. Op. Att'y Gen. (1989), 1989 WL 504451; *Walls*, Miss. Op. Att'y Gen. (1989), 1989 WL 504439).
5. 940 So. 2d 241 (Miss. Ct. App. 2006).
6. *Id.* at 242.
7. *Id.*
8. *Id.*
9. *Id.*
10. *Id.* at 245.
11. *See* MISS. CODE ANN. § 31-7-15 (2011).
12. HAW. REV. STAT. §§ 103D-1001 to -1004, -1006 (2010).
13. *Id.* § 103D-1001.
14. *Id.*
15. *Id.* § 103D-1001.5.
16. *Id.* § 103D-1002(a)(1)–(3)(A–C).
17. *Id.* § 103D-1002(c).
18. *Id.* § 103D-1002(d).
19. *Id.* § 103D-1006.
20. *Id.* § 103D-1003.
21. *Id.* § 103D-1001(2).
22. *Id.* § 103D-1003(a).
23. 974 P.2d 1033 (Haw. 1999).
24. *Id.* at 1047.
25. *See* CLIFFORD P. MCCUE ET AL., THE FRAUD/RED-TAPE DILEMMA IN PUBLIC SECTOR PURCHASING (2003), *available at* http://www.unpcdc.org/media/5316/us%20fraudred%20tape%20dilemma.pdf (last visited Oct. 8, 2011).
26. "[I]n some countries, public sector expenditure may comprise 30% to 50% of gross national product (GNP). . . . So far, governments have been able to decide for themselves how this money is to be spent, the system of procuring goods and services, and the tendering, scrutiny of applications and award of projects, subject of course to each country's laws and procedures." Martin Khor, *Government Procurement in FTAs: An Examination of the Issues*, 182/183 THIRD WORLD RESURGENCE (2005), *available at* http://www.twnside.org.sg/title2/resurgence/182-183/Cover05.doc. *See also* MCCUE ET AL., *supra* note 25

(reporting that state and local governments are spending, conservatively, 25 to 40 percent of every tax dollar on purchased materials and supplies); Matthew Potoski, *State and Local Government Procurement and the Winter Commission*, 68 Pub. Admin. Rev. S58 (2008).

27. *See* Amol Mehra, *Federalism and International Trade: The Intersection of the World Trade Organization's Government Procurement Act and State "Buy Local" Legislation*, 4 BYU Int'l L. & Mgmt. Rev. 179, 195 (2008).

28. *See U.S. Chamber Bemoans "Buy American" Costs*, 52 No. 9 Gov't Contractor ¶ 79 (2010); *see also* Benjamin C. Bair, *The Dormant Commerce Clause and State-Mandated Preference Laws in Public Contracting: Developing A More Substantive Application of the Market Participant Exception*, 93 Mich. L. Rev. 2408 (1995) (discussing the Dormant Commerce Clause in the context of domestic and local preferences); Caroline J. Hasson, *Constitutional Law—State "Buy American" Statute Held a Valid Exercise in Economic Protectionism*, 36 Vill. L. Rev. 905 (1991) (discussing Equal Protection Clause in the context of domestic and local preferences); Barton B. Clark, *Give 'Em Enough Rope: States, Subdivisions and the Market Participant Exception to the Dormant Commerce Clause*, 60 U. Chi. L. Rev. 615 (1993) (discussing the Dormant Commerce, Equal Protection, and Privileges and Immunities Clauses in the context of domestic and local preferences).

29. *See generally* Mo. Rev. Stat. § 34.353 "Missouri State Purchasing and Printing Domestic Procurement Act (Buy American Act)) (2011); N.J. Stat. Ann. § 52:32-1 (New Jersey Buy American Act) (2011); Ohio Rev. Code. Ann. § 125.09 (Ohio Buy American Act) (LexisNexis 2011).

30. *See* Okla. Stat. tit. 61, § 51(A) (2011).

31. *See id.* § 51(A)(1)–(3).

32. *Id.* § 51(B).

33. *See* Okla. Op. Att'y. Gen. No. 72-182 (May 30, 1972).

34. *See id.*

35. *See* Okla. Op. Att'y. Gen. No. 69-314 (Oct. 31, 1969).

36. It is the policy of the government to provide maximum practicable opportunities in its acquisitions to small business, veteran-owned small business, service-disabled veteran-owned small business, Historically Underutilized Business Zone (HUBZone) small business, small disadvantaged business, and women-owned small business concerns. Small business concerns must also have the maximum practicable opportunity to participate as subcontractors in the contracts awarded by any executive agency, consistent with efficient contract performance.

37. *See generally* Jeffrey L. Dunoff, *Linking International Markets and Global Justice*, 107 Mich. L. Rev. 1039 (2009).

38. A detailed discussion of the constitutional issues arising from challenges to race- and gender-conscious preferences is outside the scope of this book, but significant scholarship has been devoted to the topic. *See generally* Danielle Conway-Jones (aka Danielle M. Conway), *Department of Defense Procurement*

Practices After Adarand: What Lies Ahead for the Largest Purchaser of Goods and Services and Its Base of Small Disadvantaged Business Contractors, 39 How. L.J. 391 (1995) (analyzing, among other cases, *Adarand Constructors Inc. v. Pena* and *City of Richmond v. J.A. Croson Co.* in the context of constitutional challenges to race-conscious set-aside programs in public contracting); Ian Ayres, *Narrow Tailoring*, 43 UCLA L. Rev. 1781 (1996) (discussing *City of Richmond v. J.A. Croson Co.* and the holding that remedying past discrimination can constitute a compelling interest); Charles J. Dykhouse, *Life After Adarand: The Future Is Not Clear*, 61 Mo. L. Rev. 970 (1996).

39. *See* Small Business and Government, State Government Certifying Agencies website, http://www.sbagov.org/state_business_opportunities.htm (last visited Oct. 8, 2011) (providing a comprehensive 50 state resource offering links to Small Business and Disadvantaged Business Enterprise Programs).

40. Conn. Gen. Stat. § 4a-60g(b).

41. *Id.*

42. Ariz. Rev. Stat. §§ 41-2535 and 41-2636 (LexisNexis 2011).

43. The eligibility criteria for the small business set-aside program is set forth in N.J. Admin. Code §§ 17:13-2.1 and 17.14-2.1 (2011).

44. Robert K. Huffman and Lynda T. O'Sullivan, *Uncharted Waters: State Contracting Terms and Conditions, Intellectual Property, and the Homeland Security Era*, 33 Pub. Cont. L.J. 163, 176–77 (2003).

45. *See* Dep't of Admin. Servs., Georgia Vendor Manual, *available at* http://www.doas.ga.gov/StateLocal/SPD/Docs_SPD_Official_Announcements/GVM-A1-2010.pdf (last visited Oct. 8, 2011).

46. Ga. Comp. R. & Regs. 665-2-11-.01 (2011).

47. *Id.*

48. *Id.*

49. *See State of Idaho Special Terms and Conditions for Customized Software, available at* http://purchasing.idaho.gov/pdf/terms/special_terms_and_conditions_for_customized_software.pdf (last visited Oct. 8, 2011).

50. Huffman and O'Sullivan, *supra* note 44.

51. Fla. Stat. Ann. § 282.0041(16) (LexisNexis 2011).

52. *Id.* § 282.0041(17).

53. Md. Code Ann., State Fin. & Proc. § 3A-301(d) (LexisNexis 2011).

54. *Id.* § 3A-301(f)(2).

55. *Id.* § 3A-301(f)(3).

56. Md. Code Ann., State Fin. & Proc. § 13-402 (LexisNexis 2011).

57. Cal. Pub. Cont. Code § 12103.5 (Deering 2011).

58. Neb. Rev. Stat. Ann. § 73-102 (LexisNexis 2011).

59. *Id.* § 73-104.

60. Va. Code Ann. § 2.2-4332 (2011).

61. *Id.* § 2.2-4311.1.

62. *Id.* § 2.2-4312.

63. *See* Nooshin Mahalia, *Prevailing Wages and Government Contracting Costs: A Review of the Research, available at* http://www.inthepublicinterest.org/article/

prevailing-wages-and-government-contracting-costs-review-research (last visited Oct. 8, 2011).

64. *See id.*

65. *See* U.S. Dep't of Labor, Wage and Hour Div., *Dollar Threshold Amounts for Contract Coverage,* http://www.dol.gov/whd/state/dollar.htm (last visited Oct. 8, 2011) (reporting states without prevailing wage laws).

66. *See* Ark. Code Ann. § 22-9-301-313, *available at* http://www.arkansas.gov/labor/pdf/prevailing_wage_regs.pdf (last visited Oct. 8, 2011).

67. *See* Ark. Reg. 010.14-200(d)(1)-(6), *available at* http://www.arkansas.gov/labor/pdf/prevailing_wage_regs.pdf (last visited Oct. 8, 2011).

68. *See* Ark. Dep't of Labor, Labor Standards Div., *Prevailing Wage Laws and Regulations,* http://www.state.ar.us/labor//divisions/standards_prevailing_wage.html (last visited Oct. 8, 2011).

69. *See* U.S. Dep't of Labor, Wage & Hour Div., *McNamara-O-Hara Service Contract Act Overview,* http://www.dol.gov/whd/contracts/sca.htm (last visited Oct. 8, 2011).

70. *See* U.S. Dep't of Labor, Wage & Hour Div., *Consolidated State Minimum Wage Update Table,* http://www.dol.gov/whd/minwage/america.htm (last visited Oct. 8, 2011).

71. *See* Md. Dep't of Labor, Licensing & Regulation, *Living Wage for State Service Contracts,* http://www.dllr.state.md.us/labor/prev/livingwage.shtml (last visited Oct. 8, 2011).

72. *See* Md. Code. Ann. State Fin. & Proc. §§ 18-101 and 103 (LexisNexis 2011); *see also* Md. Code Regs. 21.11.10 (2011).

73. *See* 41 U.S.C. §§ 35 *et seq.*; 41 C.F.R. Parts 50-201, 202, 203, and 210; *see also* U.S. Dep't of Labor, *Federal Contracts—Working Conditions: Wages in Supply & Equipment Contracts, available at* http://www.dol.gov/compliance/guide/walshh.htm (last visited Oct. 8, 2011).

74. Me. Rev. Stat. Ann. tit. 5, § 1825-L(1) (2011).

75. *Id.* § 1825-L(2)(A).

76. Adequate price competition is presumed when two or more responsible competitors have participated in the formation phase of a government contract and award was made to the competitor that offered the lowest price.

77. *See* 2000 MPC § 7-101, comment (1); *see also* Md. Code Ann., State Fin. & Proc. § 13-213 (LexisNexis 2011); Ky. Rev. Stat. Ann. § 45A.215 (LexisNexis 2011); and R.I. Gen. Laws § 37-2-44 (2011).

78. *See generally* Jonas Prager, *Contracting-Out: Theory and Policy,* 25 N.Y.U. J. Int'l L. & Pol. 73 (1992). Other forms of privatization not directly falling within the scope of this book are: (1) the sale of public assets to private owners; (2) the cessation of government programs, with private enterprise taking over; and (3) the introduction of private competition in markets that were formerly public monopolies. *See generally* John E. Sanchez and Robert D. Klausner, State and Local Government Employment Liability § 7:5 (2011).

79. *See* Jeremy Barry and McKenna Long & Aldridge LLP, Georgia State and Local Gov't. Contracts § 2:8 (2010).

80. IOWA CODE §73A.1 (2011).

81. KAN. STAT. ANN. §12-5501 (2011).

82. KY. REV. STAT. ANN. §45A.551 (LexisNexis 2011).

83. UTAH CODE ANN. §63M-1-2608 (2011).

84. N.J. REV. STAT. §52:27D-124.3 (2011).

85. CONN. GEN. STAT. §4e-16 (2011).

86. KY. REV. STAT. ANN. §45A.551 (LexisNexis 2011).

87. *Id.* §45A.551(3).

88. *Id.*

89. *Id.* §107.720.

90. *Id.* §424.110 (detailing information on the nature of Kentucky's legal notices).

91. *Id.* at §107.720.

92. UTAH CODE ANN. §63M-1-2608 (2011).

93. *Id.*

94. KAN. STAT. ANN. §12-5501.

95. *Id.*

96. *Id.* §12-5502.

97. *Id.* §12-5503.

98. *Id.* §12-5504.

99. *Id.* §12-5505.

100. *Id.* §46-2701.

101. *Id.* §46-2701(d)(3).

102. *Id.* §46-2802(d)(7).

103. Kan. Op. Att'y Gen. 85-98 (Aug. 7, 1985).

104. Kan. Op. Att'y Gen. 94-27 (Mar. 4, 1994).

105. Kan. Op. Att'y Gen. 2009-1 (Jan. 13, 2009).

106. *Id.* (citing Defenders of the Christian Faith v. Horn, 254 P.2d 830 (1953)).

107. Kan. Op. Att'y Gen. 05-19 (Aug. 8, 2005).

108. United Electrical, Radio and Machine Workers of America, Local 1145, Complainant and Western Iowa Tech Community College, Respondent, 2008 WL 4154299 (IA PERB).

109. *Id.* (citing PPME and Marshall County, 86 PERB 3058 & 3085).

110. *See* 1997 WL 34674884; *see also* 2004 WL 5622821.

111. *See* Danielle Conway-Jones (aka Danielle M. Conway), *Research and Development Deliverables under Government Contracts, Grants, Cooperative Agreements and CRADAs: University Roles, Government Responsibilities and Contractor Rights*, 9 COMP. L. REV. & TECH. L. 181, 198 (2004).

112. *See generally* Nancy O. Dix et al., *Fear and Loathing of Federal Contracting: Are Commercial Companies Really Afraid to Do Business with the Federal Government? Should They Be?*, 33 PUB. CONT. L.J. 5, 7 (2003).

113. *See supra* note 125 at 198–99.

114. OHIO REV. CODE ANN. §5502.22 (LexisNexis 2011).

115. *Id.* §5913.01.

116. OKLA. STAT. ANN. tit. 45, §745.16.1 (2011).

117. Okla. Stat. Ann. tit. 82, § 1087.6 (2011).

118. Okla. Stat. Ann. tit. 70, § 17-108 (2011), *amended by* Teachers' Retirement System, 2011 Okla. Sess. Law Serv. 290 (H.B. 1002) (West 2011).

119. Mo. Rev. Stat. § 34.212 (2011).

120. *Id.*

121. Ohio Water Dev. Auth. v. W. Res. Water Dist., 776 N.E.2d 530 (Ohio Ct. App. 2002).

122. *Id.*

123. Yassin v. Schroeder, 469 N.W.2d 368 (N.D. 1991).

124. *Id.* at 369.

125. Or. Op. Att'y Gen. 7553 (Dec. 15, 1977), 38 Or. Op. Att'y Gen. 1606 (Dec. 15, 1977).

126. *Id.*

127. Or. Op. Att'y Gen. OP-5644 (June 25, 1984).

128. Ohio Op. Att'y Gen. 90-012 (Mar. 14, 1990).

129. Ohio Op. Att'y Gen. 88-039 (June 15, 1988).

130. *See* PEPPM Technology and Bidding Purchasing Program, *State Cooperative Purchasing Statutes, available at* http://www.peppm.org/services/Cooperative_Purchasing_State_Statutes_v03.pdf (last visited Oct. 8, 2011).

131. The 2007 MC PIP § 10-101 provides general model language for cooperative purchasing in connection with procurement of infrastructure facilities.

132. 5 Ill. Comp. Stat. Ann. 220/3 (LexisNexis 2011).

133. Del. Code Ann. tit. 29, § 6933 (2011).

134. Or. Rev. Stat. § 279A.220 (2011).

135. *See* U.S. Gen. Servs. Admin., GSA *Advantage!*® website, https://www.gsaadvantage.gov/advantage/main/start_page.do (last visited Oct. 8, 2011).

136. *See* U.S. Gen. Servs. Admin., State and Local Government Customers website, http://www.gsa.gov/portal/category/100631 (last visited Oct. 8, 2011).

137. *See* Public Health Services Act, 42 U.S.C. § 247d (2010).

138. *See* Tex. Office of State Purchasing, Texas Multiple Award Schedule Contracts PCC X, *available at* http://www.window.state.tx.us/procurement/pub/manual/2-9-1.pdf (last visited Oct. 8, 2011).

139. *See* Cal. Dep't of Gen. Servs., Procurement Div., *California Multiple Award Schedule Program Manual* in State Contracting manual, Vol. 2, Ch. 6, § B, *available at* http://www.documents.dgs.ca.gov/pd/poliproc/PDFCompleteSCMv2/PDFCompleteSCMv2.pdf (last visited Oct. 8, 2011).

140. *See id.*

141. *See supra* note 138.

142. *See* Ohio State Procurement, *State Term Schedules,* http://procure.ohio.gov/proc/contractsSTS.asp (last visited Oct. 8, 2011).

143. *See* State of La. Div. of Admin., Office of State Purchasing & Travel, *Brand Name or LaMAS Contracts,* http://www.doa.louisiana.gov/osp/contracts/lamas/lamas.htm (last visited Oct. 8, 2011).

8

Evaluation and Award

The ability of procuring agency personnel to evaluate bids and proposals is integral to the procurement process. Understanding the
process is also vital to prospective contractors whose offers are being
evaluated. This chapter presents fundamental principles of evaluation
and award processes that are governed by the type of solicitation and
the responsibilities of procuring agency personnel and contractors
during this phase of the procurement process. While certain topics,
such as selecting solicitation methods (Chapter 4), drafting specifications (Chapter 4), and revocation of offers (Chapter 5), have been
discussed previously, this chapter revisits these topics more comprehensively and considers what are the generally accepted practices that
occur at the evaluation and award decision states of the formation
phase of the procurement process.

Evaluation of Bids

Typically, procurement contracts are awarded to the responsible
bidder who submits the lowest responsive bid. Although this process

is ostensibly straightforward, there are numerous factors that agencies consider when evaluating bid price. As a general rule, the type of solicitation selected governs the evaluation and award processes. Typically, for most purchases over a certain amount, most states use an invitation to bid process.

Evaluation of Bid Price

Generally, the evaluation of bid price is the primary—if not only—factor considered in determining a procurement award. However, in practice, the evaluation of the bid price can be more complicated. Also, the evaluation of bid price requires consideration of several inherent factors. Proceeding through this section, note that while bid price in theory should be the only evaluation factor, states tend to require evaluation of other factors that directly affect bid price. These requirements tend to differ in scope and specificity among states. Oregon, for example, considers additional factors that affect bid price, such as "discounts, transportation costs and total costs of ownership or operation of a product over the life of the product."[1] Oregon statutes further state that "the invitation to bid must set forth the evaluation criteria to be used [and] no criteria may be used in a bid evaluation that are not set forth in the invitation to bid or in a qualified products list."[2] Similarly, Kentucky law states that the invitation for bids "shall state that the award shall be made on the basis of the lowest bid price or the lowest evaluated bid price."[3] The statute further articulates that if the lowest evaluated bid price is used, then the invitation must set forth "the objective measurable criteria to be utilized."[4] Like many other states, Kentucky articulates options available to agencies when sealed bidding is deemed inappropriate. For example, competitive negotiation is allowed when "specifications cannot be made sufficiently specific to permit award on the basis of either the lowest bid price or the lowest evaluated bid price, including, but not limited to, contracts for experimental or developmental research work, or highly complex equipment which requires technical discussions, and other nonstandard supplies, services, or construction."[5]

Evaluation of Other Price-Related Factors

Although price is the primary factor considered in procurement contracts, state statutes allow for other price-related factors to be weighed. Notably, many states provide for an "evaluated bid price,"[6] which is defined as "the price of a bid after adjustment in accordance with objective measurable criteria."[7] Like most states, Maryland requires that an invitation for bids include "whether the procurement contract will be awarded based on the lowest bid price or the lowest evaluated bid price."[8]

In Kentucky, an unsuccessful bidder on a state contract sought review of a contract award on the grounds that the relevant statutory procedures were disregarded. There, the court held that the "determination of the best bidder for a government contract involved not only the amount of the bid but also the business judgment, capacity, skill and responsibility of the bidder and the quality of the goods proposed to be provided."[9] The court further articulated "the invitation for bids indicated that the contract award would involve more than merely the highest commission on sales."[10]

In another Kentucky case, a rejected bidder with the lowest bid on a public contract to construct a water tank sued the utility commission for violation of the state's procurement code. The court of appeals held that the "Commission had the right to look beyond the bid price and consider factors such as maintenance and product life."[11] The court further articulated, "Kentucky law has long recognized that a low bidder is not necessarily the best bidder."[12]

In Mississippi, a nonresident contractor appealed a county board's award of a construction contract to a resident contractor. The court of appeals held that the board did not act arbitrarily and capriciously in determining that the resident contractor's bid was the best irrespective of whether the resident contractor was entitled to statutory preference.[13] There, the court held that "it is implicit in [the language of the statutory code] that a governing body cannot be compelled to accept a bid simply because it is the lowest, and that other factors must enter the analysis."[14] The court further articulated that "public authorities may, in making a determination of whether a bid is the lowest and best, take into consideration factors such as the

bidder's honesty and integrity, the bidder's skill and business judgment, the bidder's experience and facilities for carrying out the contract, the bidder's conduct under previous contracts, and the quality
of work previously done by the bidder."[15]

In New Jersey, a bidder for a public contract to supply road maintenance equipment brought an action challenging the county's award
of contract to an alternate bidder. The superior court subsequently
invalidated the alternate bid, rescinded the contract, and ordered the
county to advertise for new bids. The bidder then appealed, claiming
that it should have been awarded the contract as the low bidder. The
superior court held that after the trial court invalidated the county's
public contract with the alternate bidder, the county was required by
the public contracts statute to award the contract to the bidder that
had been designated the lowest responsible, responsive bidder.[16] In a
case with a similar fact pattern, the court held that the failure of the
low bidder to complete a page of the bid form was a material deviation
from the bid solicitation, rendering the bid "unresponsive." There,
the court held that the township's disqualification of the low bidder
did not justify its rejection of all bids, and the township was required
to award the bid to the lowest responsive, responsible bidder.[17]

As is apparent, there is no shortage of case law concerning the
evaluation of bid price and the injection of evaluation requirements
beyond just price. Accordingly, even a responsible bidder offering the
lowest bid will be subject to evaluation on price-related factors, and
such an evaluation will have a significant impact on a decision to
award to that bidder.

Evaluation of Equal Low Bids

When two bidders present equally low bids, state agencies
look to other price-related factors to determine the award. It is not
uncommon, for example, for state law to provide statutory preference
for local contractors. Other states may simply show a preference for
American-made products and services.

South Dakota is a good example illustrating such preferences. State statutes hold that, in the event of equal bids, the purchasing agency shall give preference to "a resident business whose principal place of business is located in the State of South Dakota, if the other equal low bid or proposal was submitted by a resident business whose principal place of business is not located in the State of South Dakota."[18] The law further provides that preference will be given "to a nonresident business offering or utilizing supplies or services found in South Dakota, if the other equal low bid or proposal was submitted by a nonresident business not offering or utilizing supplies or services found in South Dakota."[19]

Utah law provides that "if there [are] two or more equally low preferred bidders, the procurement officer shall comply with the rules adopted by the Procurement Policy Board to determine which bidder should be awarded the contract."[20] Utah law has an interesting corollary, requiring that preference be given to Utah businesses against bidders from any states that have in-state preferences of their own. The statute states that "all public procurement units shall, in all purchase[s] . . . give a reciprocal preference to those bidders . . . in Utah as against those bidders . . . in any state that gives or requires a preference to goods, supplies, equipment, materials, or printing produced, manufactured, mined, grown, or performed in that state."[21]

In addition to having statutory preference for local businesses, Florida law also contains preferences for certain business standards. The law states, "when two or more equal bids, proposals or replies are received, a preference shall be given in the award process to the business that certifies that it has implemented a drug-free workplace program."[22] Additionally, Florida law has provisions for the bids that involve commodities manufactured in the state. The relevant statute reads, "[w]henever two or more competitive sealed bids are received, one or more which relates to commodities manufactured, grown or produced in Florida, and whenever the bids are equal with respect to price, quality and service, the Florida commodities shall be given preference."[23]

Mistakes in Bid

States have clear language articulating the recourses available to contractors and state agencies when a mistake in bid is discovered.[24] Because price is the main factor considered in the competitive bidding process, mistakes in bids present a serious obstacle to the process itself. The statutory and regulatory language regarding such mistakes seeks to balance the interests of the agency and the bidder alleging the mistake, as well as the other bidders. While some of these mistakes can be clerical in nature (discussed in greater detail below), others can be significantly more complicated. Mistakes in bid were previously discussed in *Revocation of Bid* in Chapter 5 as an example of when an agency will allow a bid to be withdrawn. This section specifically discusses the process and standards applicable to these types of mistakes during the evaluation stage of the formation phase of the procurement process.

In Arkansas, statutes broadly allow for corrections in bids so long as correction does not harm the rights of other bidders. The statute states, "correction of patent or provable errors in bids that do not prejudice other bidders or withdrawal of bids may be allowed only to the extent permitted under regulations promulgated by the director and upon written approval of the Attorney General or a designee of such officer."[25] The statute states further, "no award shall be made on the basis of a corrected bid, if the corrected bid exceeds the next lowest bid of a responsible bidder."[26]

Arkansas state regulations further define the broad statutory language found in the state code. These regulations articulate, for example, that the State Procurement Director may waive minor irregularities in the bid if such mistakes "do not affect the material substance of the bids when it is in the state's best interest to do so."[27] Regulations further allow the Procurement Director to request confirmation of a bid if s/he suspects a possible mistake in the bid. If the bidder fails or refuses to clarify their bid in writing within a reasonable time, "any matter contained in its bid shall be rejected."[28] When a bidder claims a mistake in a bid prior to contract award, the bidder may be permitted to withdraw its bid if there is clear and convincing evidence that the mistake was material.[29] If a mistake is made after contract award and the awardee will likely sustain a financial loss by performing the contract, then the bidder may rescind the contract.[30]

Similarly, Colorado holds that bidders who submit flawed bids may still withdraw their bids under most circumstances before an award is issued upon clear and convincing evidence that an error was made. Colorado is indicative of most state statutes, which provide that "withdrawal of inadvertently erroneous bids before the award may be permitted pursuant to the rules if the bidder submits proof of evidentiary value that clearly and convincingly demonstrates that an error was made."[31] The statute further requires that "all decisions to permit the withdrawal of bids based on such bid mistakes shall be supported by a written determination made by the executive director or the head of a purchasing agency."[32]

Colorado regulations further hold that bids may be withdrawn after bid opening but prior to award if certain conditions are met. Included in these are "the bidder provides evidentiary proof that clearly and convincingly demonstrates that a mistake was made in the costs or other material matter provided," or "the mistake is clearly evident on the face of the bid [and] it is found to be (by the Director or head of the purchasing agency) unconscionable not to allow the bid to be withdrawn."[33]

Montana statutes also have provisions allowing for withdrawal or correction of flawed bids. As with other state laws, if the agency permits the correction, then the decision must be supported by a written determination made by the department.[34]

There is abundant case law regarding mistakes made in bids pre- and post-award. In one older Kentucky case, a bidder was offered a contract to build a dormitory but discovered an error of $22,000 in his proposal after the award was made. The court of appeals held that the contract could be cancelled "if it was entered into through the mistake of one of the parties, if the mistake is of the substance of the whole consideration, is not due to culpable negligence, and the parties may be placed [back in status quo]."[35] The court held that the contractor "made an honest mistake in his bid, and it [did not] appear that he was guilty of culpable negligence."[36]

In a Florida case, a state agency appealed the decision of a circuit court granting summary judgment to a successful bidder for reformation of a contract. The District Court of Appeals reversed the lower court's decision, holding that the contractor waived any right to reformation or rescission of the contract when it had knowledge of its own mistake at least ten days before commencement of construction and performed according to the terms of the contract for 21 months instead of seeking to withdraw the bid.[37]

Business Judgment

Generally, there is an assumption that entities contracting with state and local governments will use sound business judgment in executing their contracts. While most states do not have specific statutory language articulating what constitutes business judgment, case law in many states reveals that business judgment is a valid and important consideration in assessing bidder responsibility. For example, business judgment is crucial when assessing, among other concerns, whether or not a bidder should be allowed to correct alleged errors as discussed above.

In Kentucky, the court held that a purchasing commission, in determining who was the "lowest and best bidder" could consider not only the amount of the bid, but also the business judgment, capacity, skill, and responsibility of the bidder.[38] The court held that it was within the duty of the government agency to "take into consideration all other pertinent factors and elements in determining the lowest and best bid."[39] An Attorney General opinion echoed this same holding, stating that the "lowest and best responsible bidder" meant "not only the lowest monetary bid, but . . . that the factors of business judgment, capacity, skill, and responsibility of the bidder must be carefully assessed in awarding the bid."[40]

In a more recent Kentucky case, an unsuccessful bidder on a state contract sought review of the contract award on the ground that the relevant statutory procedures were disregarded for reasons of political patronage. There, the court held that the "determination of the best bidder for a government contract involves not only the amount of the bid but also the business judgment, capacity, skill and responsibility of the bidder and the quality of the goods proposed to be provided."[41]

Business judgment is also relevant and applicable to procuring agencies. In New Jersey, the court found that a county sewer authority was not precluded from using its business judgment in determining whether to accept an alternative bid. There, the court held that the authority "would not be precluded from considering alternative bids or circumscribed with respect to the business judgment involved in determining whether to accept one alternative as against another if the Authority included in its specifications, for comparative purposes only, the particular estimate . . . as to the average rate of inflation or price fluctuation in the Wholesale Price Index of Industrial Commodities [thereby allowing for] each bidder [to be] compared by an objective standard and the lowest bidder [to be] determined."[42] In essence, business judgment in procuring agency is another way of referring to the discretion or deference with respect to executive decision making afforded by the courts to state and local government agencies.

Clerical/Arithmetic Error

Generally, state statutes contain provisions that allow for withdrawal of bids containing clerical or arithmetic errors, provided that such errors were executed in good faith. Some states have more detailed requirements articulating when such bids may be withdrawn without forfeiture of bid security.

Georgia, for example, defines five factors for deciding whether a clerical error has been made and whether such a mistake can be the basis for withdrawal of a bid. First, the error must be documented by clear and convincing written evidence.[43] Next, the error must be clearly shown by objective evidence drawn from inspection of the original bid. Third, the contractor must serve written notice upon the agency that solicited "the work prior to the award of the contract and not later than 48 hours after the opening of bids, excluding Saturdays, Sundays, and legal holidays."[44] Fourth, the bid must have been submitted "in good faith and the mistake was due to a calculation or clerical error, an inadvertent omission, or a typographical error as opposed to an error in judgment."[45] And finally, the withdrawal of the bid must not result in "undue prejudice to the state or other bidders by placing them in a materially worse position than they would have occupied if the bid had never been submitted."[46]

New Mexico also has statutory provisions for withdrawal of bids containing clerical errors after bid opening. The relevant statute states, "[t]he contractor, as a condition to assert a claim of inadvertent clerical error in the listing of a subcontractor, shall, within four working days after the time of the prime bid opening by the using agency, give written notice to the using agency and to both the subcontractor he claims to have listed in error and the subcontractor who had bid to the contractor prior to bid opening."[47] The statute further provides that the state agency can consent to the substitution of the intended contractor if the contractor or subcontractors submits an affidavit within 12 days to the agency showing that an "inadvertent clerical error was in fact made."[48]

North Carolina has similar laws allowing for a contractor to withdraw its bid due to clerical error after the bid opening without forfeiture of its bid security. The state statute holds that such a withdrawal is permissible if "the price bid was based upon a mistake, which constituted a substantial error, provided the bid was submitted in good faith, and the bidder submits credible evidence that the mistake was clerical in nature as opposed to a judgment error, and was actually due to an unintentional and substantial arithmetic error."[49]

In an Idaho Supreme Court case, a highway contractor sued the state transportation department, alleging that it was entitled to the return of its bid bond because it made a clerical mistake in its bid. The court held that a clerical mistake for purposes of a statute allowing relief from a bid bond forfeiture could either be an error in tabulating or transcribing figures, or an error in interpreting a word used in a subcontractor's bid.[50]

In New Hampshire, a low bidder on a highway construction project who alleged a clerical error of $525,000 petitioned for equitable relief prohibiting the Commissioner of the Department of Public Works from requiring it to execute the contract. The court held that the contract could not be reformed to correct the clerical mistake after the bidder chose not to exercise its option to rescind the bid and retain its bid bond.[51] The court further held that the Commissioner did not abuse his discretion in making the award without recognizing and correcting the mistake.[52]

In another case, the city appealed a decision of the circuit court holding that a contractor was entitled to reformation of his bid after opening. There, the court of appeals held that, where the contractor submitted a bid in which there was a clerical error of over $500,000 and the contractor discovered the mistake after the opening of the bids but before acceptance and so notified the city, the contractor was entitled to a rescission of his bid and return of his deposit.[53]

Bid Opening

The procuring agency publishes dates and times for public bid openings. Generally, bidders and the public are invited, but not required, to attend the formal opening of bids. Bidders are not allowed to engage in conduct other than being physically present and taking notes on the bid opening procedures and the reading of bid prices. A bidder may be penalized with rejection, if the agency has provided prior notice of this penalty, if the bidder attempts to qualify or change its price during the bid opening procedure. Typically, prices are read aloud to the public when practical. Generally, decisions related to an award of a contract are not made at the bid opening. State and local laws usually require that bids and procuring agency documents related to the bid opening process be available for inspection during regular business hours.

Notice of Award

Once the procuring agency identifies the responsible bidder submitting the lowest bid, it will issue a notice of award or notice of intent to award to all bidders. Depending on the jurisdictions procedures, the low bid is generally examined for compliance and to confirm that it meets all required terms and conditions. This notice of award includes the name of the successful bidder, information about unsuccessful bidders' rights to seek a debriefing, and the deadline for receiving any protests. If the procuring agency receives a protest within the given time period, this protest may result in the stay of performance of the contract.

Debriefings

Debriefings occur after contract award. Also known as post-award debriefings, the procuring agency may offer debriefing in its written notification to each unsuccessful bidder. Post-award debriefings occur within a specific time period.

Generally, the contents of the bid, except for price, remain confidential until after contract award when this information may become public information. However, it is not uncommon for contract awardees to request that certain aspects of their financial information remain confidential for commercial purposes.

Evaluation of Proposals

There are various methods for evaluating proposals under competitive negotiations. Of these, three methods—best value, tradeoff, and lowest priced, technically acceptable—are discussed below because they represent the general categories that are likely to be employed by state and local government procuring agencies. Definitions for best-value and tradeoff methods vary. In fact, some jurisdictions will refer to either method interchangeably, others will use only one term exclusively, others will treat them as two distinct methods, and still others will consider tradeoff as one approach to assessing best value. While there exist points of similarity and difference between the best-value method and the tradeoff method, one important and similar feature of both methods is that they each allow for more subjective consideration of evaluation factors than the third method lowest priced, technically acceptable. What is crucial regardless of which evaluation method is chosen to evaluate proposals is that the method for evaluation must be disclosed to offerors and the factors and sub-factors to be evaluated must be included in the solicitation.

Best Value

The best-value method allows procuring agencies to evaluate proposals on quality factors rather than simply on the lowest price. Evaluators consider the combination of quality, price, and other elements of a proposal that will provide the greatest overall benefit in response to the requirements as described in the solicitation documents.[54] This process allows evaluators to select proposals that offer higher quality services or products, even if those proposals cost more. The lowest responsible proposal may be selected if it offers the best value-for-money when considered in light of all the specified evaluation factors.

Generally, the solicitation documents for this type of procurement are called requests for proposals (RFPs), which are used when competitive negotiation will be the source selection method. The offeror's response, or proposal, is generally evaluated on the technical response, in addition to cost factors.

In a best-value process, evaluation teams generally have discretion to choose whether a proposal materially complies with the solicitation. In Minnesota, a technical review committee has discretion, under the state statute governing the best-value procurement process, to determine whether an offeror's proposal was responsive rather than following the strict definition of responsiveness.[55] Gradually, state and local governments are recognizing that competitive negotiation can be a more advantageous source selection method for other than routine commodity purchases.[56] In fact, a 2002 study found that contracting agencies that used a best-value procurement pursuant to the competitive negotiation method for design-build project delivery were more satisfied when compared with agencies that used a low-bid procurement method.[57]

Tradeoff

The best value offer may not be the lowest price or the highest technical proposals; in these cases, it might be in the best interest of the government to use a tradeoff process. To ensure fair competition in this process, the solicitation documents should clearly state the relative importance, or weight, of each evaluation factor, particularly in relation to the importance of cost. An evaluation that uses the tradeoff process is not based solely on price, but rather on the weighing of criteria such as qualifications, experience, methodology, management, approach, and responsiveness to the RFP. Tradeoffs are typically used in the following circumstances:

- When the procuring agency's requirements are difficult to define, complex, or historically troublesome;
- When the procuring agency expects measurable differences in design, performance, quality, reliability, or supportability;
- When services are not clearly defined or highly skilled personnel are required; or
- When the procuring agency is willing to pay extra for capability, skills, reduced risk, or other non-cost factors, if the added benefits are worth the premium.

In a tradeoff process, the solicitation states whether all evaluation factors other than cost or price, when combined, are significantly more important than, approximately equal to, or significantly less important than cost or price. The evaluation usually involves the use of a summary, matrix, or quantitative ranking, along with an appropriate supporting narrative for each evaluated factor.[58] Evaluators, normally consisting of a team of technical or subject experts, accounting personnel, and other staff such as human resources representatives, have broad discretion to evaluate proposals.

This tradeoff process offers more flexibility and options to weigh the technical strengths, weaknesses, and risks of each offer. However, offers may not accurately reflect the actual market value of the services, and it is more subjective and difficult to evaluate and document. With the tradeoff process, it is important for the procuring agency to make an appropriate investment in the resources needed for a competent and defensible value analysis.

While tradeoffs can offer the procuring agency maximum flexibility in choosing a contractor, the procuring agency may not arbitrarily or capriciously discriminate between offerors or make choices based upon personal preference.[59] The decision of the procuring agency is subject to review through the appropriate administrative process or judicial review.

Lowest Price, Technically Acceptable

The lowest-price, technically acceptable process for selection allows the procuring agency to identify the evaluation factors that establish the minimum requirements of acceptability. Proposals are evaluated for acceptability based on qualitative factors, not cost or price. The lowest-priced proposal is awarded the contract, out of the proposals that meet or exceed the acceptability standards for qualitative factors.[60] By meeting the minimum technical requirements, the proposal with the lowest cost will offer the government the best value, usually in cases where the cost factor is paramount. There is no need to evaluate proposals based upon the tradeoff process, as a proposal will either meet or not meet the technical requirements, and only those proposals that meet the requirements will be considered. No additional credit or weight is given to proposals that exceed the minimum acceptable requirements.

The lowest-price, technically acceptable method is similar to a sealed-bid approach in that award is made to the acceptable offeror with the lowest evaluated cost or price. The major difference is that discussions can be held with offerors prior to source selection to determine acceptability and to ensure offerors understand the requirements. This process may be preferable where the technical requirements are not complex and performance risks are minimal, yet where discussions may be necessary. In some circumstances, exceptions may be made for not awarding a contract to the lowest price. In Kansas, if a negotiation committee selects a proposal that is not the lowest price on a given contract, there must be a corresponding rationale explaining why the lowest-price proposal was not awarded the contract, which is reported to the legislature.[61]

Just as lowest-price awards are seen to prevent corruption in contract award,[62] this type of evaluation process—when compared to best-value or tradeoff methods—is more objective and, thus, less subject to claims of arbitrary awards, all while allowing the procuring agency to benchmark a minimum acceptable quality requirement.

Evaluation of Factors and Sub-factors

In competitive negotiations, the solicitation must provide measurable and transparent evaluation criteria, or factors and sub-factors, to ensure fairness and to promote meaningful competition among offerors. The evaluation criteria place offerors on notice of the agency's approach to evaluating proposal submissions. As such, the evaluation criteria must reflect the essential qualities or performance requirements necessary to achieve the objectives of the contract.[63] Chapter 4 contains a table of sample evaluation criteria of quality, capability, and cost/price factors.

Generally, the cost/price factor must be evaluated in all procurements.[64] Illinois separates the evaluation by phases: phase I evaluates the qualifications of proposals resulting in a shortlist; phase II evaluates the technical and cost proposals, with cost representing 25 percent of the phase II evaluation.[65]

To ensure fairness in evaluation, the evaluation factors should reflect only the requirements specified in the solicitation document. Moreover, the solicitation should clearly inform offerors of the relative weight or importance of the significant evaluation factors and sub-factors. For example, a solicitation should express to offerors whether the agency will evaluate proposals based upon the lowest-price, technically acceptable process or whether it will use a tradeoff process. The solicitation should clearly state the consequence of failing to meet these requirements, such as reduction in evaluation score or disqualification.

The agency must fairly advise offerors that a factor is significant and will be considered. In the case of unstated factors and sub-factors, in which the procuring agency's expectation is that offerors will know to respond to these criteria because they are logically and reasonably related to stated factors or sub-factors, the best practice for a procuring agency in evaluating proposals is not to consider these evaluation criteria. Stated simply, the best practice for procuring agencies is to forego evaluating proposals against factors or sub-factors that are not included in the solicitation. For example, if evaluators expect offerors to possess national accreditation or require them to meet the unique needs of the end-user, these criteria must be included in the solicitation so that offerors know they must address these factors in order to obtain credit during the evaluation. Likewise, if this information is not requested in the solicitation, offerors who do not address these options should not be penalized.

Some agencies prefer to give more detailed information as to how each factor is broken down into sub-factors; others include a copy of the evaluation scoring sheets with the solicitation. Most states require the requests for proposals to include all evaluation factors and criteria. In New Mexico, city council members illegally introduced a new factor when evaluating proposals, as the city's own regulations stated that no criteria could be used in proposal evaluations that were not set forth in the request for proposals. In that case, the city was also found to have acted illegally when it awarded the contract to the fourth-ranked offeror. Consequently, the city was required to accept the proposal most advantageous to the city according to the evaluated factors.[66]

In South Carolina, solicitations requesting submissions of competitive sealed proposals require the procuring agency to state the relative importance of the factors to be considered, but do not require a numerical weighting for each factor.[67] States such as Illinois may require the state agency to maintain a record of the evaluation scoring to be disclosed if there is a protest regarding the solicitation.[68] It is highly advisable for all agencies to give all prospective offerors notice of the evaluation criteria and the evaluation process in the solicitation, and for the agencies to keep a detailed written record of the actual evaluation to demonstrate the fairness in competition for the solicitation.

Evaluations must assess the strengths, weaknesses, and risks of proposals, prior to assigning relative merit to competing proposals.

After assessment of proposals, each should be scored as a means of summarizing the evaluations to assist the source selection official in ranking proposals.

Clarifications and Discussions

After proposal submission and opening and before contract award, the procuring agency may choose to engage in clarifications or discussions with offerors. The procuring agency may also award the contract without conducting discussions. Clarifications and discussions promote flexibility and often result in proposals that offer more technically accurate solutions or lower costs, maximizing the procuring agency's ability to achieve a best value.

The procuring agency may request clarifications to elucidate certain aspects of proposals or to resolve minor or clerical errors. Alternately or additionally, the procuring agency may choose to engage in discussions during which the procuring officer will engage directly with each offeror and tailor the discussion to each offeror's proposal. In discussions, the procuring officer may indicate deficiencies, weaknesses, areas for improvement, or whether the proposed cost is too high or too low. The goal of discussions may be to increase the competitiveness of the proposal or to ensure that the proposal more accurately responds to the procuring agency's needs and requirements.

Generally, if a procuring agency engages in discussions, it must treat each offeror equally and provide all offerors equal opportunity to discuss and revise their proposals. All offerors must be given a fair chance to improve their respective proposals, to respond to the concerns of the procuring agency, and to submit final revised offers before contract award. In Ohio, injunctive relief was granted when an offeror was not given the opportunity to participate in face-to-face meetings to negotiate a best and final offer but other offerors were afforded this opportunity.[69]

Procuring agencies may not disclose information derived from proposals submitted from competing offerors in conducting discussions. The procuring officer or a designee from the source selection team conducting discussions may not give information that would favor one offeror over another. Such conduct might include revealing another offeror's technical solution or innovative plans, or revealing the price/cost information of another proposal without that offeror's permission.

Proposal Modifications

Proposal modification must take place before contract award. Generally, proposal modifications are accepted before the closing time and date of submission of revised proposals and before the opening and evaluation of proposals. However, modifying proposals once the submission deadline has passed would likely not prejudice a competitive offeror whose mistake may be addressed during clarifications or discussion with the procuring agency.

Decision to Award

After evaluating proposals, the procuring agency may choose to award the contract or it may choose to engage in further clarifications or discussions. Once the clarifications, discussions, and any negotiations are complete, generally each offeror will submit final revised proposals. Once the final revised proposals are evaluated, the procuring agency will then make a decision to award the contract. The procuring agency awards the contract to the responsible offeror whose proposal complies in all material respects with the solicitations requirements and who receives the highest score under the method of scoring as set forth in the request for proposals.[70]

The procuring agency will award the contract to the offeror with the best value proposal to the state or the lowest priced offer that qualifies as technically acceptable, depending upon the type of evaluation method used. In either case, the results of the evaluation and the supporting documentation should support the contract award. Generally, the award is made to the responsible offeror whose proposal is determined to be the most advantageous considering price, the evaluation factors set forth in the request for proposals, and the results of any discussions conducted with responsible offerors.[71]

If the procuring agency determines that no proposal materially complies with the solicitation requirements, or if there is lack of funding or a change in programs, the procuring officer may decide to cancel the solicitation before contract award.

Notice of Award

Once the procuring agency determines which offeror will receive contract award, it will issue a notice of award to all offerors. This notice of award includes the name of the successful offeror, information about unsuccessful offerors' rights to protect the content of their proposals, and the deadline for receiving any protests. If the procuring agency receives a protest within the given time period, this protest may result in the stay of performance of the contract.

The procuring agency may choose to include evaluation score information and supporting narrative to both successful and unsuccessful offerors along with the notice of award. The procuring agency may offer or may be required to offer debriefings to unsuccessful offerors. Absent a protest, contract negotiations may commence with the successful offeror.

Debriefings

Debriefings or post-award debriefings occur after contract award. The procuring agency may offer debriefing in its written notification to each offeror whose proposal was in the competitive range but not selected for the award. Debriefings occur within a specific time period in order to educate unsuccessful offerors about the agency's evaluation process and the weaknesses in an offeror's proposal.

The pre-award notice debriefing involves the procuring officer notifying offerors in writing that their proposals were excluded from the competitive range or otherwise eliminated from competition.

During the pre-award stage, offerors may request a debriefing from the procuring officer if the request is timely made. Pre-award debriefings usually contain: (1) the agency's evaluation of significant elements in the offeror's proposal, (2) a summary of the rationale for eliminating the offeror from the competition, and (3) reasonable responses to relevant questions about whether source selection procedures in the solicitation, applicable regulations, and other applicable authorities were followed in the process of eliminating the offeror from the competition. Pre-award debriefings will not disclose the identity of other offerors' nor how the source selection team evaluated them.

A post-award debriefing is given within a certain time period after notice of contract award. This debriefing explains the basis for the selection decision and contract award. Post-award debriefings include the following information: (1) the procuring agency's evaluation of significant weaknesses or deficiencies in the offeror's proposal, (2) the overall evaluation on cost or price and technical rating for the offeror as well as any evaluation of past performance, (3) any overall rankings that were created, (4) a summary of the rationale for award, (5) the make and model of the commercial item to be distributed by the successful offeror, and (6) reasonable responses to any relevant questions.

Generally, information regarding proposal price or contents remains confidential until after contract award when this information may become public information. It is not uncommon for contract awardees to request that certain aspects of their financial information remain confidential for commercial purposes.

Conclusion

Evaluation and contract award are crucial stages in the formation phase of the procurement process. During these stages, the procuring agency has an excellent opportunity to promote transparency and integrity by ensuring that bidders and offerors receive timely notice about the standards and methods for evaluation and award. As well, the opportunity for unsuccessful bidders and offerors to receive debriefings explaining to competitors where their bids or proposals were nonresponsive, noncompliant, or deficient will engender confidence that present and future procurements will be conducted fairly and openly and in accordance with stated laws, rules, and best practices.

Notes

1.   OR. REV. STAT. ANN. § 279B.055 (West, Westlaw through 2011 Sess.)
2.   *Id.*
3.   KY. REV. STAT. ANN. § 45A.365 (West, Westlaw through 2011 Sess.).
4.   *Id.*
5.   *Id.* § 45A.370.
6.   *See* MD. CODE ANN. § 13-111 (West, Westlaw through 2011 Sess.).
7.   *See id.* § 13-101.
8.   *See id.* § 13-103.
9.   Pendleton Bros. Vending, Inc. v. Com. Fin. & Admin. Cabinet, 758 S.W.2d 24, 30 (Ky. 1988).
10. *Id.*
11. Laurel Const. Co., Inc. v. Paintsville Util. Comm'n, 336 S.W.3d 903, 908–09 (Ky. Ct. App. 2010), *as modified* (May 28, 2010), *review denied* (May 11, 2011).
12. *Id.*
13. Billy E. Burnett, Inc. v. Pontotoc County Bd. of Sup'rs, 940 So. 2d 241 (Miss. Ct. App. 2006).
14. *Id.* at 243.
15. *Id.*
16. Bodies by Lembo, Inc. v. County of Middlesex, 286 N.J. Super. 298, 669 A.2d 254 (App. Div. 1996).
17. *Id.*
18. S.D. CODIFIED LAWS § 5-18A-25 (Westlaw through 2011 Sess.).
19. *Id.*
20. UTAH CODE ANN. § 63G-6-404 (West, Westlaw through 2011 Sess.).
21. *Id.*
22. FLA. STAT. ANN. § 287.087 (West, Westlaw through 2011).
23. *Id.* § 287.082.
24. See generally the section *Revocation of Bid* in Chapter 5.
25. ARK. CODE ANN. § 19-11-229 (West, Westlaw through 2011 Sess.).
26. *Id.*
27. Arkansas State Regulations, R9:19-11-229(a)(1) (2007), *available at* http://www.dfa.arkansas.gov/offices/procurement/Documents/lawsRegs.pdf (last visited Feb. 3, 2012).

28. *Id.*
29. *Id.*
30. *Id.*
31. Colo. Rev. Stat. Ann. § 24-103-202(6) (West, Westlaw through 2011 Sess.).
32. *Id.*
33. Colorado State Regulations, R-24-103-202a-04(b)(ii–iii), *available at* http://www.coloradomesa.edu/purchasing/documents/SOCProcurementRules.pdf (last visited Feb. 3, 2012).
34. Mont. Code Ann. § 18-4-303 (2011).
35. Bd. of Regents of Murray State Normal Sch. v. Cole, 209 Ky. 761, 273 S.W. 508, 511 (1925).
36. *Id.*
37. Dep't of Transp. v. Ronlee, Inc., 518 So. 2d 1326 (Fla. Dist. Ct. App. 1987).
38. R.G. Wilmott Coal Co. v. State Purchasing Comm'n, 246 Ky. 115, 54 S.W.2d 634, 636 (1932).
39. *Id.*
40. Ky. Att'y Gen. Op. No. 2-316 (1980).
41. Pendleton Bros. Vending, Inc. v. Com. Fin. & Admin. Cabinet, 758 S.W.2d 24, 30 (Ky. 1988).
42. A & S Transp. Co. v. Bergen County Sewer Auth., 135 N.J. Super. 117, 119–20, 342 A.2d 865, 866 (App. Div. 1975).
43. Ga. Code Ann. § 13-10-22 (West, Westlaw through 2011 Sess.).
44. *Id.*
45. *Id.*
46. *Id.*
47. N.M. Stat. Ann. § 13-4-39 (West, Westlaw through 2011 Sess.).
48. *See id.*
49. N.C. Gen. Stat. Ann. § 143-129.1 (West, Westlaw through 2011 Sess.).
50. Westway Const., Inc. v. Idaho Transp. Dept., 139 Idaho 107, 73 P.3d 721 (2003).
51. Midway Excavators, Inc. v. Chandler, 128 N.H. 654, 522 A.2d 982 (1986).
52. *Id.*
53. City of Baltimore v. De Luca-Davis Const. Co., 210 Md. 518, 124 A.2d 557 (1956).
54. Cal. Pub. Cont. Code § 20301(a) (West 2011).
55. Sayer v. Minnesota Dep't of Transp., 769 N.W.2d 305, 311 (Minn. App. 2009). *See* Minn. Stat. Ann. § 161.3426 (West 2011).
56. 44 Ill. Admin. Code § 4.2015 (West 2011) (permitting use of competitive sealed proposals for certain categories of purchases when a determination is made that competitive sealed bidding is either not practicable or advantageous); UT Admin. Code R33-3-2 (stating, "[c]ompetitive sealed proposals may be a more appropriate method for a particular procurement or type of procurement than competitive sealed bidding," after considering factors listed in the code's provision).

57. *Design-Build Effectiveness Study* prepared for The United States Department of Transportation Federal Highway Administration (Jan. 2006), *available at* http://www.fhwa.dot.gov/reports/designbuild/designbuild.pdf (last visited Feb. 3, 2012).

58. *See* MO. CODE. REGS. ANN. tit. 7, § 10-24.140 (2011).

59. *See* Emerald Correctional Mgmt v. Bay County Bd. of County Com'rs, 955 So. 2d 647 (Fla. Dist. Ct. App. 2007); *see also* FLA. STAT. ANN. § 255.20 (West 2011).

60. IDAHO CODE ANN. § 40-113(4) (West 2011).

61. KAN. STAT. ANN. § 75-37,102(e) (West 2011).

62. Istari Const., Inc. v. City of Muscatine, 330 N.W.2d 798, 800 (Iowa 1983).

63. See generally *Drafting Evaluation Criteria* in Chapter 4.

64. Following the Federal American Recovery and Reinvestment Act of 2009, the Arizona State Legislature changed the CMAR statutes to allow the contracting agency to consider price as a factor for awarding the contract if the contract involves federal funds. *See* ARIZ. REV. STAT. ANN. § 41-2578 (2011). This change applies to all requests for qualifications issued on or before December 31, 2014, after which the stimulus monies will expire and Arizona's CM-at-Risk provisions will revert to prior law. Prior to the change, price was not considered a factor in the selection process; rather, qualifications such as past performance, similar project experience, capacity to perform the work and financial strength were used in the evaluation.

65. 30 ILL. COMP. STAT. ANN. § 537/30(a) (West 2011).

66. *See* Planning and Design Solutions v. City of Santa Fe, 885 P.2d 628 (N.M. 1994); *see also* N.M. STAT. ANN. §§ 13-1-28 to 13-1-199 (West, Westlaw through 2011 Sess.).

67. S.C. CODE ANN. § 11-35-1530 (2010).

68. 30 ILL. COMP. STAT. ANN. § 537/30(b) (West 2011).

69. *See* Sequoia Voting Sys., Inc. v. Ohio Sec'y of State, 796 N.E.2d 598 (Ohio Ct. Cl. 2003).

70. ARIZ. REV. STAT. ANN. § 41-2578 (2011).

71. ARK. CODE ANN. § 19-11-230(f)(1) (West, Westlaw through 2011 Sess.).

9

Controversies over Solicitations and Contract Awards

Bid protests fulfill a vital enforcement role within the procurement process. A bid protest system provides a mechanism for efficiently resolving challenges to agency solicitation and contract award decisions. This chapter describes the types of controversies that invoke bid protest procedures, the types of protests, jurisdictional issues, remedies, taxpayer suits, and protest appeals.

Solicitation and Contract Award Controversies

Solicitation and contract award controversies are a significant component of the procurement process. Bidders and offerors who recognize that procuring agencies have not followed procurement laws, regulations, and/or procedures have the right—and some would say the responsibility—to challenge agency procurement actions. Procedures are established at various administrative and judicial levels to resolve these challenges, generally known as protests, in order to build confidence in the procurement and purchasing systems of state and local governments. The 2007 MC PIP states that "[i]t is essential that bidders, offerors, and contractors have confidence in the procedures for soliciting and awarding contracts. This can be best assured by allowing an aggrieved person to protest the solicitation, award, or related decision."[1] Protests also assist procuring agencies in policing their respective procurement systems, which ultimately results in promoting full and open competition and government compliance with acquisition laws and regulations.

There are two primary forums in which to hear protests: the procuring agency or a designated official within the state or local government.[2] With respect to the former, the protest hearing official is either the contracting officer or the head of the agency. In the latter, the hearing official is either the chief procurement officer (CPO) or someone in a division of purchasing or a department of finance. Contract formation issues are generally resolved by pre-award protests to one of the two forums listed above. Resolution of disputes about the administration of an existing contract is within the discretion of the contracting officer unless an interested party complains about an out-of-scope contract modification and demonstrates that the modification prejudicially impacts full and open competition.

The CPO, procuring agencies, or their designees are required to consider all protests filed directly with procuring agencies. If, in connection with a protest, the head of an agency determines that a solicitation, proposed award, or award does not comply with the requirements of law or regulation, the head of the agency may take remedial action. Of course, remedial action will vary by jurisdiction based upon relevant state statutes, local rules, or specific policy. As well, the timing of the remedial action will determine the remedies available to protestors. For example, if the procuring agency takes remedial action prior to award (including notice of award), a likely remedy is cancellation or amendment of the solicitation. If the procuring agency takes remedial action after award but before the start of contract performance, the head of the agency could direct the procuring officer to modify the award decision, re-evaluate bids or offers, reject all bids or offers and resolicit for bids or offers, cancel the solicitation, and/or pay reasonable costs incurred in connection with the solicitation, not to include attorneys' fees or lost or anticipated profits. In addition, the procuring agency may stay performance of a contract, unless the procuring agency determines in writing that award of a contract without delay is necessary to protect the substantial interests of the agency.

In anticipation of a protest, all parties are encouraged to use their best efforts to resolve concerns about solicitation improprieties or violations of procurement laws or regulations at the lowest level prior to contract award. In the event a bidder or offeror files a protest to the procuring agency, the agency should provide for inexpensive, informal, procedurally simple, and expeditious resolution of protests. Where appropriate, the use of alternative dispute resolution techniques should be considered acceptable protest resolution methods. Protests must be concise and logically presented to facilitate review by the procuring agency. Failure to substantially comply with the requirements to file a protest may be grounds for dismissal of the protest.

Protests

Procuring agencies have inherent authority to consider agency-level protests that challenge alleged defects in their agency procedures. Some states may even require protestors to exhaust their administrative remedies before seeking judicial review. Other states require a notice of intent to protest to the procuring agency before actually submitting a protest. For example, in Iowa a protestor, defined as a person or party who is aggrieved or adversely affected by any final agency action, is required to exhaust all adequate administrative remedies before being entitled to judicial review of such action.[3] In Florida, bidders must initiate protests by filing a notice of intent to protest with the procuring agency within 72 hours of the posting of the notice of decision or intended decision. A formal written protest must then be filed within ten days of the date the notice of intent to protest is filed.[4]

There are two basic types of bid protests. The first is the pre-award protest, which challenges the terms of a solicitation. The second is the post-award protest, which challenges an agency's evaluation of bids or proposals or the final award of a contract.

Protests Prior to Award

Protests based on solicitation improprieties that are apparent prior to bid opening or the closing date for receipt of proposals should be filed prior to bid opening or the closing date for receipt of proposals. For example, in Arizona, when feasible, protests related to solicitation improprieties are to be made before bid opening or closing dates for submittal of the proposal.[5] According to Louisiana law, "[a]ny person who is aggrieved in connection with the solicitation or award of a contract" can protest to the contracting officer, with the caveat that protests of solicitations must be made in writing two days before opening of bids.[6] The purpose of this requirement is to alert the agency to any violations of law or any solicitation improprieties or defects in a timely manner so that the agency can respond with corrective action for the benefit of all prospective bidders or offerors. The fundamental type of corrective action is either revision of the solicitation to comply with law or cancellation of the solicitation.[7]

Florida provides detailed requirements for protesting solicitations prior to award. The applicable provision states,

> [w]ith respect to a protest of the terms, conditions, and specifications contained in a solicitation, including any provisions governing the methods for ranking bids, proposals, or replies, awarding contracts, reserving rights of further negotiation, or modifying or amending any contract, the notice of protest shall be filed in writing within 72 hours after the posting of the solicitation. . . . Failure to file a notice of protest or failure to file a formal written protest shall constitute a waiver of proceedings under this chapter.[8]

According to Florida law, failure to protest a solicitation impropriety or defect results in a waiver of any issue that could have been raised prior to award. This limitation protects the agency from untimely protests and stale claims that would create unjustifiable impediments to agency contract actions that have progressed beyond the formation phase.

Protests after Award

For challenges that occur after award, protests must be filed on a designated date after the basis of the protest is known or should have been known, whichever occurs earlier. For example, in Hawai'i, protests of awards issued pursuant to an invitation for bids (IFB), multi-step IFB, small purchase, or sole source procurement must be submitted within five working days of the posting of the award to the CPO or a designee specified in the solicitation. Protests of awards issued pursuant to competitive negotiations or for professional services must be made within five working days of posting of the award, or, if pursuant to a nonselected offeror's request for a debriefing, within five working days after the last debriefing.[9] According to Louisiana law, protests of awards are made within 14 days of the date of contract award.[10] The date for protesting after contract award is based upon a constructive knowledge standard because unsuccessful bidders or offerors do not have notice of alleged agency improprieties until award has been made and possibly only become aware of such improprieties after a debriefing.

In *Telephone Associate Inc. v. St. Louis County Board*,[11] an unsuccessful offeror brought suit challenging the award to its competitor on the grounds that the latter did not comply in all material respects with the criteria in the county's request for proposals. The district court determined that the county's award procedures had been properly complied with and, therefore, refused to enjoin the county's award of a telephone system contract to the successful offeror. The court of appeals held that the county board did not comply with proper award procedures, which would have resulted in the rejection of the successful offeror's proposal for failure to comply with the material terms of the solicitation.[12]

Generally, the remedies available to a protestor who challenges a notice of award prior to the start of contract performance are modification of the award decision, re-evaluation of bids or offers, rejection of all bids or offers and resolicitation, cancellation, and/or payment of reasonable costs incurred in connection with the solicitation, not to include attorneys' fees or lost or anticipated profits. The typical remedies available to a protestor who challenges award under the scenario where contract performance has commenced are contract termination or a determination that the contract is null and void. In rare cases, contract awards can be ratified and affirmed if doing so is in the best interest of the state or local government.

Jurisdiction

Generally, aggrieved bidders, offerors, or contractors do not have a constitutional right to sue the state because of principles of sovereign immunity. Despite this limitation, states have consented to suit through the establishment of specific administrative claims procedures. Some states have placed jurisdiction to hear protests with their states' comptroller[13] or chief procurement officer,[14] administrative hearing officers or a disinterested person,[15] or directly with the procuring agency.[16] State and local governments vary widely on the question of administrative, quasi-judicial, and judicial jurisdiction to hear protests. For comprehensive guidance on jurisdictional requirements, refer to the American Bar Association's *Guide to State Procurement: A 50 State Primer on Purchasing Laws, Processes and Procedures.*[17]

Responding to protests at the lowest level is generally encouraged because it promotes cost- and time-efficient resolution of procurement-related protests for the benefit of state governments and their taxpayers. The 2007 MC PIP confirms a procuring agency's jurisdiction to hear protests in § 9-101(2), which provides that "the Chief Procurement Officer, the head of the Purchasing Agency, or a designee of either officer shall have the authority, prior to the commencement of an action in court concerning the controversy, to settle and resolve a protest of an aggrieved bidder, offeror, or contractor, actual or prospective, concerning the solicitation or award of a contract."

Standing

Although protest rules and procedures vary from state to state, there remain fundamental principles that ensure fairness to aggrieved bidders, offerors, or contractors who raise legitimate concerns about agency adherence to procurement processes, laws, and procedures. One of these principles requires identifying who has the right to challenge an agency's procurement action. Some state and local governments may provide broad and inclusive rules for who may protest by allowing both actual or prospective bidders or offerors to challenge agency procurement actions. At the other end of the spectrum, state and local governments may restrict the right to protest to only actual bidders or offerors. Still a select number of state and local governments grant the right to protest to any party who raises legitimate concerns about the manner in which a state or local government agency conducts a procurement.

In Maryland, for example, only a prospective bidder or offeror may submit a protest to the procurement officer.[18] In South Carolina, any "prospective bidder, offeror, contractor, or subcontractor who is aggrieved in connection with the solicitation of a contract" has the right to protest,[19] while only "actual bidders, offerors, contractors, or subcontractors who are aggrieved in connection with the intended award or award of a contract" have the right to protest.[20] In Massachusetts, the Office of the Inspector General's informal process for resolving procurement-related disputes allows a protest to be initiated by a phone call or letter from any individual alleging a violation of the Uniform Procurement Act.[21]

Those jurisdictions limiting standing to aggrieved actual or prospective bidders or offerors may also require a protestor to show (1) that it has a direct economic interest that will be harmed by the award of the contract or by the failure to award the contract; and

(2) that it has a substantial chance of obtaining the award. Accordingly, in *Preston Carroll Company Incorporated v. Florida Keys Aqueduct Authority*,[22] the court held that an unsuccessful bidder to a water supply contract lacked standing to protest because it lacked a substantial interest. The court upheld a general rule that in order to have a "substantial interest," the protestor must establish that it submitted the second lowest bid.

Similarly, in *Amdahl Corp. v. Georgia Department of Administrative Services*,[23] the Supreme Court of Georgia allowed an unsuccessful bidder to protest contract award because it had "allege[d] that the challenged action caused it injury in fact," and it had "asserted an interest "arguably within the zone of interests to be protected . . . by the statute." In *Amdahl*, the Georgia Department of Administrative Services allowed Amdahl's competitor, IBM, to conduct tests under a more lenient standard. Because Amdahl would have had the lowest bid but for the different standard, the court determined that it had demonstrated an "injury in fact." Additionally, because the applicable statute dealing with the agency's procurement was concerned with promoting "fair and equitable treatment of all persons who deal with the procurement system of the state," the court held that Amdahl's complaint of arbitrary and unfair review by the agency fell within the "zone of interest to be protected by procurement law." Accordingly, the Georgia Supreme Court will grant standing to any protestor who can show that it has suffered a legitimate harm because of an agency's arbitrary action in awarding a contract.

Standard of Review

The concept of "standard of review" can be described as the amount of deference given by the individual, panel, or court responsible for reviewing a decision of law or fact at a lower level. Examples of these standards include but are not limited to arbitrary and capricious, substantial evidence, and de novo. Generally, the standard of review for a bid protest is whether the agency's procurement action was arbitrary, capricious, or contrary to law.[24] Deference will be given to an agency where it is making a decision based on its special-ized experience.[25] As well, there is a presumption that a procuring agency's actions were proper.[26]

The Kentucky Model Procurement Code addresses the pre-sumption afforded to agency officials making procurement decisions as well as the standard for reviewing such decisions. Specifically, § 45A.280 provides: "[t]his state provides that the decision of any offi-cial, board, agent, or other person appointed by the Commonwealth concerning any controversy arising under, or in connection with, the solicitation or award of a contract, shall be entitled to a presumption of correctness and shall not be disturbed unless the decision was pro-cured by fraud or the findings of fact by such official, board, agent or other person do not support the decision." States can vary on the presumption of correctness and the standard of review but generally, regarding agency procurement-related decisions, reviewing officials and/or courts will show deference for the protest decisions of agency officials or their designees as long as there is no abuse of discretion and the decisions are not arbitrary and capricious.

For example, in *BECDIR Construction Company v. Proctor*,[27] a construction company submitted the low bid on a state highway construction project and sought judicial review of a decision by the Ohio Department of Transportation (ODOT) to reject all bids. On appeal, the standard of review for the trial court in determining whether a governmental body had appropriately awarded a competi-tive bidder a contract was whether the body abused its discretion. Similarly, in *Dental v. City of Salem*,[28] a bidder whose towing contract bids were rejected as nonresponsive brought an action against the city for declaratory relief. Because of the discretion granted to public contracting agencies by ORS § 279.035, the city's action had to be reviewed under the abuse of discretion standard.

Procedures

Procedures governing protests vary from state to state. The variations are largely due to the wide variety of disputes that can arise before a contract is awarded. Typically, disputes between parties are brought as civil actions in the relevant courts. In Alabama, for example, any taxpayer within the jurisdiction of the awarding authority, along with any bona fide unsuccessful bidder on a particular contract, can bring a civil action in the appropriate court if the contract violates a statutory provision.[29]

Colorado statutes also allow for civil actions of such disputes, and additionally hold that if any government body acquires "any supplies, services, or construction contrary to the provisions of this code or the rules promulgated pursuant thereto, [then] the head of such governmental body and the public employee . . . actually making such purchase shall be personally liable for the costs thereof."[30] The statute further articulates that if such services are paid with state moneys, the amount in controversy may be recovered in the name of the state in an appropriate civil action.[31]

Further, some states have specific provisions allowing concerned citizens to participate in pre-award disputes. While these statutes usually mention that such citizens must reside within the jurisdiction that would be affected by the proposed contract, many states have no such provision. Typically, state statutes are ambiguous in this regard. In Iowa, for example, any municipality that enters into a contract that is in excess of a certain competitive bid threshold must hold a public hearing in addition to giving notice by publication in at least one local newspaper at least ten days before the hearing.[32] Additionally, any interested person may "appear and file objections to the proposed plans, specifications or contract for, or cost of such improvement." Additionally, the relevant governing body of the municipality must "hear said objections and any evidence."[33]

In Maine, the Director of General Services may refuse to release plans for a project during the bidding phase to a potential contractor for a variety of reasons. The Director can refuse to release the plans if there exists evidence that the "contractor has not completed in a timely manner a prior construction project or projects and the resulting noncompletion clearly reflects disregard for the completion date and has created a hardship for the owner."[34] Significantly, the Director may also refuse to release the plan because of financial concerns, and further may require that a potential contractor submit "additional information about the contractor's resources, including identification of major claims or litigation pending and whether the contractor has sought protection under the bankruptcy laws in the past 5 years."[35]

Any contractor dissatisfied with the Director's decision pursuant to this statute may appeal the decision to the Commissioner of Administrative and Financial Services within five days of receipt of notice.[36] Further, although the appeal process is conducted at the discretion of the Commissioner, the final decision must be rendered within five calendar days after the contractor's written notice of appeal, unless extended by the Commissioner.[37] This decision by the Commissioner is final and binding.[38]

Case law differs in each state regarding remedies available through pre-award disputes. The Alabama Supreme Court heard a case in which an unsuccessful bidder on a contract for security services brought an action against the state retirement agency for judgment enjoining the agency from awarding the bid to the putative low bidder, and thereby sought award of the contract.[39] When the circuit court denied relief and the bidder appealed, the Supreme Court of Alabama held that the trial court had no power to compel an agency to award a contract to an unsuccessful bidder.[40] In another Alabama case, the district court found that a bidder for public work cannot "recover lost profits in case the contract is, contrary to the statute, awarded to a higher bidder."[41]

In an older case, the Connecticut Supreme Court determined that it was improper to permit one of three bidders on two contracts to submit a combined bid on the two contracts without informing the other two bidders of the right to do so.[42] There, the court held that by permitting a contractor to submit a conditional bid when other bidders were not afforded the same opportunity, the government "precluded the other bidders from competing on equal terms [and] defeated the object and integrity of the competitive bidding by unintentionally exhibiting favoritism to [the contractor]."[43] In a more recent case, the state's appellate court considered the claims of favoritism alleged from a contract bidder for a public school masonry restoration project. There, the court held that "the party seeking the exercise of the court's jurisdiction bears the burden of alleging facts that clearly demonstrate that it is the proper party to invoke judicial resolution of the dispute."[44] In an appellate court case, an unsuccessful bidder on a government contract brought an action against the state Department of Administrative Services and the Department's Commissioner, seeking permanent injunctive relief.[45] When the defendants were granted a motion to dismiss for lack of standing, the bidder appealed and the appellate court held that the unsuccessful bidder failed to show that the Department exhibited favoritism by excluding its proposal from consideration.[46] There, the court articulated several points relevant to procedure for unsuccessful bidders. Notably, it held that "[g]enerally, in the context of government contracting, unsuccessful bidders lack standing to pursue judicial challenges . . . because '[a] bid, even the lowest responsible one, submitted in response to an invitation for bids is only an offer which, until accepted by the [department], does not give rise to a contract between the parties.'"[47]

Remedies

Several states have statutes that specify available remedies regarding pre-award disputes. In Alabama, for example, the Attorney General, a bona fide unsuccessful or disqualified bidder, or any interested citizen "may maintain an action to enjoin the letting or execution of any public works contract in violation of or contrary to the provisions of [Alabama Code] or any other statute and may enjoin payment of any public funds under any such contract."[48] Additionally, if a bidder's action is successful, then reasonable bid preparation costs will be recoverable.[49] However, should the bidder's action prove unsuccessful, then he or she "may not sue for monetary damages under public bid law, recover bid preparation expenses, or insist upon the award of a contract."[50]

Similar to Alabama law, Alaska statutes contain a provision that "if a protest is sustained in whole or part, the protestor's damages are limited to reasonable bid or proposal preparation costs."[51] In Arizona, a state agency's chief procurement officer is given several options regarding appropriate remedies. Among the remedies, the chief procurement officer may amend the solicitation, issue a new solicitation, or render "such other relief as determined necessary to ensure compliance with procurement statutes and regulations."[52]

South Carolina has specific provisions addressing remedies in pre-award disputes. The law states that if, prior to the award, "a solicitation or proposed award of a contract is in violation of law, then the solicitation or proposed award may be: (a) canceled; (b) revised to comply with the law and rebid; or (c) awarded in a manner that complies with the provisions of this code."[53]

Maryland code articulates a wide range of remedies. If an administrative law judge sustains an allegation in such a dispute, he or she may find that "the respondent business entity is not a 'responsible bidder' . . . with respect to specific contracts that the State has put out for bids or intends to put out for bids."[54] Additionally, the judge may refer the matter "for criminal prosecution of fraud and other violations under State law if appropriate under the circumstances."[55]

Case law varies with regard to pre-award remedies. In a recent Pennsylvania case, an unsuccessful bidder petitioned for review of the Department of Revenue's award of a contract to provide terminal-based games for the state lottery and sought declaratory and injunctive relief against further advancement of the government contract. There, the court held that the exclusive remedy to a substantive challenge of the Department's selection was the bid protest procedure articulated in the Procurement Code.[56]

In Virginia, a bidder who was to be awarded a contract filed an action against a protesting bidder for tortious interference with contract expectancy and for conspiracy to injure its business and reputation.[57] The state supreme court held that statements made by the protesting bidder pursuant to Virginia's Public Procurement Act procedure for protesting award of a government contract were not entitled to absolute privilege, and that the bidder was precluded under law of the case doctrine from relitigating the conspiracy claim.[58] Further, the court held that because the protesting bidder did not prove that it could not recoup its pro rata home office expenses, it was not entitled to recover unabsorbed overhead expenses.[59]

In an older case of first impression, an unsuccessful bidder on a state contract sought review of a contract award on the grounds that Kentucky's relevant statutory procedures were disregarded for reasons of political patronage.[60] There, the Kentucky Supreme Court held that, following enactment of the state's model procurement code, an unsuccessful bidder could challenge contract award even absent allegations of specific acts of fraud, collusion, or dishonesty.[61]

The Attorney General found that amendments or modifications to competitive bid contracts were permissible as long as they were "not material to the central purpose of the contract."[62] There, the AG reasoned that the underlying issue was whether the proposed changes subverted the purpose of competitive bidding.[63] In making this determination, the AG considered several factors, including the reasons for the change, the unforeseeability of the change, the timing, and the extent of the change relative to the original contract.[64]

Taxpayer Suits

Although most statutes do not specifically mention taxpayer suits, states have enjoyed a long history of protecting taxpayer standing. This is due, in no small part, to the longstanding principle that taxpayers have a right to know how their government uses public money in awarding contracts.[65] The promulgation of procurement codes typically does not preclude the ability of a taxpayer to file for an injunction when the state violates the requirements of competitive bidding. Pennsylvania, for example, determined that such taxpayer standing was proper even after the creation of the state's Commonwealth Procurement Code.[66]

Pennsylvania case law is rife with examples of taxpayer suits regarding government contracts. In a recent case, the court found that enactment of the state's Procurement Code did not take away the right of taxpayers to bring an action in equity to enjoin the award of a contract when the relevant bidding requirements were not followed.[67] The court held that the aggrieved taxpayer, who lacked standing to file a protest under the Procurement Code, could nonetheless still file an equity action in the court's original jurisdiction to protest the award of the contract.[68] In another case, Pennsylvania courts found that employees of subcontractors who worked for an unsuccessful bidder had standing.[69] Here, the court made its determination based on the fact that the employees were taxpayers in the Commonwealth.[70]

Conversely, in a different case, Pennsylvania courts held that a taxpayer did not have standing when he failed to show that "redress through other channels [was] *available at multiple levels*."[71] Here, the court reiterated the general rule that taxpayers lacked standing if their interest in the outcome of the suit did not surpass that of other taxpayers.[72] The court then outlined the exceptions to this rule, holding that a taxpayer may show that "(1) the government action would otherwise go unchallenged; (2) those directly and immediately affected by the complained use of expenditures are beneficially affected and not inclined to challenge the action; (3) judicial relief is appropriate; (4) redress through other channels is unavailable; and (5) no other persons are better situated to assert the claim."[73]

In yet another case, Pennsylvania courts held that a taxpayer of the public entity funding a public contract has standing to enjoin its award to anyone other than the lowest responsible bidder.[74] Here, the court reasoned that a taxpayer, having an interest in public funds, may maintain an action aimed at preventing the unauthorized or unlawful expenditure of money.[75]

Like Pennsylvania, New York also has a wide variety of case law on taxpayer suits. In one case, the court held that taxpayers had standing to bring an action challenging the legality of a contract under which a public building was constructed in alleged violation of public bidding requirements.[76] Similarly, the court held that where the city's actions allegedly violate state and municipal law bidding and procurement procedures, non-union transit employees had taxpayer standing to sue to enjoin the city from transferring certain transit operations to the Metropolitan Transportation Authority.[77]

Conversely, several New York cases have denied relief to taxpayer parties. In one such case, the city sought to purchase a snowplow when the town's snow removal equipment was destroyed by fire.[78] Here, although the accepted bid was $1,247 higher than the only other valid bid, the lower bidder was unable to furnish the truck and snowplow for six weeks. Consequently, the court held that an emergency existed, and because evidence established that there had been compliance with relevant provisions in the Highway Law code, the taxpayers' motion for continuation of temporary injunction would be denied on the grounds of irreparable injury.[79]

Oklahoma also has clear case law on the issue of taxpayer standing. In an early case from 1915, the Oklahoma Supreme Court held that payment for bridges for which a contract had been illegally made could be enjoined in a taxpayer suit without any appeal from the action of the court in issuing a warrant in payment.[80]

In New Hampshire, the court decided a case that presented an interesting twist on the typical taxpayer standing case. In *Clapp v. Town of Jaffrey*, petitioning taxpayers sought to restrain the town from contracting to use city equipment to plow the driveways of certain private individuals and also from performing certain other functions for hire for private individuals.[81] The Supreme Court of New Hampshire considered "whether it [was] lawful for the town to rent equipment to or perform services for private individuals on their property."[82] The court concluded that "taxpayers are entitled to injunctive relief if the acts of the town are ultra vires even though they cannot show any financial loss to the town."[83]

In an older case from New Mexico, a county was given money by the state, which it used to purchase a road grader.[84] The plaintiff taxpayer sued, claiming that the purchase violated the state procurement procedures because the road grader was not purchased from the lowest responsible bidder. The trial court sustained the defendant's motion to dismiss, reasoning that because the money was in effect a gift, the taxpayer had no business dictating how it should be spent. On appeal, the New Mexico Supreme Court agreed with the plaintiff that the source of the funds made no difference at all and permitted the taxpayer to maintain his suit.[85]

Protest Appeals

Prior to commencement of administrative or court action, most jurisdictions provide an opportunity for the Chief Procurement Officer or a designee to settle and resolve protests. When settlement is not reached, most state and local government procurement codes or rules require the CPO, head of the procuring agency, or a designee to issue a final and conclusive written decision on the protest. From this final decision, the protestor or the procuring agency may appeal to a higher administrative tribunal or court. The protestor must inform the head of the purchasing agency within a prescribed time of the intention to administratively or judicially appeal the final and con-clusive decision of the CPO, head of the agency, or a designee.[86]

In Arizona, for example, appeals of bid protest decisions are made to the Director of the Department of Administration within 30 days of the procurement officer's decision on the protest. The pro-curement officer must furnish the appellant with an agency report including all related documents as well as a statement summarizing findings, actions, recommendations, and any other evidence to assist in the appeal decision. Upon receipt of the agency report, the appel-lant then has five days to file an answer to the report with the Direc-tor. If the Director finds an appeal has merit, he or she may either decide the appeal on the protest or assign the matter to an Admin-istrative Law Judge.[87] Similarly, in Utah, adverse decisions from the chief procurement officer may be appealed to the Procurement Appeals Board[88] or the district court.[89]

The 2007 MC PIP is in line with jurisdictions that allow pro-test appeals to be made to administrative or judicial bodies. Spe-cifically, § 9-107, Access to Courts, provides that "[t]he [designated court or courts of the State] shall have jurisdiction over an action between the [Purchasing Agency] and a bidder, offeror, or contrac-tor, prospective or actual, to determine whether a solicitation or award of a contract is in accordance with the Constitution, statutes, regulations, [operational procedures], and the terms and conditions of the solicitation. . . ."

Conclusion

Bid protest systems encourage transparency and integrity by offering a means for unsuccessful bidders and offerors, citizens, and independent third parties to review procuring agency solicitation and contract award decisions. A well-functioning bid protest system promotes confidence among contractors and the public that state and local governments are committed to having agency actions reviewed for compliance with procurement laws and rules. Furthermore, a properly functioning bid protest system facilitates the resolution of solicitation and contract award controversies at the lowest levels, thereby protecting financial investments made by taxpayers.

Notes

1. 2007 MC PIP, § 9-101, comment (1).
2. Some states have invested in more formal protest systems where bid protests are heard by administrative judges who are independent from the procuring agency. The State of Maryland Board of Contract Appeals is illustrative. *See* MD. CODE REGS. 21.02.02.01 & .02 (2011).
3. IOWA CODE § 17A.19(1) (2011).
4. FLA. STAT. § 120.57(3)(b) (2011).
5. ARIZ. ADMIN. CODE § R2-7-A901 (2011).
6. LA. REV. STAT. ANN. § 39:1671(A) (2011).
7. *See* ARK. CODE ANN. § 19-11-247 (2011).
8. FLA. STAT. § 120.57(3)(b) (2011).
9. HAW. REV. STAT. § 103D-701(a) (2011); HAW. CODE R. § 3-126-4 (Weil 2011).
10. *See supra* note 6.
11. 350 N.W.2d 398 (Minn. Ct. App. 1984).
12. *Id.* at 398.
13. *See* Office of the State Comptroller for N.Y. State, *Contract Award Protest Procedures*, http://www.osc.state.ny.us/vendrep/protestprocedures.htm (last visited Oct. 8, 2011).
14. 34 TEX. ADMIN. CODE § 20.384 (2011).
15. VA. CODE ANN. § 2.2-4365 (2011).
16. WIS. ADMIN. CODE ADM. § 10.15(1) (2011) (any bidder or proposer who is aggrieved by a solicitation or notice of intent to award a contract may protest to the procuring agency).
17. MELISSA J. COPELAND, GUIDE TO STATE PROCUREMENT: A 50 STATE PRIMER ON PURCHASING LAWS, PROCESSES AND PROCEDURES (2011).
18. MD. CODE ANN. STATE FIN. & PROC. § 15-217(a)(1) (LexisNexis 2011).
19. *See* S.C. CODE ANN. § 11-35-4210(1)(a) (2011).
20. *See id* § 11-35-4210(1)(b).
21. *See* MASS. ANN. LAWS Ch. 30B (LexisNexis 2011); *see also* Massachusetts Office of the Inspector General, *Procurement Assistance and Enforcement*, *available at* http://www.mass.gov/ig/igch30b.htm (last visited Oct. 8, 2011).

22. 400 So. 2d 524 (Fla. Dist. Ct. App. 1981).

23. 398 S.E.2d 540 (Ga. 1990).

24. Equitable Shipyards, Inc. v. State, 93 Wn. 2d 465, 471, 611 P.2d 396, 400 (Wash. 1980) ("The court shall hear any such appeal on the administrative record which was before the [Commission]. The court may affirm the decision of the [Commission] or it may reverse the decision if it determines the action of the [Commission] is arbitrary or capricious.").

25. Everett Concrete Prods. v. Dep't of Labor & Indus., 109 Wn. 2d 819, 823, 748 P.2d 1112, 1114 (1988) ("[The court] may engage in de novo review, but should accord substantial weight to the agency interpretation (internal citation omitted).").

26. *See* Ghilotti Construction Co. v. City of Richmond, 45 Cal. App. 4th 897 (1996) (quoting 47 Ops. Cal. Att'y Gen. 129 (1966)).

27. 144 Ohio App. 3d 389, 760 N.E.2d 437 (2001).

28. 196 Or. App. 574, 103 P.3d 1150 (2004).

29. ALA. CODE § 41-16-31 (2011).

30. COLO. REV. STAT. § 24-109-404 (2011).

31. *Id.*

32. IOWA CODE § 73A.2 (2011).

33. *Id.* § 73A.3 (2011).

34. ME. REV. STAT. ANN. tit. 5, § 1747(1) (2011).

35. *Id.* § 1747(3).

36. *Id.* § 1749.

37. *Id.*

38. *Id.*

39. Vinson Guard Serv., Inc. v. Ret. Sys. of Alabama, 836 So. 2d 807 (Ala. 2002).

40. *Id.* at 810.

41. Urban Sanitation Corp. v. City of Pell City, 662 F. Supp. 1041, 1044 (N.D. Ala. 1986).

42. Spiniello Const. Co. v. Town of Manchester, 189 Conn. 539, 456 A.2d 1199 (1983).

43. *Id.* at 544–45, 456 A.2d at 1201.

44. Capasso Restoration, Inc. v. City of New Haven, 88 Conn. App. 754, 759, 870 A.2d 1184, 1187 (2005).

45. AAIS Corp. v. Dep't of Admin. Servs., 93 Conn. App. 327, 888 A.2d 1127 (2006).

46. *Id.*

47. *Id.* at 331, 888 A.2d at 1130 (citing John J. Brennan Constr. Corp. v. Shelton, 187 Conn. 695, 702, 448 A.2d 180, 184 (1982)).

48. ALA. CODE § 39-5-4 (2011).

49. *Id.*

50. *Id.*

51. ALASKA STAT. § 36.30.585(c) (2011).

52. ARIZ. ADMIN. CODE § R2-7-A904(C)(6) (2011).

53. S.C. CODE ANN. § 11-35-4310 (2011).

54. MD. CODE ANN. STATE FIN. & PROC. § 19-110(b)(5) (2011).

55. *Id.* § 19-110 (b)(6).

56. GTECH Corp. v. Commw., Dep't of Revenue, 965 A.2d 1276 (Pa. Commw. Ct. 2009).

57. Lockheed Info. Mgmt. Sys. Co., Inc. v. Maximus, Inc., 259 Va. 92, 524 S.E.2d 420 (2000).

58. *Id.*

59. *Id.* at 115, 524 S.E.2d at 433.

60. Pendleton Bros. Vending, Inc. v. Commw. Fin. & Admin. Cabinet, 758 S.W.2d 24 (Ky. 1988).

61. *Id.*

62. Ky. Op. Att'y Gen. No. 04-009 (Oct. 13, 2004).

63. *Id.*

64. *Id.*

65. *E.g.,* Jennifer Zimmerman, *On-Point Technology Systems, Inc. v. Commonwealth, Department of Revenue: The Commonwealth Court of Pennsylvania Upholds the Rights of Taxpayers After the Enactment of the Commonwealth Procurement Code,* 10 WIDENER J. PUB. L. 345, 354 (2001).

66. *See* On-Point Tech. Sys., Inc. v. Commw., Dep't of Revenue, 753 A.2d 911 (Pa. Commw. Ct. 2000).

67. Direnzo Coal Co. v. Dep't of Gen. Services, Bureau of Purchases, 779 A.2d 614 (Pa. Commw. Ct. 2001).

68. *Id.*

69. Balsbaugh v. Commw., Dept. of Gen. Servs., 815 A.2d 36, 40 (Pa. Commw. Ct. 2003), *aff'd,* 815 A.2d 628 (2003).

70. *Id.* at 40.

71. Reich v. Berks County Intermediate Unit No. 14, 861 A.2d 1005, 1011 (Pa. Commw. Ct. 2004) (emphasis in original).

72. *Id.*

73. *Id.* at 1009.

74. Nat'l Const. Services, Inc. v. Philadelphia Reg'l Port Auth., 789 A.2d 306 (Pa. Commw. Ct. 2001).

75. *Id.*

76. Reilly v. Town of Brookhaven, 34 A.D.2d 1001, 313 N.Y.S.2d 72, 73 (2d Dep't 1970).

77. Andre v. City of New York, 47 A.D.3d 602, 604, 850 N.Y.S.2d 148 (2d Dep't 2008).

78. Bloomfield v. Dunkel, 129 N.Y.S.2d 629 (N.Y. Sup. Ct. 1954).

79. *Id.* at 635–36.

80. Bd. of Comm'rs of Kay County v. Smith, 47 Okla. 184, 148 P. 111 (1915).

81. Clapp v. Town of Jaffrey, 97 N.H. 456, 91 A.2d 464 (1952).

82. *Id.* at 458, 91 A.2d at 465.

83. *Id.* at 461, 91 A.2d at 468.

84.   Shipley v. Smith, 45 N.M. 23, 107 P.2d 1050 (1940).

85.   *Id.,* 107 P.2d at 1053.

86.   *See* VA. CODE ANN. § 2.2-4365(B) (providing that any party, including the public body, may institute judicial review within 30 days of receipt of the written agency decision); *see also* MICH. CONST. art. 6, § 28 (providing that protestors may appeal an adverse decision by the chief procurement officer to Michigan's District Courts; appeals from trial court decisions involving bid protests follow normal civil appellate practice).

87.   ARIZ. ADMIN. CODE § R2-7-A905 (2011).

88.   UTAH CODE ANN. § 63G-6-807 (2011).

89.   *Id.* § 63G-6-810 (2011).

10

Contract Administration

While contract formation encompasses the activities that occur in the procurement process before a procuring officer awards a contract, contract administration governs the entire contractual relationship between the procuring agency and the contractor from the time of contract award through contract performance and ending with completed and accepted contract work. The contract administration phase of the procurement process presents distinct situations and issues that largely focus on assessing the legal rights of the parties to a validly executed government contract and the manner and mechanism to enforce contract obligations such as contract changes, contract adjustments, and contract claims.

Contract Modifications

Changing a contract for new or different requirements is a recurring issue in contract administration. Contract modifications are often effectuated by the issuance of change orders. The definition of a change order varies from one jurisdiction to the next, but most provide that a change order means a properly prepared document authorized by the procuring agency that directs and authorizes a contractor providing goods, construction, or performing services to change the quantity or character of goods or construction provided or services performed from that originally specified or estimated. Specifically, change orders can alter the following: description of services to be performed; time of performance; place of performance; or drawings, designs, or specifications. These changes may be required if the procuring agency or the contractor incorrectly estimates the work, encounters unforeseen obstacles, or wishes to add features or options. Major differences in the definition of a change order that may exist among the jurisdictions depend on what kinds of change in work clauses apply to goods, services, or construction; whether or not a contractor is entitled to a change in payment based upon the changed work to be performed; and the nature of the change (i.e., unilateral, bilateral, or constructive).

Generally, contract modifications fall into three categories: unilateral, bilateral, and constructive changes. Unilateral change orders require approval and signature from only the contracting officer. Unilateral change orders allow a procuring officer to make administrative or performance changes that fall within the scope of the contract without a requirement to negotiate with the contractor. Bilateral changes (more commonly referred to as contract amendments) are negotiated and require approval and signature from both the contractor and the contracting officer. Bilateral changes may reflect any agreement made between the parties that memorializes the modification of the terms of the original contract. Constructive changes occur when a contractor performs additional work beyond the contract requirements due to informal orders by the government or as required because of government fault.

Unilateral Changes

Generally, standard change of work clauses in government contracts allow procuring officers to make unilateral changes to contracts. Change orders may affect or alter the original requirements of a contract by adding or deleting work, readjusting delivery schedules, or directing the method or manner of performance. How the parties intend to handle changes is determined from the entire contract and all its provisions must be given meaning if that can be accomplished consistently and reasonably.[1]

A unilateral change order is exclusively a government privilege that advances the flexibility in administering a government contract.[2] The following contract clause illustrates a typical unilateral change of work clause,

> § 13.1 The OWNER may at any time, as the need arises, order changes within the scope of the WORK without invalidating the Agreement. If such changes increase or decrease the amount due under the CONTRACT DOCUMENTS, or in the time required for performance of the WORK, an equitable adjustment shall be authorized by CHANGE ORDER.

When this change of work clause appears in a government contract, it allows the procuring agency to unilaterally order changes for which an equitable adjustment shall be authorized.

A unilateral change order is almost always in writing and becomes a part of and conforms to the existing contract. Unless otherwise stipulated, all work is performed under the same terms and conditions specified in the original contract. The change order details all changes to the original contract, particularly those that result in a change to the contract price.[3] If a change in the contract price occurs, then the change order will typically require the signatures of both the authorized procuring official and the contractor before becoming effective. For example, Arizona law states that the procurement administrator of the Assistant Director of General Services must approve in writing any change order exceeding $100,000.[4]

Although unilateral change orders are exclusively issued by the procuring agency, a contractor may submit a request for a change order to the appropriate procuring official. If a contractor fails to submit a request for a change order, the contractor may not be paid for the additional costs incurred in doing work not yet approved by the procuring official. In *Seneca Valley, Inc. v. Village of Caldwell*,[5] a contractor who did not submit a request for a change order for fill and gravel replacement beyond the fixed price set forth in its bid was not entitled to payment for excess materials used in the project.[6] The contractor agued that the solicitation contemplated a unit price for all necessary work, including fill and asphalt replacement, and, as such, a change order was not required because payment for work was based upon unit pricing with no set number of units.[7]

In affirming the trial court's summary judgment in favor of the procuring agency, the Court of Appeals of Ohio interpreted the contract as requiring lump-sum pricing for specifically listed work that was inclusive of labor and materials as opposed to unit pricing, which was the interpretation urged by the contractor. Furthermore, the appeals court agreed with the procuring agency's interpretation of the contract's change in work clause that supported a determination that pre-negotiated unit prices were included in the contract to deal with measuring post-contractual increases resulting from written and executed change orders authorized by the proper procuring official.[8] Specifically, the contract changes clause stated,

> 13.2 The ENGINEER, also, may at any time, by issuing a FIELD ORDER, make changes in the details of the WORK. The CONTRACTOR shall proceed with the performance of any changes in the WORK so ordered by the ENGINEER unless the CONTRACTOR believes that such FIELD ORDER entitles the CONTRACTOR to a change in CONTRACT PRICE or TIME, or both, in which event the CONTRACTOR shall give the ENGINEER WRITTEN NOTICE thereof. . . . Thereafter the CONTRACTOR shall document the basis for the change in CONTRACT PRICE or TIME within thirty (30) days. The CONTRACTOR shall not execute such changes pending the receipt of an executed CHANGE ORDER or further instruction from the OWNER.[9]

The appeals court concluded that the contractor misinterpreted the contract as well as oral statements made by individuals representing the agency. Furthermore, the appeals court concluded that the contract unambiguously required a written change order in advance of any additional pay items. By failing to follow the designated procedure for requesting written explanations of prebid requirements and failing to file for change orders once approved work was already underway, the contractor bore the sole risk of the changes made and thus was not entitled to additional payment in the form of an equitable adjustment.[10]

Contract interpretation of unilateral change order clauses can work a hardship on contractors not responsible for changed conditions or delays in performance. These hardships may occur when contracts include "no damages for delay" clauses and the government as opposed to the contractor is responsible for subsequent delays. For example in *R & R, Incorporated of Louisville v. Commonwealth*,[11] the procuring agency unilaterally ordered a change that revised the contractor's completion date in order to accommodate another contractor that fell substantially behind schedule on its portion of a fast track procurement.[12] The procuring agency advised the delayed contractor that the revised completion date would not result in any increase to the contract amount.[13] After the procuring agency denied the contractor's claim for additional compensation based on the delay, the contractor filed an action in court seeking damages for delay, including extended job site costs, added labor costs, lost productivity, acceleration costs, and forfeiture of other business opportunities.[14]

The complaining contractor cited Article 14 of the contract titled "Changes in Work" to support its contention that this clause and not the "no damages for delay" clause in Article 16 of the contract controlled the issue of additional compensation for delays unilaterally ordered by the procuring agency where the contractor was not at fault.[15] Specifically, Article 14 stated in relevant part,

> [T]he [procuring agency], without invalidating the contract, may as the need arises, unilaterally order changes in the work in the form of additions, deletions or other revisions. Such changes in the work shall be authorized by Change Order signed by the [procuring agency] and Architect. The Contract Sum and the Contract Completion Time will be adjusted accordingly.[16]

The procuring agency argued, and both the trial court and the Court of Appeals of Kentucky agreed, that Article 16 of the contract was controlling because it specifically addressed delays and time extensions, whereas Article 14 addressed unilateral change orders.[17] Article 16 titled, "Delays and Extensions of Time," provided in relevant part,

> the Contractor shall not be charged with liquidated damages or any access cost when the delay in completion of the work is due to:
>> (1) any preference, priority, or allocation order duly issued by the government;
>> (2) unforeseeable cause beyond the control and without the fault or negligence of the Contractor, . . . or
>> (3) any delays of subcontractors or suppliers occasioned by any of the causes specified in subsection (1) and (2) of this article:
> on condition that the Contractor shall, within fifteen (15) calendar days of the occurrence of the event, notify the Architect in writing. The Architect shall ascertain the facts and extent of the delay and notify the Contractor within a reasonable time of its decision in the matter. Any change in the contract time resulting from any such claim shall be incorporated in a change order. An extension of time shall not be construed as cause for extra compensation under the contract. . . .[18]

In affirming a grant of summary judgment in favor of the procuring agency, the Court of Appeals of Kentucky concluded that Article 16's "no damages for delay" clause was dispositive on the issue of additional compensation because that article specifically addressed changes in contract completion times and, in cases of ambiguity, specific contractual clauses are controlling.[19]

Bilateral Changes (Contract Amendments)

Bilateral changes, sometimes referred to as mutually agreed change orders,[20] to a contract typically require negotiation between the parties, a written instrument, and signatures from both the procuring officer and the contractor to execute any amendments, modifications, or waivers of contract terms.[21] Rarely are oral modifications to contracts permitted when public contracts contain clauses that require mutual written consent of the parties to execute bilateral changes.[22] Bilateral changes may cover price, delivery schedule, quantity, key personnel, terms and conditions, and specifications or designs.[23]

New Mexico procurement law refers to a contract modification, which necessarily includes, among other actions, bilateral changes, and defines the former term as "any written alteration in the provisions of a contract accomplished by mutual action of the parties to the contract."[24] The Georgia Procurement Manual refers to a bilateral change as a substantive change that can be requested by the contract administrator or the supplier that must be processed through a bilateral amendment that requires signatures of authorized representatives from both parties.[25] In Texas, the Local Government Code states that after award of a contract but before the contract is made, the county official who makes purchases for the county may negotiate a bilateral change to a contract if the change is in the best interests of the county and does not substantially change the scope of the contract or cause the contract amount to exceed the next lowest bid. According to the county code, to be effective, the commissioner's court must approve the bilateral change and the resulting contract modification.[26] Rhode Island's purchasing statute deals with bilateral changes under the term "contract amendments," which means,

> any written alteration in the specifications, delivery point, rate of delivery, contract period, price, quantity, or other contract provisions of any existing contract, whether accomplished by unilateral action in accordance with a contract provision, or by mutual action of the parties to the contract. It includes bilateral actions, such as supplemental agreements, and unilateral actions, such as change orders, administrative changes, notices of termination, and notices of the exercise of a contract option.[27]

A bilateral changes clause has several purposes. First, it is there to provide operating flexibility by giving the procuring agency the ability to negotiate a change of work to accommodate advances in technology. Second, it provides the contractor a means of proposing changes to the work, thereby facilitating more efficient performance and improving the quality of the contract and the products. A contract clause allowing for a bilateral change also furnishes authority to the procuring officer to order additional work within the "general scope" of the contract without using the procedures required for a new procurement. It is important to ensure that both parties properly approve a bilateral change. In Oklahoma, a bilateral change was struck down because the proper authority, the Office of Public Affairs, did not authorize it.[28]

Even if a contractor has customarily performed work at the direction of a government official before the execution of a bilateral change order, the contractor may be precluded from receiving compensation for extra work costs incurred as a result of an oral authorization. For example, in *P & D Consultants, Inc. v. City of Carlsbad*, the contractor argued that the contract's written change order requirement was modified by the procuring official's oral authorization of the extra work for which it sought payment, and by the parties' conduct in handling prior contract amendments.[29] In deciding against the contractor, the California Court of Appeal determined that "[t]he plain language of the contract limits the [procuring agency's] power to contract to the prescribed method[, i.e., written change as opposed to changes by oral authorization or conduct]. By ostensibly relying on [the procuring official's] oral authorization or direction to begin or perform extra work without a written change order, [the contractor] acted at its peril."[30] The court reasoned that "the purpose for including a written change order requirement in a . . . contract was obviously to protect the public fisc" from unmonitored overspending by contractors in excess of funds appropriated for the work.[31]

Constructive Changes

Constructive changes are those that are informally ordered by the government or required by government fault despite the absence of a formal change order.[32] A "change" is established when the actual performance goes beyond the minimum standards required by the contract. An "order" can be shown whenever a government representative, by words or deeds that go beyond mere advice, comment, suggestion, or opinion, requires the contractor to perform work that is not a necessary part of the contract.[33] A distinct feature of constructive changes is that the procuring agency does not acknowledge the change. In this respect, a constructive change amounts to a breach of contract.

Generally, this type of contract change occurs when a contractor (1) performs additional work beyond the contract requirements, without a written or express change order from the procuring official; (2) receives an informal order by the procuring official; or (3) must alter performance to address the government's faulty specifications or miscalculations.[34] The principle of a constructive change exists to address contractor claims for compensation for changed work resulting from the conduct or actions of the procuring agency. For example, if the contractor followed the procuring agency's plans, although these plans were faulty in achieving the desired result, the contractor in fairness should be paid for the work, even if an unintended result was achieved. The unintended final result is considered a constructive change, and the contractor would be paid, in theory, as if it were a unilateral change order under the contract.

Contractors should present constructive changes to procuring agencies before any final payment is rendered. Once the procuring agency issues its final payment, it can act as a bar to any claims for constructive changes. Generally, there are four instances where constructive changes will allow the contractor to recover additional payment: (1) if the specifications are defective, requiring the contractor to perform additional work; (2) if the procuring official misinterprets the contract and rejects work that conforms to the contract's requirements; (3) if the procuring official requires a higher standard of performance beyond the terms of the contract; or (4) if the procuring official denies a justifiable time extension.[35]

Procuring agencies generally protect against the advent of constructive change claims by requiring that all changes in work comply with the requirement for written authorization. Thus, in *Foster Wheeler Enviresponse, Inc. v. Franklin County Convention Facilities Authority*,[36] the Supreme Court of Ohio cited as a general rule that when a building or construction contract stipulates that changes in work requirements must be in writing, then there is no recovery without a written directive, unless waived by the contracting official.[37] In *Foster*, the procuring agency awarded a contract to remove coal tar waste from a construction site on a fixed-price basis with one line item encompassing a base bid and an attachment providing a prenegotiated unit price that would adjust the contract sum in the event of an increase or decrease in the amount of contamination actually excavated at the construction site.[38] During the course of remediation, the contractor removed a significant excess of contamination above what was contemplated in the base price; however, the contractor did not receive written authorization to embark on the additional work. Instead, the contractor performed the work allegedly in reliance upon oral representations by the procuring agency's consultant that the unit price would be paid by the procuring agency for the additional work.[39] The court framed the issue as whether the contract between the procuring agency and contractor should be interpreted to contain a requirement for written authorization where more than the base amount of contaminated materials was found on site.

In concluding that a written authorization was required, the court interpreted the contract's changes clause as providing,

> that "[n]o *alterations* shall be made in the work shown or described by the plans and specifications, except upon the written order of the Owner." Only after the alteration is made pursuant to a written order is the "value of the work added . . . [to] be computed . . . , and the amount so ascertained [to] be added to . . . *the base bid amount*." Article 7, Section b of the general conditions makes clear that the term "alterations" is intended to encompass "increases . . . in the quantity of work." Whatever legal significance there may be in other contexts of defining "scope of work," and regardless of whether the removal of excess contaminated waste falls within that definition, such work constitutes an "alteration," as that term is used in this contract, for which a written order is required.[40]

With respect to the unit price contract attachment, the court determined after construing the agreement as a whole that

> the parties' intent in inserting the footnote was to set forth a prenegotiated unit price for adjusting the contract sum in the event an alteration involving an increase or decrease in the

quantity of work was ordered in writing. The unit price [was] a preset method of calculating the value of additional work to be used to adjust the contract sum where the amount of waste [was] found to be more than [that contemplated by the base price]. It is not a prenegotiated waiver of the requirement for written authorization.

Placing this case outside the application of the constructive change doctrine, the court held that "[t]he compensation to be paid was . . . based upon a price fixed as a result of competitive bidding, and was not left to the subsequent agreement of the parties. . . ."[41]

Also determining the nonexistence of a constructive change, the court concluded that "[t]here [was] no evidence in the record that [the procuring agency] ordered the contractor to remove and transport more than the base amount of contaminated waste. The most that can be inferred from the record [was] that [the procuring agency] had knowledge that alterations involving increases in the quantity of work were being made, and asserted no objection. However, mere knowledge, and even acquiescence, is not enough for recovery."[42] Accordingly, the court held that a written order was required in order for the contractor to remove excess contamination materials from the site, and the contractor should not have relied on the consultant's on-site monitor who claimed there was no need for a written order.[43] Thus, if the contractor stipulates that alterations or changes must be in writing, such language is binding, and a constructive change will not be deemed to have occurred unless the proper authority waives the written requirement.

While the overarching policy to protect the public fisc from runaway expenditures that could result from an onslaught of claims for constructive changes is prudent, some courts have recognized and applied the doctrine to respond to cardinal changes imposed by procuring agencies. For example, in *Global Construction Inc. v. Missouri Highway and Transportation Commission*,[44] the Missouri Court of Appeals recognized the constructive change doctrine as a generally accepted rule of public contract law. The court explained that a

contractor who has agreed to construct a public improvement for a stated price is entitled to additional compensation

for expenses incurred by reason of the fact that the public officials in control of the work have insisted upon the contractor
doing work not fairly embraced in the contract; however, the
contractor is not entitled to additional compensation where it is
shown that the contract actually contemplated his performing
the work for which further remuneration is sought. . . . When
the public or authorized officials direct performance of work
which is, in fact, beyond contract requirements, the direction to
perform such work has been defined in some jurisdictions as a
. . . constructive change.[45]

The court explained further "there are three categories of constructive [changes]. The first category is where the specifications
are defective and, as a result, the contractor is required to perform
extra work. The second category is where the public official[]
misinterpret[s] the contract by erroneously rejecting work that conforms to the contract's requirements, or where the public official[]
require[s] a higher standard of performance that is not within the
terms of the contract. The third category is where the public official[] den[ies] the contractor a justifiable time extension, requiring
the contractor to adhere to the original contract schedule to complete the contract."[46]

Applying the constructive change doctrine and going further
to award a contractor damages, *Housing Authority of City of Texar-
kana v. E.W. Johnson Construction Co. Inc.*[47] recognized a viable claim
by the contractor for cardinal changes and delays occasioned by the
procuring agency's conduct that prevented a construction project
from being completed on schedule.[48] The procuring agency did not
include housing unit roof repairs in the original contract but later
issued a change order requiring the contractor to undertake such
additional work without an extension of time and without allowance for extra labor and materials.[49] As such, the contractor rejected
the change order and was told to stop all other work until a decision was made about the roofing repair.[50] As a further consequence
of the delay caused by the roofing defects and other change orders
received from the procuring agency either adding or deleting certain items of repair and the failure of the procuring agency to make
timely decisions involving changes and corrections in defective plans

and specifications, the contractor experienced substantial delays in its project completion schedule.[51] The Supreme Court of Arkansas determined that where delays result from faulty specifications and plans, the procuring agency will have to respond in damages for the resulting additional expenses realized by the contractor.[52] "Moreover, the owner's breach of its implied warranty may not be cured by simply extending the time of the performance of a contractor's assignment."[53] Based on this reasoning, the court concluded that the failures, delays, and inaction by the procuring agency amounted to cardinal changes that resulted in additional expense to the contractor and a delay in the completion of the original contract, all of which justified affirming the damage award to the contractor.[54]

Public policy considerations favor scrutinizing contractors' claims for constructive changes, particularly when contractors do not follow the processes set forth in change of work clauses. The standard processes outlined in contracts for addressing changes give procuring officials timely notice of deviations and any additional expenses incurred by contractors in order to make fiscally responsible decisions that will mitigate or avoid additional expenditure of public funds.[55] Regardless, the doctrine of constructive changes is a generally accepted rule of public contract law.

Scope of Changes

Change orders should not be used to substantially change the quality or character of the items or work to be provided, inasmuch as these types of changes would have been a determining factor in the original bidding. Changes that are deemed substantial or material as measured against the requirements of the original contract are referred to as "out of scope" or "cardinal" changes and are not permitted because they are inconsistent with full and open competition principles. Most jurisdictions allow change orders for additional work falling within the scope of the original contract but require re-solicitation of the change requirement if it is determined to be out of scope.[56] For example, Delaware procurement law provides in part:

> [w]here, because of changed situations, unforeseen conditions, strikes or acts of God, a change order is determined to be necessary and is requested by the agency and not specified in the agency's solicitation or advertisement for bids and in the contract, as awarded, the awarding agency may issue a change order setting forth the change, addition or extra work required to be undertaken by the contractor on a contract, which shall not: . . .
>
> (2) Invalidate the contract; provided, that such change is within the scope of the contract as set forth in the standard specifications, special provisions or similar publication of the agency.[57]

Similarly, the Utah Procurement Code requires the inclusion of clauses in construction contracts that relate to possible changes and may require or permit such clauses in contracts for supplies and services that govern change order within the scope of the original contract. Specifically, the Utah Procurement Code provides,

> (1) Rules and regulations shall require for state construction contracts and may permit or require for state contracts for supplies and services the inclusion of clauses providing for adjustments in prices, time of performance, or other appropriate contract provisions, and covering the following subjects:
>
> (a) the unilateral right of the state to order in writing changes in the work within the scope of the contract and changes in the time of performance of the contract that do not alter the scope of the contract work;
>
> (b) variations occurring between estimated quantities of work in a contract and actual quantities;
>
> (c) suspension of work ordered by the state; and
>
> (d) site conditions differing from those indicated in the construction contract, or ordinarily encountered, except that differing site conditions clauses required by the rules and regulations need not be included in a construction contract when the contract is negotiated, when the contractor provides the site or design, or when the parties have otherwise agreed with respect to the risk of differing site conditions.

(2) Adjustments in price pursuant to clauses promulgated under Subsection (1) shall be computed in one or more of the following ways:

(a) by agreement on a fixed price adjustment before commencement of the pertinent performance or as soon thereafter as practicable;

(b) by unit prices specified in the contract or subsequently agreed upon;

(c) by the costs attributable to the events or situations under the clauses with adjustment of profit or fee, all as specified in the contract or subsequently agreed upon;

(d) in any other manner as the contracting parties may mutually agree; or

(e) in the absence of agreement by the parties, by a unilateral determination by the state of the costs attributable to the events or situations under the clauses with adjustment of profit or fee. . . .[58]

Some jurisdictions apply price limits based on a percentage increase or decrease in contract work to establish whether a change is within the general scope of a contract. For example, in Oklahoma, change orders for construction contracts of $1,000,000 or less shall not exceed a 15 percent cumulative increase in the original contract amount; for contracts over $1,000,000, change orders shall not exceed the greater of $150,000 or a 10 percent cumulative increase in the original contract amount.[59] If the change order or if cumulative change orders exceed these amounts, then the statute requires a re-advertising for bids on the incomplete portions of the contract.[60] This restriction in price increase does not apply to changes in the unit price.[61] Similarly, in Indiana, the amount of a construction contract plus the amount of all change orders may not exceed the cost as estimated by the county surveyor by more than 20 percent.[62]

The provisions cited above all address and authorize change orders that are within the scope of the original contract. When the procuring agency seeks to add additional work that falls outside of the scope of the original contract, such changes are viewed as out of scope or "cardinal" changes that materially or substantially alter the character or the nature of the work contemplated by the parties and based upon a reasonable interpretation of the original solicitation's statement of work, specifications, and contract requirements and conditions. Accordingly, a cardinal change is a change that exceeds the original scope of the contract work that formed the basis of the solicitation and ensuing competition.[63] Cardinal or out-of-scope changes may result in a determination that a contract is void.[64] To void the contract, the aggrieved party, often an unsuccessful bidder or a performing contractor, would have to show that such changes would materially change or alter the scope of work contemplated by the original contract. Thus, in *Ray Sattler Construction Inc. v. City of Bossier City*,[65] the Court of Appeals of Louisiana concluded that in a contract to clear a tract of land, an amendment to include removal of subsurface debris was outside of the scope of the original solicitation requirements and violated the statute. As well, the changed work violated another statute requiring that out-of-scope changes in excess of $100,000 be let out for public bid.[66] Despite these violations, the appeals court recognized that the procuring agency agreed to pay the contractor's cost of hauling excess debris and determined that it would be unjust to allow the procuring agency to reap the benefits and escape liability because of the statutory prohibitions.[67] Accordingly, the appeals court concluded that the contractor would only be entitled to the expenses it incurred in performing the work created by the out-of-scope change.[68] Thus, because it was already paid in excess of its incurred expenses, no additional compensation would be forthcoming.[69]

Equitable Adjustments

Equitable adjustments are a type of corrective measure that responds to an increase or a decrease in the cost of a contractor's performance after the issuance of a change. Equitable adjustments, sometimes referred to as payment changes in state and local administration of procurement contracts, are appropriate in three types of situations: (1) when the contractor assumes additional obligations under the contract; (2) when some of the contractor's original obligations are canceled; and (3) when new obligations are substituted for pre-existing obligations.[70] An equitable adjustment is said to be "the difference between what it would have reasonably cost to perform the work as originally required and what it reasonably cost to perform the work as changed."[71]

Equitable adjustments are permitted on all three types of changes. A contractor may present a claim for equitable adjustment by submitting a demand for payment in writing, asserting its request for compensation as a matter of right under the changes clause of the contract along with supporting documentation. The claim for equitable adjustment is a mechanism common in government contracts to afford a contractor compensation for costs incurred in performing changes work and provides a remedy in lieu of seeking damages. In establishing the total amount of the equitable adjustment, the party claiming entitlement to the adjustment must bear the burden of proof. The submission of actual cost data to the court or reviewing agency is the preferred method of establishing the amount of the adjustment.[72]

A heavily cited equitable adjustment case is *M.J. Paquet, Inc. v. New Jersey Department of Transportation.*[73] In *Paquet*, the Supreme Court of New Jersey considered "whether an equitable adjustment should be awarded to a successful bidder of a public contract whose performance [was] rendered impracticable during the course of the contract."[74] The contactor submitted an unbalanced bid to the DOT for highway and bridge rehabilitation, including painting. Because a subcontractor submitted a lower, yet late bid before the contractor submitted its final bid, the contractor, instead of adjusting its pricing, allowed the painting costs to absorb other costs in the bid. After a year of work, the Occupational Safety and Health Administration (OSHA) revised regulations regarding the painting of bridges with lead-based paint. These new regulations would require more work for the painting portion of the contract, and hence a higher cost. Because the painting cost item could no longer absorb the other contract costs, the contractor submitted a claim for an equitable adjustment. The parties did not agree on the price increase, and the DOT cancelled the painting portion of the contract through a change order. After alternative dispute resolution, the contractor filed an action seeking an equitable adjustment.[75]

The court found that the DOT did not breach the contract when it cancelled the painting portion of the contract because painting amounted to "extra work" that could be contracted out separately with another bidding process, rather than "changed work" that would be included in the contract on a "force account" basis. Contract specification 101.03 defined "extra work" as "new and unforeseen work found essential to the satisfactory completion of the Project" and specification 104.08 provided that "the Contractor shall do such Extra Work . . . upon receipt of a Change Order . . . and in the absence of such [the contractor] shall not perform, nor be entitled to payment for, such Extra Work." Furthermore, specification 109.03 allowed the DOT Commissioner, if the contractor and the engineer could not agree, "[when] inadvisable to have such work completed on a Force Account basis . . . , [to exercise the discretion] to have such work completed by others, and the Contractor shall not interfere therewith nor have any claim for additional compensation as the result of such election."[76] The court concluded that the OSHA regulations required "new and unforeseen" work, which amounted to extra work. As such, the DOT could have negotiated with the contractor to perform the extra work, issued a change order that required the contractor to perform the extra work by force account, or it could decide not to have the contractor perform the extra work. The DOT chose not to have the contractor perform the work, which it was permitted to do under the contract specifications, and, thus, the DOT was not liable for breach of contract.[77]

The court examined whether the deletion of the entire painting portion of the contract, due to the unforeseen extra work, entitled the contractor to an equitable adjustment where the painting was now impracticable. Because the contract specifications did not provide for an equitable adjustment, and New Jersey case law had not adopted equitable relief, the court looked to federal law. According to the court, an equitable adjustment was defined as "the difference between what it would have cost to perform the work as originally required and what it cost to perform the work as changed"[78] with the purpose "to keep a contractor whole when the Government modified a contract."[79] The court also briefly noted several other states that allow equitable adjustments in contracts, such as Florida, Louisiana, Maryland, New York, Ohio, Oregon, and Texas.[80]

The court held that the contractor was entitled to an equitable adjustment for several reasons. First, the absence of an equitable adjustment clause in the contract did not prevent the contractor from receiving one. Regarding contract specification 102.08 that did not allow unbalanced bids, the Court found this term to be ambiguous and therefore construed it against the drafter, the DOT. Furthermore, the court would grant the contractor equitable relief despite finding an unbalanced bid because of the special circumstances of the case.[81] The contractor did not seek additional compensation for the extra work or the painting work; rather, it sought an equitable adjustment only for the completed work apart from the painting part of the contract. The court made a special exception for the contractor for submitting an unbalanced bid because there was no evidence of fraud or collusion. The special circumstances surrounding the bid submission and the subsequent unforeseen change in regulations placed the contractor in a unique position in which an equitable adjustment was necessary to make the contractor "whole."[82]

However, courts will not always extend equitable adjustments in circumstances of unforeseen risks, as in *Kilgore Pavement Maintenance v. West Jordan City*.[83] In *Kilgore*, the Court of Appeals of Utah distinguished the facts from *Paquet*. Specifically, the contractor submitted a bid for road reconstruction when the price for liquid asphalt oil was $350 per ton, which increased to $1,005 per ton after contract execution. The contractor submitted a claim for equitable adjustment after it completed the work. Upon presentation of the claim, the city council rejected it.[84] The appeals court distinguished this case from *Paquet* because it did not deal with "an equitable adjustment of the contract price after an unforeseen event had prompted the parties to modify the contract requirements."[85] Rather, *Kilgore* "assumed the risk of supply cost increases," which precluded its claim for equitable adjustment.[86]

Inspection

A fundamental goal of the procurement process is to obtain quality goods and services. In furtherance of this goal, procuring agencies inspect tendered supplies and services to ensure conformance with contract requirements. Inspection is defined as examining and testing supplies or services to determine whether they conform to contract requirements. Furthermore, testing encompasses that degree of inspection that determines the properties or elements of products, including the functional operation of supplies or their components, by the application of established scientific principles or procedures. While the right to inspect and test is very broad, it is not without limits. Inspections governed by either state commercial code provisions or specific government procurement provisions and contract clauses must reasonably relate to the determination of whether performance is in compliance with contractual requirements.[87]

Inspection clauses in state contracts are generally considered to be remedy-granting clauses that vest state and local governments with significant rights and remedies. The procuring agency generally has the right to inspect to ensure that it receives conforming goods and services. The particular inspection clauses contained in a contract, if any, determine the procuring agency's right to inspect a contractor's performance. The purpose of inspection provisions and contract clauses is to ensure that supplies, services, and construction provided by contractors conform to state and local government contract testing, quality, and quantity requirements.

State and local procurement laws or codes vest authority in the chief procurement officer to establish and maintain programs for inspection and testing of supplies and services. It is important to note that most state and local governments do not require the inclusion of inspection and testing provisions and contract clauses in solicitations and contracts; rather, these provisions and contract clauses may be included at the discretion of the procuring agency.

For example, Arkansas procurement rules provide that "the State Procurement Director, within the limitations of this subchapter and the rules and regulations promulgated under authority of this subchapter . . . may establish and maintain programs for the inspection, testing, and acceptance of commodities and services."[88] Maryland has a comprehensive regulatory scheme covering the inclusion of inspection and testing provisions and clauses in solicitations, the procedures for testing, and the method for conducting inspections. Specifically, in Maryland, contracts may provide for the inspection of labor or goods at the contractor's or subcontractor's facility and testing to determine whether there is conformance with solicitation or contract requirements. The inspections and tests shall be conducted in accordance with the terms of the solicitation or the contract. Furthermore, in terms of procedures for testing, the procurement officer may establish operational procedures governing the testing and trial use of labor or goods and the application of resulting information and data to specifications or procurements. Finally, with respect to conducting inspections, inspections or tests shall be performed so as not to unduly delay the work of the contractor or subcontractor. Also, no inspector other than the procurement officer may change any provision of the specifications or the contract without written authorization. The presence or absence of an inspector does not relieve the contractor or subcontractor from any requirements of the contract.[89]

Where jurisdictions follow the principles of the jurisdiction's version of the uniform commercial code, the rights afforded to a buyer in accordance with general inspection rights will govern. For example, according to Oklahoma sales law, "the buyer has a right before payment or acceptance to inspect goods at any reasonable place and time and in any reasonable manner."[90] Similarly, Oregon has adopted the uniform commercial code as part of its code, thus incorporating the general principles regarding inspection, which provide that "[i]nspection is a right of the buyer."[91]

Whether based on specific sections of procurement codes or the uniform commercial code, procuring agencies have several options if goods or services are found to be defective upon inspection. The purchasing law in Nevada illustrates the procuring agency's options when presented with defective goods or services. Specifically, the chief of the purchasing division may, before final acceptance, require rejection of defective goods or services and require strict performance without additional charge or take delivery of defective goods or services at a reduced price.[92]

Acceptance

Acceptance is the act of an authorized representative of the procuring agency asserting ownership of identified supplies tendered or approved specific service performed in partial or complete fulfillment of contractual requirements.[93] Acceptance is conclusive except for latent defects, fraud, or gross mistakes amounting to fraud, or as otherwise provided for in the contract. Acceptance entitles the contractor to payment and is the event that marks the passage of title from the contractor to the procuring agency. The government may impliedly accept goods or services by making final payment, unreasonably delaying acceptance, or using or changing the product.

Delivery, inspection, acceptance, and warranties are closely linked concepts. Most procuring agencies will inform contractors that delivery of goods or services does not constitute acceptance.[94] Instead, delivery subjects supplies, materials, and equipment to potential inspection and testing. Even if inspection and testing does not occur immediately upon delivery, contractors are not relieved of liability. In addition, if solicitations and contracts include warranty clauses or if contracts incorporate provisions of the Uniform Commercial Code, contractors warrant that any goods supplied to procuring agencies meet or exceed specifications set forth in solicitations or contracts or come with implied warranties of merchantability and fitness for a particular purpose.[95]

As a general rule, contractors bear the risk of loss or damage to the contract work prior to acceptance. But, once the government accepts the goods or services, the risk of loss shifts to it. Despite government acceptance, latent defects may enable it to recover, even after acceptance. To be latent, a defect must have been unknown to the government, in existence at the time of acceptance, and not discoverable by reasonable inspection. This framework for evaluating latent defects was the central issue in *School Board of Pinellas County v. St. Paul Fire & Marine Insurance Company*.[96] The Second District Court of Appeal of Florida held that a surety of a contractor who was accused of breaching its contract upon the discovery of a latent defect in the construction of a roof would be estopped from claiming that acceptance of contract performance and payment by the school board constituted a waiver of a claim for damages for such latent defects.[97]

In addition, contract fraud allows the government to avoid the finality of acceptance. To establish fraud, the government must demonstrate that the contractor intended deceit and misrepresented a material fact, and that the government relied on the misrepresentation to its detriment. As well, a gross mistake may rise to the level of fraud and allow the government to avoid the finality of acceptance. The elements of a gross mistake amounting to fraud are a major error, without intent to deceive, causing the government to accept nonconforming performance, the contractor's misrepresentation of a fact, and detrimental reliance.

Warranties

State and local government contracts may contain provisions and contract clauses that require written guarantees from contractors that the goods supplied or the services rendered are suitable and meet or exceed the procuring agency's specifications.[98] These guarantees are commonly known as warranties. Express warranties are affirmative promises about the quality and features of the goods being sold. Implied warranties allow buyers to purchase goods and be confident that they meet certain minimum standards. The two implied warranties created by the Uniform Commercial Code are the warranty of "merchantability" of the goods being sold and the warranty that the goods are "fit for a particular purpose." Under the Uniform Commercial Code's definition of "merchantability," goods must be of at least average quality, properly packaged and labeled, and fit for the ordinary purposes they are intended to serve. The implied warranty of fitness for a particular purpose applies if the seller knows or has reason to know that the buyer will be using the goods he or she is buying for a certain purpose.

The enforcement of warranty clauses is not without limit. Warranties can be limited by the finality of acceptance of incomplete or defective performance. For example, in *Grass Range High School District No. 27 v. Wallace Diteman, Incorporated*,[99] the Montana Supreme Court held that where the school district without reservations, objections, or conditions on final acceptance ratified its architects' acceptance of a gymnasium floor that was patently defective and the subject of dissatisfaction during final inspection, a one-year warranty contained in the contract would not be extended to cover defects existing and known to be in the floor at the date of acceptance.[100] The court concluded that the floor was defective at the date of acceptance; the acceptance and payment were made without equivocation. The school district had a right to withhold payment or issue it with qualification, but it chose to rely upon the warranty for latent defects, and as a matter of law it waived its rights to later require the contractor to rebuild the accepted floor.[101]

Indemnification

Indemnification agreements are risk-shifting measures that set forth an obligation in which one party agrees to compensate or hold harmless another party for existing and/or future loss, damage, or injury liability sustained under a contract. Indemnification clauses in state and local contracts typically inure to the benefit of state and local governments and cover a promise by the contractor to hold the procuring agency harmless for the acts or omissions of the contractor.

More problematic and likely less enforceable are indemnity agreements that run from the government to the contractor for the contractor's benefit.[102] Such is the case because state and local governments incurring open-ended contingent liabilities in the use of public funds in the event a government act or omission would create the need to use public funds to cover the costs of holding a contractor harmless.[103]

The more common and enforceable type of indemnification clause is examined in *R. Zoppo Company, Inc. v. City of Manchester.*[104] The City of Manchester hired an engineering firm to prepare plans for enclosing a stream, and once complete, the plans were used as the basis of a solicitation for bids. After award, and shortly after construction began, a dispute arose concerning the extent of the so-called "cofferdamming." The contractor claimed that a short cofferdam would be sufficient and in compliance with the specifications, while the City wanted much more extensive (and expensive) structures. As the contract required, the issue was submitted to the engineer, who decided that the more extensive cofferdamming was required.

The contractor proceeded under protest and eventually sued the City for *quantum meruit*. The City brought a third-party claim against the engineer, alleging that the firm was required by the contract to indemnify the City for claims such as the contractor's. A master appointed by the court agreed with the City. On appeal, the reviewing court determined that the contract required the architect-engineer to hold the City harmless for all suits and claims arising out of or in consequence of the acts or failure to act of the architect-engineer.

Contract Terminations

Procuring agencies normally employ standard termination clauses with each contract, in accordance with contract administration policies and procedures. Termination clauses bestow broad rights that allow procuring agencies to discontinue contract performance. There are several good reasons for allowing such broad rights, including when a procuring officer determines that circumstances warrant discontinuing contract performance in the best interest of the state or local government or when a contractor fails to perform or has engaged in conduct that threatens the integrity of the procurement process.

A procuring officer possesses the authority and responsibility to terminate the contract in whole or in part and to give notice of the termination. The termination notice contains the extent of the termination and the effective date. Contractors must stop work as specified in the notice; place no further subcontracts for materials, services, or facilities, except as necessary to complete the continued portion of the contract; terminate all subcontracts to the extent that they relate to the work terminated; assign appropriate rights, title, and interests to the state and local government; and settle all outstanding liabilities. Termination clauses set forth the general procedures for a settlement agreement between the parties in the event of a termination. There are two types of termination clauses that benefit the government: (1) termination for convenience and (2) termination for default. Both types of termination clauses are rights that may be exercised; however, the difference between the two is that the former does not call into question the contractor's performance.

Terminations for Convenience

Termination for convenience clauses bestow broad rights that allow procuring agencies to discontinue contract performance without incurring liability for breach of contract damages.[105] The procuring officer has broad discretion to determine when to terminate a contract for convenience. The basis for such a termination is whether such action is in the best interest of the government. In the event a procuring officer terminates a contract for the convenience of the government, the procuring agency is obligated to compensate the contractor for work performed; however, the agency is not liable for expectation damages.

While the Model Procurement Code and the Model Code for Public Infrastructure Procurement do not set forth detailed provisions and clauses treating termination for convenience actions, the requirements for the broad right of termination for convenience are understood as a function of state and local governments' responsibility as the representative of the public interest. For example, at the federal level, the principles supporting the broad right to terminate a contract for the convenience of the government are well understood as originating from the winding down of wartime contracts that clearly no longer need to be performed at war's end.[106] Thus, for the benefit of the public interest, the federal government developed the innovation of termination for convenience to permit it the right to unilaterally cancel contracts for supplies, services, and construction without being deemed to have breached them.[107] The wartime justification for termination for convenience later expanded to include such terminations of peacetime contracts that were in the best interests of the government.[108]

At the state level, the same principle of protecting the public interest has been applied to justify termination for convenience clauses in state and local government contracts. For example, in *A.J. Temple Marble & Tile, Inc. v. Long Island Railroad*,[109] a cleaning contractor sued a public railroad after the railroad terminated its contract under the convenience provision. The New York appellate court based its decision to uphold the railroad's termination on the termination for convenience developments in federal courts.[110] The court outlined the rights, obligations, and remedies following a decision to terminate for convenience as follows:

> A standard "termination for convenience" clause in a government contract provides the government with broad rights to terminate a contract whenever the government deems that termination is in its interest. These clauses limit a contractor's recovery to the costs incurred as a result of the termination, payment for completed work, and the cost of preparing a termination settlement proposal. They often preclude . . . recovery of punitive damages or anticipated profits. . . . Thus, a termination for convenience clause limits the government's liability for a termination action that would otherwise constitute a breach of contract.[111]

The court addressed when there would be no limitation on the recovery of breach of contract damages. The standard for such recovery would depend on a showing that the procuring agency acted in bad faith or abused its discretion in invoking the termination for convenience clause, where bad faith would be demonstrated by a showing of malicious intent or animus toward the contractor.[112] Based on these rules applicable to termination for convenience, the court determined that the procuring agency did not act in bad faith in issuing a decision to terminate the cleaning contract when there was no evidence to show that it acted beyond the scope of its own termination for convenience procedures.

Similarly, the court in *Capital Safety, Inc. v. State Division of Building and Construction*[113] found that breach of contract damages will not be awarded absent a showing of bad faith and that such a showing cannot be made if a procuring agency is simply exercising its discretionary authority under the contract for ordinary business purposes that are reasonably within the contemplation of the parties.[114] In *Capital*, an asbestos removal contractor sued the public agency that terminated its contract for convenience. The "termination for convenience clause" provided, "[t]he State may, at any time, by written order terminate the Contract or any portion thereof for convenience after determining that for reasons beyond the Contractor's control, the Contractor is or will be unable to proceed with or complete the Project as contracted for, or that termination is otherwise in the public interest."[115] The Superior Court of New Jersey acknowledged that there were no state decisions and, thus, decided to follow federal termination for convenience case developments.[116] The court found that the contractor failed to show that the public agency acted in bad faith when it decided that its own conduct would cause delays in contract performance and, therefore, decided to terminate for convenience in order to avoid exposure to such a claim. The court concluded that a termination for convenience provision should be construed similarly to authorize termination of a contract even though the occasion for invoking this right is a government agency's unreasonable delay in providing the contractor access to the work site.[117]

The best interest of the state government and the propriety of statewide contract originally solicited under an invitation to bid procurement method was the primary issue in *Roth Produce Company v. Ohio Department of Administrative Services*.[118] In *Roth*, the procuring agency decided it was in the best interest of the government to terminate a multimillion-dollar produce contract for convenience and then reprocure the government's produce requirements using competitive negotiations because the original solicitation documents contained irregularities regarding how historical costs and contract prices were to be evaluated.[119] Moreover, the procuring agency's selection of the lowest bidder based on the original solicitation was called into question by an unsuccessful bidder who challenged the propriety of the competition and the ultimate contract award.[120] In response to the unsuccessful bidder's challenges and the irregularities in the solicitation documents, the procuring agency determined that terminating the contract for convenience and reprocuring the agency's requirements using competitive negotiations was more suitable.

The unsuccessful bidder, however, urged that it was the second low bidder and, thus, should have been awarded the contract under the original invitation to bid method.[121] The Ohio Court of Common Pleas found that "[g]iven the evidence . . . [and] the demands placed upon the [procuring agency], the [decision] . . . to terminate [the performing contractor's contract] for convenience and then go back and clarify both process and language while reletting a new contract was sensible."[122] The court found that "the [] contract documents did not [preclude the procuring agency from reserving the right to . . . terminate for convenience."[123] It further found that nothing assured the unsuccessful bidder or any other competitor that an award would be made to the next low bidder or that all bids would not be thrown out in favor of reprocurement.[124] Accordingly, the court determined that the procuring agency did not abuse its discretion in proceeding as it had in its effort to assure that the process of awarding an important, multimillion-dollar contract was transparent, reasonable, and in furtherance of full and open competition principles.[125]

The process for fair and equitable discontinuation of contract performance must take into account the government's rights and also the contractor's expectations. Accordingly, procuring agencies establish procedures and remedies that are as unique as termination provisions and contract clauses themselves. Generally, procuring agency procedures permit a contractor to submit a final termination settlement proposal to the procuring officer. The contractor and the procuring officer may agree upon the whole or any part of the amount to be paid or remaining to be paid because of the termination. The contractor is entitled to a monetary remedy. The remedies recoverable include the contract price for completed supplies or services accepted by the procuring agency; reasonable costs incurred in the performance of the work terminated, which may include a reasonable allowance for profit on work done; and reasonable costs of settlement of the work terminated.[126] Usually, the contractor's recovery may not exceed the total cost or price of the contract.

If the procuring officer and the contractor fail to agree on the whole amount to be paid because of the terminated work, the procuring officer may unilaterally make the determination of the amount to be paid. The contractor generally then has the right to file an appeal or to bring suit in a trial court.

A procuring officer may reinstate all or a portion of a terminated contract. The procuring officer must determine in writing that there is a requirement for the terminated items and that reinstatement is advantageous to the government. Once the procuring agency terminates a contract for convenience, it cannot later substitute this termination for a default termination.[127] As well, state and local governments and their procuring agencies are advised to use best practices in classifying a termination as one for convenience or default because the latter determination has dire consequences for a contractor and thus should be used consistent with agency procedures that protect the due process rights of the contractor. A contract clause that protects against wrongful or erroneous default terminations provides for conversion to a termination for convenience.[128] A typical termination conversion clause provides, "[i]f after notice of termination of the contractor's right to proceed under the provision of this clause, it is determined for any reason that the contractor was not in default under the provisions of this clause, or that the delay was excusable, the rights and obligations of the parties shall be the same as if the notice of termination had been issued pursuant to the termination for convenience clause."[129]

Terminations for Default

Termination for default is an extraordinary measure that should only be utilized in the most compelling circumstances. A termination for default, while not always considered a penalty, carries harsh consequences for a contractor, such as loss of bonding capacity, negative performance evaluations in future competitions for government work, and potential loss of business opportunities. Because of this, procuring agencies should proceed cautiously to ensure appropriate use of this government remedy and use best practices to assess the ability of a contractor to cure performance deficiencies before resorting to a default termination. There are several grounds to support a procuring officer's decision to terminate a contract for default. These include failure to deliver or perform on time; failure to make progress such that performance is endangered; notice of debarments, suspensions, or other responsibility determinations; and anticipatory repudiation. It is the procuring agency's burden to prove, by a preponderance of the evidence, that a termination for default is proper.

Once the procuring agency has met its burden of demonstrating the appropriateness of the default, the contractor has the burden of proof that its failure to perform was the result of causes beyond its control and without fault on its part.

Default termination rules and procedures only slightly vary by jurisdiction. Maryland's termination for default provision is comprehensive and illustrative. The provision states,

> [i]f the Contractor fails to fulfill its obligation under this contract properly and on time, or otherwise violates any provision of the contract, the State may terminate the contract by written notice to the Contractor. The notice shall specify the acts or omissions relied upon as cause for termination. All finished or unfinished work provided by the Contractor shall, at the State's option, become the State's property. The State shall pay the Contractor fair and equitable compensation for satisfactory performance prior to receipt of notice of termination, less the amount of damages caused by Contractor's breach. If the damages are more than the compensation payable to the Contractor, the Contractor will remain liable after termination and the State can affirmatively collect damages. Termination hereunder, including the determination of the rights and obligations of the parties, shall be governed by the provisions of COMAR 21.07.01.11B.[130]

Courts hold procuring agencies to a high standard when terminating a contract for default because of the adverse impact such an action has on a contractor. Unfortunately, procuring officials frequently fail to follow prescribed procedures, rendering default terminations subject to reversal on appeal. Prior to issuing default termination notices, procuring officers must (1) have a valid basis for the termination, (2) issue proper notices, (3) account for the contractor's excusable delay, (4) act with due diligence, and (5) make a reasonable determination while exercising independent judgment. Attorneys play a critical role in the process, ensuring that all legal requirements are met and that every termination decision receives the attention it deserves.

The procuring agency must notify the contractor, in writing, of its failure to progress, and in most jurisdictions, the procuring officer is required to give the contractor an opportunity to promptly correct nonperformance. The opportunity to promptly correct performance is called a cure notice. A proper cure notice informs the contractor in writing that the procuring agency intends to terminate the contract for default, the reason for the termination, and the contractor's opportunity to cure the specified deficiencies within a prescribed time period. Generally, a cure notice is not required before terminating for failure to deliver goods timely, anticipatory repudiation, or failure to perform under a construction contract. If the contractor does not respond with a defense, the procuring officer can, based on his or her discretion, issue a default termination notice. In summary, the default termination must state clearly the following: the specific contract under review for default termination; the acts or omissions constituting the default; the right to proceed under the contract if it is terminated; notice to the contractor of the right to appeal; and notice of the procurement agency's remedies.

The contractor can promptly correct nonperformance, accept the termination, and/or provide a defense to the proposed termination action. There are several defenses that a contractor can offer in response to a termination or cure notice. The contractor should analyze the situation to determine if its delay was excusable, with no fault or negligence attributable to it, or if unforeseeable causes exist in construction contracts for which the contractor had no responsibility or control over. The contractor has the burden of proving the existence of an excusable delay. Typical examples of excusable delays are acts of God, acts of government in its sovereign capacity, fire, strikes, or epidemics.

A case illustrating a procuring agency's proper steps in pursuing a default termination is *Dano Resource Recovery, Inc. v. District of Columbia*[131] This case analyzes the relevant elements of a termination for default: breach, notice, opportunity to cure, and remedies. In *Dano*, the District of Columbia Court of Appeals reviewed whether the procuring agency properly terminated a contract for default where the contractor was required to process and dispose of sludge and waste. The appeals court considered whether the contractor breached the contract by not performing the required work within a specified time frame.[132] Despite the contractor's protestations that the contract contained no time requirement for performance, the appeals court determined that the contractor was in breach of contract because it was on notice that the waste removal requirement was carefully drafted and the contract clearly expressed the 21-day performance time frame.[133] The appeals court reasoned that the 21-day requirement applied, otherwise "it would largely leave the District without performance standards by which to judge the contractor's timely processing and removal of waste after the demonstration period."[134]

The appeals court next considered whether the procuring agency properly terminated the contractor under the termination clause of the contract. The contractor and the District carefully negotiated these clauses, as the District had previously terminated other contracts awarded to the contractor; as well, the current project was considered a large investment.[135] There were two termination clauses within the contract: one, subsection (a)(i), which allowed for termination without an opportunity to cure if the services were not performed "within the time specified";[136] and the other, subsection (a)(ii), the sales provision, which required notice and a ten-day opportunity to cure period. The appeals court concluded that because the termination provisions were carefully negotiated by the parties, subsection (a)(i) must have a specific purpose and application, and that application was to cover the specific circumstance of failure to perform within the contractually specified time frame.[137] Moreover, the appeals court rejected the contractor's argument that the "time specified" in the termination clause applied to the "end product" of the contract as opposed to the 21-day time requirement because the disposal of waste was the purpose of the contract and the 21-day requirement was an essential condition.[138] Because the appeals court concluded that the contractor had a long-term and continuous inability to follow the removal procedures within the 21-day time requirement, resulting in an "environmentally serious and costly problems of waste accumulation," it concluded that the contractor breached the contract through "repeated non-compliance with the removal requirement," amounting to "substantial nonperformance." Accordingly, the appeals court affirmed the decision to terminate the contractor for default.[139]

The appeals court also considered whether the procuring agency could terminate for default when it waited several months before giving notice of termination rather than immediately terminating when the breach first became apparent. On this issue, the contractor argued that the procuring agency waived its right to terminate when it approved the contractor's initial demonstration period. The appeals court acknowledged that if the contractor detrimentally relied on this alleged waiver, the government had a "greater burden to act expeditiously when the contractor continue[d] to incur expenses in performing a contract. . . . On the other hand, there is obvious tension between this requirement and the government's duty not to act precipitously in declaring a default termination."[140] The appeals court assessed the behavior of the parties in the months preceding termination and determined that the procuring agency gave the contractor adequate notice that the removal requirement would be enforced and that it insisted on compliance.[141]

The appeals court also considered whether the procuring agency's failure to perform its responsibilities caused the contractor to breach the contract, thereby excusing the contractor's nonperformance. Specifically, the contractor claimed that the procuring agency materially contributed to the circumstances giving rise to the default when the procuring agency provided it with sludge that had too high a water content, which violated the contract term that sludge contain no more than approximately 80 percent water, and when the site flooded due to the procuring agency's failure to provide an adequate water leaching system. The appeals court concluded that the contractor's claims did not meet the standard required to excuse the contractor due to fault or interference by the procuring agency because the sludge water content only marginally deviated from the approximate requirement of 80 percent. Instead, the appeals court cited evidence that "the default resulted from [the contractor's] own failures because the contractor repeatedly and continuously failed to remove the waste within the time requirements when the water leaching system was working properly."[142]

Finally, the appeals court considered whether the government acted in good faith when it terminated the contract for default. Although the contractor claimed that the procuring agency terminated a project "involving major capital investment for essentially technical violations without giving the project a chance to succeed,"[143] the court held that the procuring agency terminated the contract in good faith for "substantially more than 'technical' violations."[144] The appeals court noted that a termination for default is a "severe remedy" and "the requirement of good faith and sound judgment underlying termination has 'special application for a default-termination [that] has the drastic consequences of leaving the contractor without further compensation."[145] Here, the appeals court determined that the termination for default "followed a pattern of recurrent assurance from [the contractor] that it would comply with the removal, no-storage, and permit requirements, followed by its failure to do so—all of which convinced the [procuring agency] that [the contractor] would not [] be able to overcome the defects in its operation."[146] Accordingly, the appeals court held that the procuring agency's decision to terminate the contractor for default was proper.

A contractor may succeed in defending against a default termination if it can show an excuse for nonperformance or that its nonperformance was waived by the procuring agency. For example, in *Alexander & Shankle, Inc. v. Metropolitan Government of Nashville and Davidson County*,[147] the Court of Appeals of Tennessee examined whether a government agency could waive its requirement that "time is of the essence" in the construction of two schools. The procuring agency terminated the contract for default, claiming the contractor defaulted on the "time of the essence" provision. The termination for default or "cause" clause allowed the procuring agency to terminate for failing to complete work in a timely manner, and allowed the procuring agency to take possession of the site and complete the work, with the defaulting contractor being liable for any costs in excess of the contract price.[148] In *Alexander & Shankle* various causes delayed the work: for example, a house that was onsite delayed the project by 15 days; soil conditions were not as expected, leading to the issuance of a change order providing for a 50-day extension; masonry work slowed because the work had to take place in the winter months due to the extensions; and the procuring agency issued a change order that requested additional work without allowing any additional time extensions. As the procuring agency continued to make additional work requests, the contractor wrote letters requesting more time, which the procuring agency did not grant. Instead, the procuring agency responded by writing "proceed" on the contractor's letters.[149] The procuring agency further modified the scope of work three times after the completion of performance date; however, 15 days after that date, the procuring agency sent the contractor a termination letter for failure to perform by the "substantial completion date."[150]

The appeals court analyzed whether or not the government had waived its substantial completion date requirement. The appeals court held,

> [t]he non-defaulting party may . . . by conduct indicating an intention to regard the contract as still in force after the other party's default, waive a provision in the contract making time of the essence. Thus, [when a procuring agency], knowing construction will not be completed before the deadline, [] allows the contractor to continue working after the deadline and encourages the contractor to finish the job, [the procuring agency] waives [the] right to terminate under a "time is of the essence" provision.[151]

Because the procuring agency made several changes to the scope of the work, the contractor notified the procuring agency of the need for extensions, and the procuring agency allowed the contractor to continue working beyond the completion date and even made further modifications beyond that date, the appeals court determined that the procuring agency waived its rights under the "time is of the essence" provision and, therefore, did not properly terminate the contract for default.[152] *Dano* and *Alexander & Shankle* illustrate when a default termination has been properly issued and when it has not. These cases analyze the substance of a default termination. *Dano* also highlights that a proper termination for default provides remedies for the procuring agency.

Upon termination of a contract for default, the contractor is liable to the procuring agency for any excess costs incurred in acquiring supplies or services. These include excess reprocurement costs, liquidated damages (agreed upon damages in lieu of actual damages), common law damages, and unliquidated damages (advance or progress payments). As explained in the previous subsection, a wrongful default termination gives way to remedies for the contractor.

Specifically, a procuring agency's erroneous termination of a contractor for default is converted to a termination for convenience. This conversion is sometimes referred to as a constructive termination for convenience. At the time of conversion, the contractor becomes entitled to the remedies provided for by the contract's termination for convenience clause.

One case covering constructive termination for convenience is *Peterson & Associates v. Dayton Metropolitan Housing Authority*.[153] In *Peterson*, a contractor complained that the procuring agency wrongfully terminated its contract for default while the procuring agency argued that the contractor failed to complete the work.[154] The contractor argued that project delays were the result of excusable delays, and the procuring agency failed to investigate these claims as required by the contract. The Court of Appeals of Ohio adopted its magistrate's interpretation of the contract, which precluded the procuring agency from terminating a contract for default if "(1) the delay arose from unforeseeable causes beyond the control and without the fault of the contractor; and (2) the contractor timely notified [the procuring agency] of the causes of the delay." Specifically, the contractor sent the State timely notice of excusable delays, which the procuring officer failed to properly investigate. The procuring agency claimed the contractor was partially responsible for the delay and failed to set up a reasonable completion date. The procuring agency also claimed in its appeal that if the court found that termination for default was improper, then that default termination should be converted into a termination for convenience.

The procuring agency relied on the termination conversion language to argue for a limit on the contractor's recovery. The contract language for conversion provided "[i]f, after termination of the Contractor's right to proceed, it is determined that the Contractor was not in default, or that the delay was excusable, the rights and obligations of the parties will be the same as if the termination had been for the convenience of the [procuring agency]."[155] While the appeals court determined that the procuring agency's termination by default was improper, it did accept the argument that the termination for default should be converted to a termination for convenience because there was no proof presented at trial that the procuring agency acted in bad faith or clearly abused its discretion in rendering its termination decision.[156] Therefore, the contractor's recovery was limited to items allowed under the termination for convenience clause; specifically, the procuring agency would be liable upon receipt of a properly presented claim setting out in detail (1) the cost of work performed to the date of termination; (2) the cost of settling subcontractor claims; (3) the cost of preserving work; (4) the cost of presenting the termination claim; and (5) reasonable profit on the work performed.[157]

Suspension and Debarment

Suspension

States typically outline statutory guidelines for suspending prospective bidders on a government contract. While the statutory language varies from state to state, most codes include provisions articulating the reasons for suspension and include the relevant authority and procedures for appeals.

Authority and Procedure

Colorado's procurement code is indicative of many states' statutory language regarding suspension of prospective bidders. State law gives authority to the head of a purchasing agency or designee to suspend a person from consideration for award of a contract if there is probable cause that such person has engaged in activities that may lead to debarment.[158] Colorado law further requires that the purchasing agency consult with the attorney general and the using agency.[159] Further, suspension cannot exceed the three-month limit defined by statute.[160] However, if a criminal charge has been issued for an offense that would lead to debarment, the attorney general may request that the suspension remain in effect until after the trial of the suspended person.[161]

New Mexico law allows a state purchasing agent to recommend to a state agency that a business be suspended from consideration of a public contract.[162] As in Colorado, the suspension cannot exceed a three-month statutory period.[163] As with many states, New Mexico requires that the suspension be in accordance with relevant rules regarding reasonable notice and fair hearing. First, the governing authority of a state agency must issue a written determination that includes the reasons for the action taken and the information regarding the suspended party's rights to judicial review.[164]

With respect to suspension procedures, in the event that an appeal is submitted, Colorado's debarment and suspension statute requires the executive director to "promptly decide . . . debarment or suspension."[165] Additionally, this decision must be in writing and issued within 30 days after receipt of the appeal.[166] In the case of an appeal to the executive director from a decision regarding suspension, the aggrieved contractor must file an appeal within 20 working days of the receipt of the decision.[167] Colorado also sets forth time limitations for appeals to the district court, holding that a judicial review of a decision of the executive director must be initiated within six months after the receipt of the decision.[168]

Reasons for Suspension

Because many statutes state that suspensions are appropriate where there is probable cause that a contractor has engaged in activities that may lead to debarment, it is not unusual that the reasons for suspension are much the same as the reasons for debarment. Among the reasons listed in Colorado's statutes are the conviction of a criminal offense as an incident to obtaining or attempting to obtain a public or private contract; conviction under state or federal statutes of embezzlement, theft, forgery, bribery, falsification or destruction of records, or receiving stolen property; and conviction under state or federal antitrust statutes arising out of the submission of bids or proposals.[169] The statute additionally lists that a history of material failure to perform, materially unsatisfactory performance, or debarment by any other governmental entity that is based upon a settlement agreement can justify suspension.[170]

New Mexico has statutes articulating causes for suspension. While the statute is not exhaustive, it lists among the causes conviction of a bidder for a criminal offense relating to obtaining a public or private contract and conviction under state or federal statutes of embezzlement, theft, and antitrust activities. The statute also allows suspension based on a "history of failure to perform, or of unsatisfactory performance of [] one or more contracts."[171] New Mexico affords a general three-year time limit from the date of procurement to issue suspensions.[172]

There is ample case law concerning suspension in government contracts. In one New Jersey case, for example, the Commissioner of Transportation temporarily suspended a government contractor from a list of responsible bidders, and the contractor appealed. The Supreme Court held that the Commissioner of Transportation did not act unreasonably when he issued the suspension on the basis of an indictment charging that the corporate contractor's majority stockholder conspired with another to bribe a member of the state police.[173]

In another New Jersey case, the lowest bidder for a state lottery advertising contract sought review of the Director of Division of Purchase and Property's determination denying the award to the lowest bidder. When the Superior Court determined that the contract should be awarded to the lowest bidder, the Director petitioned for certification. The Supreme Court held that the Director did not abuse his discretion in awarding the contract to other than the lowest bidder, and that the Director was not obligated to initiate debarment or suspension proceedings against the low bidder.[174] The court noted, "[w]hen a bid is rejected based on grounds or for reasons that are similar to those that could, under other circumstances, support debarment or suspension, the procedures followed must generate the same assurance that the public interest has been met as attends the conduct of debarment and suspension proceedings."[175]

Debarment

State statutes typically discuss debarment and suspension together, sometimes explicitly outlining that a bidder can be suspended for any activity that may lead to debarment.[176] When discussed together, debarment is virtually always considered the more severe punishment, though there is often overlap in the numerous causes that can trigger the two penalties.

Authority and Procedure

Maryland procurement statutes contain a separate chapter devoted entirely to debarment and suspension procedures. Notably, the code states that the provisions of the chapter are "broadly applicable to all contracts with public bodies, except where a section refers only to the State."[177] Maryland gives authority to both the Board of Public Works and the Attorney General to institute debarment proceedings.[178]

Interestingly, Maryland statutes provide conditions for mandatory and permissive debarment. By operation of law, a person is debarred from entering into a contract with a public body if the person has been "convicted under the laws of the State for bribery, attempted bribery, or conspiracy to bribe, committed in furtherance of obtaining a contract with a public body."[179] The statute then articulates that permissive debarment is applicable where a person has been "convicted under the laws of the State for bribery, attempted bribery, or conspiracy to bribe, committed other than in furtherance of obtaining a contract with any public body, [or] has been convicted under the laws of another state."[180] Finally, the statute allows for debarment proceedings when a person has admitted during an investigation, in writing or under oath, "acts or omissions that would constitute bribery, attempted bribery, or conspiracy to bribe, under the laws of the State, another state or the United States."[181]

If an entity is to be mandatorily debarred, the Board of Public Works must give reasonable opportunity for that person to be heard on whether the stated basis for debarment exists."[182] Maryland statutes also articulate procedure for the termination of debarment, stating, "[i]f the conviction that is the basis for a debarment or suspension is reversed or otherwise rendered void, the debarment or suspension terminates automatically."[183] The statute also allows any person to submit a petition for removal of debarment to the Board of Public Works five years from the date of debarment.[184] The Board, in turn, must make a determination within 90 days whether to conduct a hearing regarding the petition.[185]

Colorado, similar to other jurisdictions, articulates several procedural requirements for initiating debarment proceedings. Generally, debarment proceedings permit the head of a purchasing agency, after issuing reasonable notice to the person involved and after consultation with the attorney general, to debar a person from consideration for award for any statutorily defined reason.[186] State law also provides that debarment shall not be for a period of more than three years.[187] Utah, for example, also allows the chief procurement officer or head of a purchasing agency to debar a person after reasonable notice has been issued, and after consultation with the attorney general.[188] Utah's debarment period is also three years.[189]

Reasons for Debarment

Maryland law allows for debarment proceedings for several offenses. In addition to the mandatory debarment proceedings discussed above, the state also has provisions concerning fraud, embezzlement, and theft-related offenses.[190] Significantly, Maryland statutes allow debarment if the person commits the prohibited activity, or if such acts are committed by "an officer, partner, controlling stockholder or principal of that person, or any other person substantially involved in that person's contracting activities."[191] Among the various causes for debarment, Maryland statutes include criminal offenses incident to obtaining a public or private contract, criminal convictions for violating an antitrust statute of any state, and convictions for violating the Racketeer Influenced and Corrupt Organization Act.[192] There is currently proposed legislation in the Maryland state senate regarding minority business participation. Under this proposed bill, the Board of Public Works would be authorized to "debar a person from contracting with the State for one year if the Board finds that the person knowingly violated a contract clause requiring a specified degree of minority business enterprise participation."[193]

Utah law articulates several causes for debarment. As in most states, chief among these causes is the conviction of a "criminal offense as an incident to obtaining or attempting to obtain a public or private contract or subcontract or in the performance of such contract or subcontract."[194] The law also states several other causes, among them conviction under state or federal statutes for embezzlement, theft, forgery, bribery, falsification, destruction of records, or any other offense indicating a lack of business integrity.[195] The law also lists conviction under antitrust statutes, failure without good cause to perform in accordance with the terms of the contract, or debarment by another governmental entity for any cause listed by state rules and regulations.[196]

New Mexico statutes contain residual language that includes the violation by a bidder of contract provisions of a nature and character "reasonably regarded by the state purchasing agent or a central purchasing office to be so serious as to justify a suspension or debarment action."[197] New Mexico statutes also permit debarment of delinquent bidders with "a history of failure to perform, or of unsatisfactory performance of, one or more contracts, provided that this failure or unsatisfactory performance has occurred within a reasonable time preceding the decision to impose debarment and provided further that failure to perform or unsatisfactory performance caused by acts beyond the control of the contractor shall not be considered to be a basis for debarment."[198] Finally, New Mexico law contains a catch-all provision that any unlisted cause that the state purchasing agent determines is "so serious and compelling as to affect responsibility [of] a contractor" may be a basis for debarment, provided the cause occurred within three years of a procurement.[199]

There are numerous cases relating to debarment issues. In a New Jersey case, a paving and construction company appealed a decision from the Commissioner of Labor and Industry who placed the contractor's name on a list of ineligible firms for public works contracts because the contractor failed to pay prevailing wages. There, the Superior Court held that debarment provisions cover both intentional and unintentional violations, and that the debarment was not an abuse of discretion, notwithstanding that the amount of monies underpaid was small with respect to the aggregate amount of monies involved in public contracts.[200] The court noted that "although the amount of monies underpaid is relatively small . . . appellant's conduct represents a breach of his statutory duty to safeguard the interests of his employees [that] the statute seeks to protect, as well as the interests of the State."[201]

Similarly, in a Wisconsin case, a construction contractor appealed a decision of the state Department of Workforce Development (DWD) that debarred the contractor from bidding on state and municipal public works projects for six months for failure to abide by prevailing-wage laws.[202] The Circuit Court essentially upheld the DWD's decision, holding that the contractor could be debarred from municipal but not state projects. There, the Court of Appeals held that a 15-month delay in issuing the debarment determination did not violate the contractor's due process rights.[203]

Conclusion

The contract administration phase is arguably the last opportunity for the procuring agency to exercise oversight over the procurement process. In some cases, contract administration is overlooked as too costly or administratively burdensome. These concerns should not discourage the procuring agency from exercising its authority to observe, test, inspect, and approve of contract work. The administrative contracting officer plays a vital role in interpreting contract clauses, managing unilateral changes and contract amendments, making pricing adjustments, and referring contractors for termination, suspension, or debarment when necessary to protect the integrity of the procurement process. Contract administration is the final opportunity to ensure that the procuring agency receives the goods, services, or construction necessary to accomplish agency minimum needs.

Notes

1. *See* Prunty Const., Inc. v. City of Canistota, 682 N.W.2d 749, 757 (S.D. 2004); *see also* Carstensen Contracting, Inc. v. Mid-Dakota Rural Water Sys., Inc., 653 N.W.2d 875, 877 (S.D. 2002).
2. *See* R.I. CODE § 37-2-42; UTAH ADMIN. CODE § R 33-6-102; S.C. CODE OF LAWS § 11-35-3410; M.G.L.A. 7 § 42E.
3. 10 ME. REV. STAT. ANN. § 1488 (West, Westlaw through 2011 Sess.).

4. ARIZ. ADMIN. CODE § R2-7-604.

5. 156 Ohio App. 3d 628, 808 N.E.2d 422 (2004).

6. *Id.*, 808 N.E.2d at 432.

7. *Id.* at 427–28.

8. *Id.* at 429.

9. *Id.* at 430.

10. *Id.* at 431.

11. 2005 WL 626391 (Ky. App.).

12. *Id.* at *1.

13. *Id.*

14. *Id.*

15. *Id.* at *3.

16. *Id.*

17. *Id.* at *4.

18. *Id.* at *2

19. *Id.* at *4.

20. DiGioia Bros. Excavating, Inc. v. Cleveland Dept. of Pub. Util., Div. of Water, 135 Ohio App. 3d 436, 734 N.E.2d 438, 447 (1999).

21. P & D Consultants, Inc. v. City of Carlsbad, 190 Cal. App. 4th 1332, 1336, 119 Cal. Rptr. 3d 253, 256 (2010).

22. *Id.* at 1340, 119 Cal. Rptr. at 259.

23. 64 AM. JUR. 2D *Public Works and Contracts* § 96 (2011).

24. N.M. STAT. ANN. § 31-1-42. Contract modifications can also include administrative changes, supplemental agreements, notices of exercising an option, or notices of termination; *see also* M.G.L.A. 7 § 42E.

25. GEORGIA PROCUREMENT MANUAL § 7.6.1.2. Substantive Change, *available at* http://pur.doas.ga.gov/gpm/MyWebHelp/GPM_Main_File.htm (last visited July 28, 2011).

26. TEX. LOC. GOV'T CODE ANN. § 262.0305 (West, Westlaw through 2011 Sess.).

27. R.I. CODE § 37-2-7.

28. Indiana Nat. Bank v. State Dep't of Human Services, 857 P.2d 53 (Okla. 1993).

29. 190 Cal. App. 4th at 1337, 119 Cal. Rptr. at 257.

30. *Id.* at 1341–42, 119 Cal. Rptr. at 260–61.

31. *See id.* at 1342, 119 Cal. Rptr. at 261.

32. District of Columbia v. Organization for Environmental Growth, Inc., 700 A.2d 185, 203 (D.C. App. 1997).

33. *Id.*

34. 64 AM. JUR. 2D *Public Works and Contracts* § 181 (2011).

35. Global Const., Inc. v. Missouri Highway and Transp. Comm'n, 963 S.W.2d 340 (Mo. App. 1997).

36. 78 Ohio St. 3d 353, 678 N.E.2d 519 (1997).

37. *Id.* at 360, 678 N.E.2d at 525.

38. *Id.* at 356, 678 N.E.2d at 523.

39. *Id.* at 358, 678 N.E.2d at 524.
40. *Id.* at 362–63, 678 N.E.2d at 527.
41. *Id.* at 363, 678 N.E.2d at 527.
42. *Id.* at 364, 678 N.E.2d at 528 (explaining further that "[t]he primary purpose of requiring written authorization for alterations in a building or construction contract is to protect the [procuring agency] against unjust and exorbitant claims for compensation for extra work. It is generally regarded as one of the most effective methods of protection because such clauses limit the source and means of introducing additional work into the project at hand. It allows the [procuring agency] the means to investigate the validity of a claim when evidence is still available and to consider early on alternative methods of construction that may prove to be more economically viable. It protects against runaway projects and is, in the final analysis, a necessary adjunct to fiscal planning.").
43. *Id.* at 364–65, 678 N.E.2d at 528.
44. 963 S.W.2d 340 (Mo. App. 1997).
45. *Id.* at 343.
46. *Id.*
47. 264 Ark. 523, 573 S.W.2d 316 (1978).
48. *Id.* at 534, 573 S.W.2d at 322–23.
49. *Id.* at 527, 573 S.W.2d at 319.
50. *Id.*
51. *Id.* at 528, 573 S.W.2d at 319–20.
52. *Id.* at 533, 573 S.W.2d at 322.
53. *Id.*
54. *Id.* at 534, 573 S.W.2d at 323.
55. A.H.A. Gen. Const., Inc. v. New York City Hous. Auth., 699 N.E.2d 368 (N.Y. 1998).
56. *See* Roy Sattler Constr., Inc. v. City of Bossier City, 903 So. 2d 503, 505 (La. App. 2005) (citing La. Rev. Stat. Ann. § 38:2212(A)(6), which provides that any change order outside the scope of the contract in excess of $100,000 shall be let out for public bid).
57. 29 Del. C. § 6904(f).
58. Utah Code Ann. § 63G-6-601.
59. Okla. Stat. Ann. § 61-121A & B; *see also* C.G.S.A. § 4e-46.
60. Okla. Stat. Ann. § 61-121A & B.
61. *Id.* § 61-121C.
62. Ind. Code Ann. §§ 36-1-12-18, 36-9-27-80.5 (West, Westlaw through 2011 Sess.).
63. *See* Roy Sattler Constr., Inc. v. City of Bossier City, 903 So. 2d 503, 505 (La. App. 2005) (citing La. Rev. Stat. Ann. § 38:2211(A)(5), which states that "[a] change order outside the scope of the contract means a change order [that] alters the nature of the thing to be constructed or [that] is not an integral part of the project objective").
64. *See* La. Rev. Stat. Ann. § 38:2220(A); *see also Ray Sattler*, 903 So. 2d at 505.

65. 903 So. 2d 503, 505 (La. App. 2005).

66. *See id.* at 505.

67. *See id.*

68. *See id.*

69. *See id.*

70. District of Columbia v. Org. for Envtl. Growth, Inc., 700 A.2d 185, 203 (D.C. App. 1997).

71. *Id.*

72. *See id.; see also* AM. JUR. 2D *Public Works and Contracts* § 185 (2011) (if the contractor appeals a claim for equitable adjustment in a court, the contractor bears the burden of proof to show that the government ordered or created the need for changed work under the contract).

73. 794 A.2d 141 (N.J. 2002).

74. *Id.* at 143.

75. *See id.* at 143–45.

76. *Id.* at 146–47.

77. *See id.*

78. *Id.* at 149 (citing General Ry. Signal Co. v. Washington Metro. Area Transit Auth., 875 F.2d 320, 325 (D.C. Cir. 1989), *cert. denied*, 494 U.S. 1056 (1990)).

79. *Id.*

80. *Id.* at 150; *see* Hendry Corp. v. Metro. Dade Cnty., 648 So. 2d 140, 141 n.2 (1994), *review denied*, 659 So. 2d 1087 (Fla. 1995); Ronald Adams Contractor v. City of New Orleans, 764 So. 2d 1149, 1152 (2000), *writ denied*, 768 So. 2d 1287 (La. 2000); State Highway Admin. v. David Bramble, Inc., 351 Md. 226, 717 A.2d 943, 948 n.7 (1998); Tempforce Inc. v. Mun. Hous. Auth. of Schenectady, 263 A.D.2d 926, 694 N.Y.S.2d 240, 242 n.1 (1999), *appeal dismissed*, 94 N.Y.2d 838, 702 N.Y.S.2d 586, 724 N.E.2d 378 (1999); Sherman R. Smoot Co. v. Ohio Dep't of Admin. Servs., 136 Ohio App. 3d 166, 736 N.E.2d 69, 74–75 (2000); State v. Triad Mech., 144 Or. App. 106, 925 P.2d 918, 920 (1996), *review denied*, 324 Or. 488, 930 P.2d 852 (1996); Texas Natural Res. Conservation Comm'n v. IT Davy, 998 S.W.2d 898, 899 (Tex. App. 1999), *abrogated on o.g.,* General Servs. Comm'n v. Little-Tex Insulation Co., 39 S.W.3d 591 (2001).

81. *See Paquet,* 794 A.2d at 151.

82. *See id* at 153–54.

83. 2011 WL 1886812 (Utah App.).

84. *See id.* at *1.

85. *Id.* at *4.

86. *Id.*

87. With respect to sections *Inspections, Acceptance,* and *Warranties,* UCC provisions only apply to sales of goods, not construction or services contracts. With regard to construction and services contracts, common law and other statutes, policies, and rules apply.

88. ARK. CODE ANN. § 19-11-217.

89. Md. Code Regs. 21.06.08.02, *available at* http://www.dsd.state.md.us/comar/comarhtml/21/21.06.08.02.htm (last visited July 17, 2011).

90. Okla. Stat. Ann. tit. 12A, § 2-513.

91. Or. Rev. Stat. § 72.5130.

92. Nev. Rev. Stat. § 333.190.

93. *See* Georgia Vendors Manual § 7.11 (2010), *available at* http://doas.ga.gov/StateLocal/SPD/Docs_SPD_Official_Announcements/GVM-A1-2010.pdf (last visited July 17, 2011).

94. *See id.*

95. *See id.* § 7.19.

96. 449 So. 2d 872, 17 Ed. Law Rep. 727 (Fla. Dist. Ct. App. 1984).

97. *See id.*, 449 So. 2d at 873–74.

98. *See* Ga. Code Ann. §§ 11-2-314 and 11-2-315 (Georgia's general and specific warranty provisions adopted from the Uniform Commercial Code).

99. 155 Mont. 10, 465 P.2d 814 (1970).

100. *See id.* at 14–15, 465 P.2d at 817.

101. *See id.* at 16, 465 P.2d at 817.

102. *See, e.g.,* Ariz. Rev. Stat. § 34-226, Indemnity agreements in construction and architect-engineer contracts void.

103. *See* Fla. Att'y Gen. Op. No. 84-103 (1984). Governmental entities, including school districts, are limited by constitutional mandate from entering into certain contracts. These limitations are placed on governmental entities through constitutional restrictions on the use of public funds and public credit.

104. 453 A.2d 1311 (N.H. 1982).

105. *See* Utah Admin. Code R. 33-6-108.

106. *See generally* Torncello v. United States, 681 F.2d 756, 764 (Ct. Cl. 1982). The age-old tension in upholding a decision to terminate for the convenience of the government has been centered around two tests: the changed circumstances test offered in *Torncello* and the bad faith or abuse of discretion test offered in *Kalvar Corp. v. United States*, 543 F.2d 1298 (Ct. Cl. 1976), the latter case having been affirmed and reinstated as the majority test for determining the sufficiency of a contracting officer's decision to terminate for the convenience of the government by *Krygoski Constr. Co., Inc. v. United States*, 94 F.3d 1537 (Fed. Cir. 1996). *See also* Ram Eng'g & Constr., Inc. v. Univ. of Louisville, 127 S.W.3d 579, 583 (Ky. 2003) (explaining the concept of termination for the government's convenience at the federal level).

107. *See Torncello*, 681 F.2d at 764.

108. *See* Questar Builders, Inc. v. CB Flooring, L.L.C., 410 Md. 241, 266, 978 A.2d 651, 666 (2008).

109. 172 Misc. 2d 422, 659 N.Y.S.2d 412 (N.Y. Supp. 1997).

110. *Id.*, 659 N.Y.S.2d at 424.

111. *Id.* (citations omitted).

112. *Id.*, 659 N.Y.S.2d at 425; *but see* Ram Eng'g & Constr., Inc. v. Univ. of Louisville, 127 S.W.3d 579, 585 (Ky. 2003) (reasoning that the government right

to "terminate contracts for convenience . . . cannot supersede the good faith duty to do 'everything necessary' to carry out the contract. Kentucky's recognition of good faith as 'a duty to do everything necessary to carry [the contract] out' . . . limits the contracting officer's discretion to terminate a contract for convenience and indicates that a change of circumstances standard is best for Kentucky.").

113. 369 N.J. Super. 295, 848 A.2d 863 (App. Div. 2004); *see* Stony Brook Constr. Co. v. College of New Jersey, 2008 WL 2404174, at *7 (N.J. Super. App. Div.).
114. *Capital*, 369 N.J. Super. at 301, 848 A.2d at 866.
115. *Id.* at 298, 848 A.2d at 864.
116. *Id.* at 300, 848 A.2d at 866.
117. *Id.* at 304–05, 848 A.2d at 869.
118. 160 Ohio Misc. 2d 117, 940 N.E.2d 672 (Com. Pl. 2010).
119. *Id.* at 119, 940 N.E.2d at 674.
120. *Id.* at 122, 940 N.E.2d at 675–76.
121. *Id.* at 122, 940 N.E.2d at 676.
122. *Id.* at 125, 940 N.E.2d at 678.
123. *Id.*
124. *Id.*
125. *See id.*
126. *See Stony Brook*, 2008 WL 2404174, at *6 (explaining that "[a] termination for convenience, whether constructive or otherwise, limits a contractor's recovery to costs incurred, a reasonable profit for the work performed, and termination costs.").
127. *See* Public Bldg. Auth. of City of Huntsville v. St. Paul Fire, 2010 WL 3937962, at *7 (Ala.) (explaining that the effect of a termination for convenience is the discharge of contractual obligations. Thus, on the issue of whether a termination for convenience could be conditional and later converted into a termination for cause, the Supreme Court of Alabama decided that "[u]nder the terms of the contract, a termination for convenience unequivocally terminates the contract and relieves [the contractor] from incurring any further obligation associated with the project. There is no language in the contract allowing a termination for convenience to be converted into a termination for cause, and the [procuring agency] offered no applicable legal authority to support [the] position that a termination for convenience may be converted to a termination for cause absent contractual language allowing such a conversion." Therefore, the court held "[i]n light of the unambiguous terms of the contract, there [was] no basis for reading the contract in such a way as to allow the [procuring agency] to resuscitate a dead contract so that it may re-terminate it.").
128. UTAH ADMIN. CODE R. 33-6-106; MD. CODE REGS. 21.07.01.11, *available at* http://www.dsd.state.md.us/comar/comarhtml/21/21.07.01.11.htm (last visited July 31, 2011); *see Stony Brook*, 2008 WL 2404174, at *6 (explaining

that "if the government terminates a contract for an improper purpose, the termination can be 'constructively' converted into a termination for convenience if such a clause is present in the contract").

129. UTAH ADMIN. CODE R. 33-6-106; MD. CODE REGS. 21.07.01.11(B)(4).
130. MD. CODE REGS. 21.07.01.11.
131. 620 A.2d 1346 (D.C. 1993).
132. *See id.* at 1352.
133. *Id.*
134. *See id.* at 1356.
135. *See id.* at 1357.
136. *Id.*
137. *See id.* at 1356–57.
138. *See id.* at 1357.
139. *See id.* at 1357–58.
140. *Id.* at 1359.
141. *See id.*
142. *See id.* at 1360.
143. *Id.*
144. *Id.* at 1361.
145. *Id.* (citing Darwin Contr. Co. v. United States, 811 F.2d 593, 597 (Fed. Cir. 1987) and Schlesinger v. United States, 390 F.2d 702, 709, 182 Ct. Cl. 571 (1968)).
146. *Id.*
147. 2007 WL 2316391 (Tenn. Ct. App.).
148. *Id.* at *2.
149. *Id.* at *3–4.
150. *Id.* at *4.
151. *Id.* at *9 (citing LauLin Corp. v. Concord Properties, 1995 WL 511947, at *4 (Tenn. Ct. App.)); *see also* Shepherd v. Perkins Builders, 968 S.W.2 832, 833 (Tenn. Ct. App. 1997).
152. *Id.* at *9–10.
153. No. 17306, 2000 WL 1006562 (Ohio Ct. App.).
154. *Id.* at *1.
155. *Id.* at *4.
156. *Id.* at *12–13.
157. *Id.* at *7.
158. COLO. REV. STAT. ANN. § 24-109-105(1)(b) (West).
159. *Id.*
160. *Id.*
161. *Id.*
162. N.M. STAT. ANN. § 13-1-177 (West).
163. *Id.*
164. N.M. STAT. ANN. § 13-1-179 (West).
165. COLO. REV. STAT. ANN. § 24-109-204(1) (West).
166. *Id.*

167. COLO. REV. STAT. ANN. § 24-109-203 (West).
168. COLO. REV. STAT. ANN. § 24-109-206(1)(b) (West).
169. COLO. REV. STAT. ANN. § 24-109-105(2) (West).
170. *Id.*
171. *Id.*
172. *Id.*
173. Trap Rock Indus., Inc. v. Kohl, 59 N.J. 471, 284 A.2d 161 (1971).
174. Keyes Martin & Co. v. Dir., Div. of Purchase & Prop., Dep't of Treasury, 99 N.J. 244, 491 A.2d 1236 (1985).
175. *Id.,* 99 N.J. at 264.
176. *See, e.g.,* COLO. REV. STAT. ANN. § 24-109-105 (West).
177. MD. CODE ANN., State Fin. & Proc. § 16-201 (West).
178. *See id.* § 16-303.
179. *Id.* § 16-202.
180. *Id.*
181. *Id.*
182. *Id.* § 16-304.
183. *Id.* § 16-310.
184. *Id.*
185. *Id.*
186. COLO. REV. STAT. ANN. § 24-109-105 (West).
187. *Id.*
188. UTAH CODE ANN. § 63G-6-804 (West).
189. *Id.*
190. MD. CODE ANN., State Fin. & Proc. § 16-203 (West).
191. *Id.*
192. *Id.*
193. H.B. No. 194, 428th Sess. of the Gen. Assemb. (Md. 2011) (as of publication, there have been no votes on this bill).
194. UTAH CODE ANN. § 63G-6-804 (West).
195. *Id.*
196. *Id.*
197. N.M. STAT. ANN. § 13-1-178 (West).
198. *Id.*
199. *Id.*
200. Dep't of Labor & Indus., Div. of Workplace Standards v. Union Paving & Const. Co., Inc., 168 N.J. Super. 19, 401 A.2d 698 (App. Div. 1979).
201. *Id.,* 168 N.J. Super. at 32–33.
202. Kruczek v. Wisconsin Dep't of Workforce Dev., 692 N.W.2d 286 (Wis. Ct. App. 2004).
203. *Id.*

11

Controversies during Contract Performance

Government contract disputes can be timely and expensive. Many state and local governments attempt to manage the cost and risk of disputes by implementing dispute resolution procedures. The type and scope of these procedures vary greatly among jurisdictions. Despite these variances, however, many of the goals for dispute resolution procedures are uniform, namely keeping the lines of communication open between the procuring agency and the contractor, quickly addressing and resolving disputes when they arise, and reaching settlements that are fair to both contracting parties. This chapter describes various dispute resolution processes, ranging from alternative dispute resolution to lawsuits. The purpose of all of these resolution techniques is to resolve disputes quickly so that work can continue and so that the relationship between the procuring agency and the contractor remains amicable. When disputes cannot be resolved, they should be allowed to proceed to a final determination by a competent agency or judicial body.

Alternative Dispute Resolution

Alternative dispute resolution (ADR) is a technique designed to help parties settle issues in controversy without resorting to timely

275

and costly litigation. The term "alternative dispute resolution" encompasses many different processes with many different traits. All of the processes are alternatives to trial, but individual processes have distinct characteristics. The contracting community has viewed ADR not as an imposition, but rather as a powerful tool to navigate issues in controversy in expedient, cost-effective ways. The 2007 MC PIP acknowledges the importance of ADR in comment (2) to Article 9, Appeals and Remedies. In providing a model structure that authorizes the chief procurement officer to settle and resolve protests, comment (2) provides that "[n]othing in this Article is intended to preclude the use of alternative dispute resolution methods in the resolution of procurement-related disputes, or in the use of contract clauses that provide for the avoidance, negotiation, or mediation of disputes."

Alternative dispute resolution refers to a wide variety of non-binding and binding dispute resolution methods that involve the use of third-party neutrals to aid the parties in resolving issues in controversy according to a structured settlement process. ADR methods exist on a continuum, ranging from dispute avoidance to litigation. When considering employing an ADR method, parties in controversy must consider the appropriateness of resorting to alternative dispute resolution, the availability of a structured alternative dispute mechanism, and the effectiveness of alternative dispute resolution methods. It is imperative to remember that ADR, although a powerful tool, has its own set of limitations; therefore, ADR techniques should not be viewed as a panacea for all contract controversies. Alternative dispute resolution is just one technique to resolve controversial issues before they grow into insurmountable problems.

The purpose and goals of ADR are primarily to reduce the costs of litigation, maximize the efficiency of the administrative and judicial dispute systems, minimize disruptions to agency actions, and increase the satisfaction of parties in controversy by resolving disputes. As relates to government contractors, most state and local governments' express policies stress resolving all contract disputes at the contracting officer level. To achieve this policy, agencies are encouraged to use alternative dispute resolution procedures to the maximum extent practicable.

No community has embraced the purpose and goals of ADR more than the government contracting community. As with the federal government, many states have specifically imposed requirements for their agencies to use alternative dispute resolution in an effort to settle disagreements between their agencies and their contractors. For example, in North Carolina, § 143-128 directs certain state agencies to use dispute resolution processes. This provision states,

> (f)(1) Dispute resolution.—A public entity shall use the dispute resolution process adopted by the State Building Commission pursuant to G.S. 143-135.26(11), or shall adopt another dispute resolution process, which shall include mediation, to be used as an alternative to the dispute resolution process adopted by the State Building Commission. This dispute resolution process will be available to all the parties involved in the public entity's construction project including the public entity, the architect, the construction manager, the contractors, and the first-tier and lower-tier subcontractors and shall be available for any issues arising out of the contract or construction process. . . . The public entity may require in its contracts that a party participate in mediation concerning a dispute as a precondition to initiating litigation concerning the dispute.[1]

Some jurisdictions, such as South Carolina, take a global approach to ADR, requiring the majority of all civil litigation to first go through court-ordered mediation.[2] This means that controversies between a governmental body and a contractor or subcontractor that arises under or by virtue of a contract between them in South Carolina are subject to ADR processes.[3] Specifically, § 11-35-4230 provides,

> Applicability. This section applies to controversies between a governmental body and a contractor or subcontractor, when the subcontractor is the real party in interest, which arises under or by virtue of a contract between them including, but not limited to, controversies based upon breach of contract, mistake, misrepresentation, or other cause for contract modification or recession. The procedure set forth in this section constitutes the

exclusive means of resolving a controversy between a governmental body and a contractor or subcontractor, when the subcontractor is the real party in interest, concerning a contract
solicited and awarded pursuant to the provisions of the South
Carolina Consolidated Procurement Code.

Duty and Authority to Attempt to Settle Contract Controversies. Before commencement of an administrative review as
provided in subsection (4), the appropriate chief procurement
officer or his designee shall attempt to settle by mutual agreement a contract controversy brought pursuant to this section.
The appropriate chief procurement officer has the authority to
approve any settlement reached by mutual agreement.

This provision of South Carolina law has been interpreted by
the federal district court in *Hass Construction Co. v. Thomas*,[4] where
contractors brought an action alleging a violation of their constitutional right to due process. In that case, a state engineer indefinitely
suspended contractors from participating in the state's construction
projects until they complied with the state engineer's written opinion
regarding contract disputes and until they could provide evidence of
financial stability. Plaintiffs first argued that the defendant did not
have jurisdiction to act because he had no statutory authority to conduct a hearing. The court ruled that a chief procurement officer has
the sole authority to resolve contract and breach of contract controversies between contractors or subcontractors and state agencies. If a
dispute arises, either party may initiate resolution proceedings before
the chief procurement officer "by submitting a request for a resolution
to the appropriate chief procurement officer in writing setting forth
the general nature of the controversy and the relief requested with
enough particularity to give notice of the issues to be decided.[5] The
chief procurement officer must then attempt to mediate a resolution.

The district court determined that South Carolina Code
§ 11-35-4230 directs the chief procurement officer to settle contractual disputes arising between contractors and state agencies. The
court explained that this is the exclusive means of resolving a controversy between the state and a contractor or a subcontractor concerning a contract solicited and awarded under the provisions of the
South Carolina Consolidated Procurement Code.

Similarly, in *Unisys Corporation v. South Carolina Budget and Control Board Division of General Services Information Technology Management Office,*[6] in response to a contractor's action against state for breach of contract and declaratory judgment on inapplicability of the Consolidated Procurement Code, the state, among other defenses, submitted a request for a resolution of various contract controversies pursuant to the South Carolina Consolidated Procurement Code.[7] Further, it alleged fraud in the inducement of the contract and unfair and deceptive acts in violation of the South Carolina Unfair Trade Practices Act. The contractor responded to the state's request for resolution by moving for dismissal on several grounds, asserting essentially that the chief procurement officer lacked jurisdiction. The court held that the procedure set forth in the Code was the exclusive means of resolving the controversy and the circuit court thus lacked jurisdiction.

In those states where no specific ADR statute or regulations exist, general rules of contract interpretation govern. Accordingly, in *FCI Group, Inc. v. City of New York,*[8] in a construction contract controversy between the City of New York and its contractor, the court rejected the defendants' alternative theory that the dispute fell within the contract's narrow ADR clause so as to require dismissal of the action in favor of arbitration. The court ruled that the contractor's claim against the City and its agency for the balance due under a construction contract did not fall within scope of the contract's ADR provision. The contract limited ADR as a recourse only for those disputes involving the scope of work delineated in the contract, interpretation of contract documents, amounts to be paid for extra or disputed work, and acceptability and quality of the contractor's work. The dispute between Group and the City did not involve any of these.

Furthermore, the court ruled that arbitration and alternative procedures for resolving disputes are creatures of contract, and while the law favors such alternatives to litigation, a party will not be denied judicial resolution of a controversy unless it falls within the governing ADR provision. Moreover the court ruled that the constitutional right to seek redress before the courts cannot be waived by implication but must be relinquished in a clear and unequivocal manner. The court held that the contractor's claim did not fall within scope of the contract's ADR provision and public policy did not bar enforcement of contract's forfeiture provision based on attempted bribes of city employees.

State Procurement Appeals Boards

An indication of a sophisticated and fair state procurement system is the constitution of a functional and independent appeals board that "can provide informal, expeditious, and inexpensive procedures for the resolution of controversies."[9] The 2000 MPC sets forth guidelines for a procurement board's composition, its jurisdiction, its substantive scope, and the weight and value of its precedence on future executive and judicial decisions. Executive decision makers and state courts often turn to decisions of procurement boards for guidance when these boards have, over time and experience, "advance[d] the development of a uniform set of precedents in [the state's] procurement law."[10]

Some courts recognize that state procurement boards are the initial and proper forum to resolve contract disputes. For example, in *District of Columbia v. Greene*,[11] the District of Columbia Court of Appeals interpreted the District of Columbia Procurement Practices Act as establishing the District of Columbia Contract Appeals Board as the exclusive hearing tribunal for determination of government contract disputes of the kind underlying this controversy.

The court of appeals cited D.C. Code § 2-308.03(a)(1), which stated that, in the first instance, "[a]ll claims by the District government against a contractor arising under or relating to a contract shall be decided by the contracting officer. . . ."[12] In like fashion, § 2-308.05(a) provided that "[a]ll claims by a contractor against the District government arising under or relating to a contract shall be . . . submitted to the contracting officer for a decision."[13] Further, in § 2-309.03(a), the statute declared that "[t]he [Contract Appeals] Board shall be the exclusive hearing tribunal for, and shall have jurisdiction to review and determine de novo: . . . (2) Any appeal by a contractor from a final decision by the contracting officer on a claim by a contractor, when such claim arises under or relates to a contract; and (3) Any claim by the District against a contractor, when such claim arises under or relates to a contract."[14] Accordingly, the court of appeals agreed with the District of Columbia "that the proper forum to resolve the question of whether there [was] an agreement to arbitrate [was], in the first instance, the Contract Appeals Board, with recourse to this court. . . ."[15]

Another robust state procurement appeals board can be found in Maryland. The Board is an executive branch agency of the State of Maryland that has jurisdiction over most appeals involving bid protests and contract disputes between the State and contractors doing business with the State.[16] The Board consists of three members appointed by the governor to five-year terms. The Board members serve a similar role to administrative law judges. As with other final administrative agency decisions, final decisions of the Board of Contract Appeals are subject to judicial review by the trial court. Final decisions of the Board are used as precedent by State agencies and the contracting community. Most final decisions of the Board issued after 1996 are posted on the website;[17] as well, published opinions of the Board are available at the Board's office, at circuit courts, and through the Maryland Institute for the Continuing Professional Education of Lawyers.

Contract Disputes and Claims

Filing claims and processing disputes with the contracting agency are just other forms of dispute resolution meant to encourage parties to negotiate before resorting to litigation, promote fair and equitable treatment between contracting agencies and their contractors, and equalize the bargaining power between contracting agencies and contractors.

Claims and dispute procedures are triggered by activities and events that occur after contract award. Procedures vary among states and even among contracting agencies within a particular state, but there are some basic principles and characteristics shared by all. These basic principles and characteristics include, but are not limited to, the following:

- There is a requirement of privity between the contracting agency and the contractor;[18]
- Claims must be made in writing;[19]
- Claims must be sent to the proper government official;[20]
- Claims may seek the kinds of remedies available in contract actions between private parties, which can include the payment of money damages, the interpretation of a contract clause, or some other relief arising under or related to the contract;[21] and
- Claims must be timely and supported with data and/or documentation.[22]

Many states have not adopted specific rules for handling contract claims and disputes, but some states have rules that govern the procedures for claim submission and contract dispute resolution. For example, the Arizona Procurement Code provides for the director to adopt rules of procedure governing the expeditious administrative review of all contract claims or controversies both before the purchasing agency and then through an appeal heard before the director.[23] A contract claim can be made to the agency's chief procurement officer within 180 days of the issue arising.[24] A decision by the chief procurement officer must be issued within 60 days. The claimant then has 30 days to appeal to the director of the Department of Administration.[25] Any decision made by the director can be vetted by judicial review at the superior court level.[26]

A case reinforcing the statutory scheme for fair and equitable claims and dispute resolution procedures is *R.L. Augustine Construction Co. v. Peoria Unified School District No. 11*.[27] In *R.L. Augustine*, a contractor appealed the dispute rules of the state Board of Education as being inconsistent with the enabling legislation. The Board of Education had established contract dispute procedures where the governing board either heard themselves or appointed the hearing officer for the primary hearing and then again heard the appeal themselves. The court held that these contract dispute rules were invalid because, although in theory they met the two-tiered requirement of the state procurement code, there was no meaningful appeal within the agency since both the primary hearing and the appeal were heard by the governing board, making the governing board both the interested party and the adjudicator. In addition, the procurement code required judicial review of the agency director's decision but the board of education did not have that avenue in their rules.

In Hawai'i there is no state procurement appeals board but there is a procedure to file claims and seek negotiation of contract disputes. Specifically, a controversy between a governmental body and a contractor must first be brought within the agency and will be dealt with by the chief procurement officer, whose opinion is final unless judicial action is pursued. If the contractor and procurement officer cannot resolve the issue, the chief procurement officer issues a decision justifying the agency's actions and informing the contractor of his or her right to judicial action.[28] If the contractor or government agency is dissatisfied with the chief procurement officer's decision, either or both can take their action to the circuit court. This statutory scheme is illustrated in *Koga Engineering & Construction, Inc. v. State of Hawai'i*.[29]

Remedies

Contracting parties can seek remedies if there has been any compensable change during contract performance, any modification to the scope of the contract, or a termination of the contract. Remedial relief can be achieved through the lodging of claims or contract disputes to contracting agencies, chief procurement officers, state procurement appeals boards, or the courts.

As discussed in the previous section, many states do not have formal claims or contract disputes procedures. As such, contractors and contracting agencies must resort to the standard remedies that can be pursued by private litigants in traditional, garden-variety breach of contract actions. To reduce the occurrence of litigation within the courts, some of these states rely upon required or suggested ADR procedures to resolve these disputes before resorting to judicial remedies.

A New Jersey case discussing remedies is *M.J. Paquet, Inc. v. New Jersey Department of Transportation.*[30] In *Paquet*, a contractor was awarded a contract, but it could not complete performance because the state rendered such performance impracticable. The contractor sought equitable adjustment as relief. The court held that it was appropriate for the Department of Transportation to render the performance impracticable but that equitable adjustment was required for the work that the contractor did perform. The court reasoned that the remedy was appropriate because equitable adjustment keeps "[the] contractor whole when the Government modifies [a] contract."[31] An equitable adjustment is defined as being the difference between what it would have cost to perform the work as originally required and what it cost to perform the work as changed.

Conclusion

Dispute resolution procedures can be viewed as another method for managing the risk of performance of a government contract. Generally, the procedures should not be viewed as points for controversy; instead, procedures should be viewed as opportunities to resolve differences while continuing to maintain good contractual relationships. Disputes will always arise; the trick is to make sure that procedures are in place to deal with them efficiently, quickly, fairly, and cost effectively.

Notes

1. SARAH RUDOLPH COLE ET AL., MEDIATION LAW, POLICY & PRACTICE, Appendix C-34 (2008 ed.); John J. Borer Jr., *Representing the Government Contractor*, 14 AM. JUR. TRIALS 437 (2011); Mary Elizabeth Moore, *A. Bolton Corp. v. T.A. Loving Co.: The Reservation of Rights Clause in Settlement Agreements*, 65 N.C. L. REV. 1207, 1219 (1987); and Daniel M. Gaylord and William Grainger Wright, *Public Utilities*, 21 CAMPBELL L. REV. 425, 431 (1999).

2. Alternative dispute resolution in South Carolina is regulated under Rule 3 on Actions Subject to ADR within the Alternative Dispute Resolution Rules of Code of Laws of South Carolina 1976 Annotated.
3. Section 11-35-4230 concerning Authority to Resolve Contract and Breach of Contract Controversies, under Article 17 of Legal and Contractual Remedies, Subarticle 1 of Administrative Resolution of Controversies, Code of Law of South Carolina 1976 Annotated Chapter 35 South Carolina Consolidated Procurement Code, Title 11 on Public Finance.
4. 183 F. Supp. 2d 800 (2001).
5. *Id.* at 803; *see also* S.C. CODE ANN. § 11-35-4230(2) (West, Westlaw 2011 Sess.).
6. 346 S.C. 158, 551 S.E.2d 263 (2001).
7. S.C. CODE ANN. § 11-35-4230.
8. 54 A.D.3d 171, 862 N.Y.S.2d 352 (2008).
9. 2000 ABA MPC, Chapter 9, Optional Part E, Comment (1).
10. *See id.*
11. 806 A.2d 216 (D.C. 2002).
12. *Id.* at 220.
13. *Id.*
14. *Id.*
15. *Id.* at 218.
16. *See* COMAR 21.02.02.02 and 21.02.02.03, *available at* http://www.dsd.state.md.us/comar/getfile.aspx?file=21.02.02.02.htm and http://www.dsd.state.md.us/comar/getfile.aspx?file=21.02.02.03.htm, respectively (last visited May 8, 2011); *see also* Kahns, Smith & Collins, P.A., Frequently Asked Questions About the Maryland Board of Contract Appeals, *available at* http://www.marylandprocurementlawyer.com/maryland-state-board-of-contract-appeals/ (last visited May 8, 2011).
17. *See* Maryland State Board of Contract Appeals, Origins and Functions, *available at* http://www.msbca.state.md.us/origins.html (last visited May 8, 2011).
18. A contractor can sue a government agency for breach of contract if privity exists between the two entities. C & W Enterprises, Inc. v. Sioux Falls, 635 N.W.2d 752, 756 (S.D. 2001).
19. A contractor with a claim against the State of New Jersey must first, according to N.J. STAT. ANN. § 59:13-5 (Presentation and consideration of claims), "promptly" notify the State in writing of any situation or occurrence that could result in the submission of a claim against the State. Generally, a notice of claim for breach of contract must be filed with the contracting agency within 90 days after the accrual of such claim. A notice of claim must include: the name of the claimant, the nature of the claim, specific reasons for making the claim, and the total dollar amount of the claim if known. After the expiration of 90 days from the date that the notice of claim is received by the contracting agency, the claimant may file suit in a court of competent jurisdiction of the State of New Jersey.
20. *Id.* Any contract claim will be barred if the contractor/claimant fails to notify the appropriate contracting agency within 90 days of accrual of his or her claim.

21. Georgia and Florida are examples of states that do not have statutes or regulations that govern a dispute arising between a contractor and the State during the performance of a public contract. In these jurisdictions, either the contractor or the State is permitted to bring an action in state court for breach of contract, unless the contract states otherwise.

22. The Washington Court of Appeals ruled that notice requirements in contracts strictly limiting the time period for providing notice and documentation of claims by contractors would be enforced. Mike M. Johnson, Inc. v. County of Spokane, 112 Wash. App. 462, 78 P.3d 161 (2003).

23. ARIZ. REV. STAT. ANN. §41-2611 (2008).

24. ARIZ. ADMIN. CODE §R2-7-B901 (2008).

25. *Id.* §R2-7-B902 and §R2-7-B904.

26. ARIZ. REV. STAT. ANN. §41-2614 (2008).

27. 188 Ariz. 368, 936 P.2d 554 (1997).

28. HAW. REV. STAT. §103D-703 (2008).

29. 122 Haw. 60, 222 P.3d 979 (2010).

30. 171 N.J. 378, 794 A.2d 141 (2002).

31. *Id.*, 171 N.J. at 392.

12

Ethics in Government Contracting

[handwritten annotations: protect integrity of the procurement process   protect against the appearance of impropriety in the procurement process]

State and local governments protect the public purse and guard the public trust in many ways when conducting their procurement functions. Responsibility determinations and prequalification requirements serve a preventative function by ensuring that contract awards are not made to unqualified contractors. Bonding and insurance requirements minimize the risk of contract breaches. Tax clearances protect the public against unscrupulous contractors. And licenses and permits assure the public that a contractor is operating at an acceptable threshold of competency. State and local governments rely on both general and specific ethical rules to govern the conduct and activities of government procurement personnel. The cornerstone of ethics in government contracting is not only to protect the integrity *[handwritten: ①]* of the procurement process but also to protect against the appearance *[handwritten: ②]* of impropriety in the procurement process.

To this end, state and local governments have explicit and extensive ethical requirements and standards for their employees, especially those performing purchasing and procurement functions. Chapter 12 of the 2007 MC PIP provides six specific standards of ethical conduct, which are likely incorporated, in one form or another, in the laws or rules of most state and local governments. The six standards of ethical conduct are: (1) prohibition against employee *where we will spend most of our time* conflict of interest, (2) employee benefit disclosure requirements, (3) gratuities and kickbacks, (4) prohibition against contingent fees, (5) restrictions on employment of present and former employees, and (6) employee use of contractor confidential information. In addition to these six standards, several state and local governments regulate *regulate lobbying* lobbying in an effort to preserve transparency in the procurement process. As well, most state and local governments have both crim- *criminal civil sanctions* inal and civil sanctions for violations of public trust and integrity, conflicts of interest, gratuities and kickbacks, restrictions on employment, and uses of confidential information. This chapter provides a general examination of the spectrum of ethical rules related to procurement at the state and local government levels.

Prohibition against Employee Conflicts of Interest and Disclosure Requirements

Most state and local government laws, rules, and standards of ethical conduct relating to conflicts of interest are broad in scope and are meant to apply to all government personnel, including procurement personnel. Conflict of interest rules and standards of conduct generally encompass financial conflicts and personal conflicts. The 2007 MC PIP primarily addresses financial conflicts of interest. Specifically, § 12-104(1) provides,

[i]t shall be a breach of ethical standards for any employee to participate directly or indirectly in a procurement when the employee knows that:

(a) the employee or any member of the employee's Immediate Family has a Financial Interest pertaining to the procurement;

(b) a business or organization in which the employee, or any member of the employee's Immediate Family, has a Financial Interest Pertaining to the procurement; or

(c) any other person, business, or organization with whom the employee or any member of the employee's

> Immediate Family is negotiating or has an arrangement concerning prospective employment is involved in the procurement.

Pennsylvania's restriction reads simply "[n]o public official or public employee shall engage in conduct that constitutes a conflict of interest."[1] This law, however, has been further defined by State Ethics Commission rulings that "[a] conflict of interest is defined as use by a public official or public employee of the authority of his office or employment or any confidential information received through his holding public office or employment for the private pecuniary benefit of himself, a member of his immediate family, or a business with which he or a member of his immediate family is associated."[2]

In addition, Pennsylvania's ethics laws specifically address conflicts in the context of contracts. One law states, [n]o public official or public employee or his spouse or child or any business in which the person or his spouse or child is associated shall enter into any contract valued at $500 or more with the governmental body with which the public official or public employee is associated or any subcontract valued at $500 or more with any person who has been awarded a contract with the governmental body with which the public official or public employee is associated, unless the contract has been awarded through an open and public process, including prior public notice and subsequent public disclosure of all proposals considered and contracts awarded. In such a case, the public official or public employee shall not have any supervisory or overall responsibility for the implementation or administration of the contract. Any contract or subcontract made in violation of this subsection shall be voidable by a court of competent jurisdiction if the suit is commenced within 90 days of the making of the contract or subcontract.[3]

Like Pennsylvania, the 2007 MC PIP is relatively narrower in scope than the financial conflict of interest rules enacted by other states. The 2007 MC PIP considers financial conflicts of interest to exist when employees or their immediate family members have a financial interest, while many states will extend the conflict to relatives. For example, Arizona provides in § 38-503,

[a]ny public officer or employee of a public agency who has, or whose relative has, a substantial interest in any decision of a public agency or any contract, sale, purchase or service to such public agency shall make known that interest in the official records of such public agency and shall refrain from voting upon or otherwise participating in any manner as an officer or employee in such contract, sale or purchase.[4]

Financial conflict of interest rules generally apply to public officials and employees. Routinely, questions arise regarding whether consultants or independent contractors working on behalf of a state or city are public officials or employees for the purposes of application of the financial conflict of interest rules. For example, in *Hub City Solid Waste Services, Inc. v. City of Compton*,[5] a consultant/independent contractor defended against an alleged violation of § 1090 by asserting that he was not a public official or employee. California's prohibition against conflicts of interest in contracts, §§ 1090 and 1092, provides in pertinent part, "'city officers or employees shall not be financially interested in any contract made by them in their official capacity, or by any body or board of which they are members.' Any contract in which an official is financially interested is void."[6] The court explained further that "[a] person in an advisory position to a city may fall within the scope of section 1090. In particular, independent contractors whose official capacities carry the potential to exert considerable influence over the contracting decisions of a public agency may not have personal interests in that agency's contracts.[7]

In holding that there existed sufficient evidence that the defendant fell within § 1090, the court reasoned that "[p]ursuant to the management agreement between defendant and Compton, defendant supervised city staff, negotiated contracts, and purchased equipment and real estate on behalf of the city. His activities served a public function, and he was intricately involved in the city's waste management decisions."[8] Based on these facts the court determined that the defendant had a financial stake in the franchise agreement that he proposed and ultimately negotiated on behalf of a company within which he held the ownership interest. The court concluded that the defendant's "interest was neither remote nor speculative, and resulted in an immediate and obvious conflict of interest. It cast doubt on whether the defendant was acting in Compton's best interest when he proposed franchising the city's waste management services to [defendant's] company and licensing city-owned equipment and facilities."[9]

(2) A personal conflict of interest exists when an employee's ability to act impartially can be questioned. Circumstances that may raise a personal conflict of interest include matters having specific parties that evidence a relationship. These relationships are often referred to as organizational conflicts of interest. Examples of personal or organizational conflicts of interest include: (1) someone with whom an employee has or is seeking employment, or a business, contractual, or other financial relationship; (2) a relative with whom an employee has a close relationship; (3) a present or prospective employer of a spouse, parent, or child; or (4) an organization that an employee now serves or has served as an employee or in another capacity.

In *Medco Behavioral Care Corporation of Iowa v. Department of Human Services*,[10] the Supreme Court of Iowa affirmed a district court determination of an existence of an organizational conflict of interest in the award of negotiated contracts. The Iowa Department of Human Services (DHS) awarded a managed care policy analysis contract to Lewin, a subsidiary of Value Behavioral Health. The policy analysis contract led to a determination that managed care for Medicaid patients should be pursued, thus calling for the Iowa DHS to issue an RFP. Along with other competitors, another subsidiary of Value submitted an offer in response to the RFP, even though Lewin represented to the Iowa DHS that it was unlikely that its parent company would submit an offer. After notice that Value would submit an offer, Lewin surreptitiously engaged another company to draft the RFP and to define bidder evaluation criteria and review proposals. The Iowa DHS's award to Value was challenged by one of Value's competitors through the administrative process and on judicial review.

Applying federal law on the issue of the existence of an organizational conflict of interest, the district court found and the Supreme Court of Iowa agreed that the "evidence convincingly demonstrate[d] an 'appearance of impropriety' that tainted the procurement process. The interrelationships between [Lewin, Value, and Value's subsidiaries], coupled with the unique position each entity occupied, create[d] what one authority described as 'a certain aroma that is hard to purify.'"[11] Iowa statutory law directed the DHS to award a contract for Medicaid managed healthcare through a competitive bidding process. According to state law, the DHS was required to follow federal law concerning the procurement process, which included prohibitions against organizational conflicts of interest. Thus, according to federal law,

> [c]ontracting officials are directed to identify potential organizational conflicts of interest early in the procurement process and to avoid, neutralize, or mitigate those conflicts before awarding the contract. . . . Disqualification of a bidder is appropriate where the existence of a conflict of interest cannot be avoided or mitigated. . . . Recognizing that allegations of conflicts may arise in factual situations not expressly addressed in the FAR sections [], contracting officials are advised to examine each situation individually and to exercise "common sense, good judgment, and sound discretion" in resolving the matter . . . . The underlying goal is to prevent (1) the existence of conflicting roles that might bias a contractor's judgment, and (2) unfair competitive advantage.[12]

Lewin raised conflict of interest issues first by having a related company perform a contract when it had a hand in setting the ground rules for competition; and second by having access to nonpublic information as part of its performance of an earlier government contract that potentially could provide it with a competitive advantage in the contested contract. In holding that an appearance of impropriety was the correct standard applied by the district court in finding the existence of a conflict, the Supreme Court of Iowa identified that the standard stemmed from the federal government's strict policy in avoiding conflicts of interest. The Supreme Court of Iowa determined that direct evidence of a conflict was unnecessary to support a violation of an ethical standard where impaired objectivity would likely result because of the parties' involvement in the procurement process and their direct and indirect relationship to the successful offeror.

[handwritten margin note: provide contractor a competitive advantage]

[handwritten margin note: bias a contractor's judgment]

According to the Supreme Court of Iowa, "each occupied a position to advise DHS in a potentially biased manner so as to enhance Value's chances of obtaining the contract. It therefore appears that an organizational conflict of interest existed that provided Value with an unfair competitive advantage in the procurement process."[13]

A public official or employee who receives a benefit as a result of a financial conflict of interest has a disclosure obligation. According to the 2007 MC PIP § 12-105,

> (1) Any employee who has, or obtains any benefit from any [Purchasing Agency] contract with a business in which the employee has a Financial Interest shall report such benefit to the [Ethics Commission]; provided, however, this Section shall not apply to a contract with a business where the employee's interest in the business has been placed in a disclosed Blind Trust.
>
> (2) Any employee who knows or should have known of such benefit, and fails to report such benefit to the [Ethics Commission], is in breach of the ethical standards of this Section.

Generally, state and local government officials and employees are required to execute and submit disclosure forms annually to their respective ethics offices. These forms are referred to as Financial disclosure statements. *[handwritten margin note: FDS]* Financial disclosure statements serve an oversight function. The purpose of the disclosure requirement is to remind public officials and employees of their obligation to identify and disclose financial interests that may conflict with their duties and to assist agencies in monitoring potential conflicts of interest. Along with general personal information, most Financial disclosure statements request the following information from filers: all sources of income; investments valued over a designated amount; businesses in which the filer is an officer or board member; sources of travel expenses incurred in connection with official duties; sources of meals, food, and beverages incurred in connection with official duties over a prescribed amount; sources of gifts valued over a designated amount; and real estate investments. The National Conference *[handwritten margin note: resource]* of State Legislators provides a comprehensive online searchable list of States' Legislative Ethics Laws.[14]

Gratuities, Kickbacks, and Anti-bribery Statutes

Statutes prohibiting unlawful gratuities/compensation, bribery, and kickbacks in the context of procurement are enacted to fight corruption. Unlawful gratuities/compensation focuses on offering extra compensation for work that a public servant is already authorized to perform. Generally, a gratuity is a payment, loan, subscription, advance, or deposit of money; a service; or a promise of such given in return for a favor or in expectation of a favor. A gratuity may include any tangible and intangible benefit in the nature of gifts, favors, entertainment, discounts, or kickbacks. Also included are passes, transportation, accommodations, hospitality, or offers of employment in connection with any decision, approval, disapproval, recommendation, influence, investigating, auditing, rendering advice, request for ruling determination, or claim. A gratuity implies a further obligation on the recipient to provide favorable action to the person who provides the gratuity. The 2007 MC PIP § 12-106(1) similarly provides,

> [i]t shall be a breach of ethical standards for any person to offer, give, or agree to give any employee or former employee, or for any employee or former employee to solicit, demand, accept, or agree to accept from another person, a gratuity or an offer of employment in connection with any decision, approval, disapproval, recommendation, preparation of any part of a program requirement or a purchase request, influencing the content of any specification or procurement standard, rendering of advice, investigation, auditing, or in any other advisory capacity in any proceeding or application, request for ruling, determination, claim or controversy, or other particular matter, pertaining to any program requirement or a contract or subcontract, or to any solicitation or proposal therefor.

Bribery is defined as the giving or receiving of anything of value to influence a person in the discharge of his or her official duties. A kickback is a type of bribe; it is defined as a payment made by a payer to a person in a position of trust in exchange for the official action or inaction for the benefit of the payer. Where procurement personnel are concerned, bribes and kickbacks are given in exchange for favor- *in procurement context* able results regarding contract awards or other contract actions, such as improper disclosure of bid information; narrow tailoring of specifications to benefit a particular bidder or offeror; improper disqualification of competitors from the formation phase of the procurement process; supporting or voting for the bribing bidder or offeror; or approval of false invoices, improper change orders, or cost overruns on behalf of the bribing contractor.

The 2007 MC PIP § 12-106 establishes a prohibition against kickbacks geared toward subcontractors, but arguably the section could apply to any person depending on the manner in which the provision is adopted by a jurisdiction. In *Commonwealth v. Tobin*,[15] a case that predates the 2007 MC PIP yet demonstrates the reach of anti-bribery statutes, a private individual was deemed to be the agent of a public official who was found guilty of bribery for compelling contractors and vendors to make campaign contributions in exchange for public contracts.[16] The private individual was a "bag man" for the mayor whose first bribery scheme sought a $25,000 kickback from the contractor who was selected by the mayor to provide the specifications for the various categories of furnishings and interior equipment for a public high school. The second scheme required the chosen contractor to solicit additional contractors interested in bidding for contracts and to determine whether—and how much—these individual contractors would be willing to pay as a kickback to city officials in return for being awarded contracts with the city. It is the first scheme that gave rise to the indictments against the private individual, the alleged agent or "bag man" for the mayor, who allegedly collected a $25,000 kickback from the contractor. Even though the agent was a private individual, the court determined that there was sufficient evidence of criminal joint enterprise to show that his conduct coupled with the conduct of the mayor was done by public employees for the purpose of soliciting and obtaining kickbacks from contractors in return for contract awards.[17]

Virtually all states and U.S. territories have enacted laws that prohibit unlawful gratuities, kickbacks, and bribes.[18] Arizona's anti-bribery statute is illustrative of those state statutes that attempt to *a bribe can occur in either direction —*

contractor to official

or

official to contractor

cover gratuities, kickbacks, and bribery. In Arizona, bribery of a public servant occurs if, with corrupt intent, a person offers, confers, or agrees to confer any benefit upon a public servant with the intent to influence the public servant's vote, opinion, judgment, exercise of discretion, or other action in his or her official capacity as a public servant; or if while a public servant, such person solicits, accepts, or agrees to accept any benefit upon an agreement or understanding that his or her vote, opinion, judgment, exercise of discretion, or other action as a public servant may thereby be influenced.[19] Bribery is punishable as a Class 4 felony; as well, it serves as one cause for debarment or suspension.[20]

Some states specifically address gratuities, kickbacks, and bribery in government contracting. For example, in Virginia, public employees with "official responsibility for a procurement transaction" may not "solicit, demand, accept, or agree to accept from a bidder, offeror, contractor or subcontractor any payment, loan, subscription, advance, deposit of money, services or anything of more than nominal or minimal value, present or promised, unless consideration of substantially equal or greater value is exchanged."[21] Like-

donut example v. mangua spread

wise bidders, offerors, contractors, and subcontractors are prohibited from "confer[ring] upon any public employee having official responsibility for a procurement transaction any payment, loan, subscription, advance, deposit of money, services or anything of more than nominal value, present or promised, unless consideration of substantially equal or greater value is exchanged."[22] Specifically, the code prohibits contractors and subcontractors from inducing anything of value from their suppliers or subcontractors in exchange for the award of a subcontract or order.[23]

giving something of value to induce another competitor not to bid/offer

Similar to the bribery statute, the kickback statute prohibits both receiving and giving kickbacks.[24] Additionally, "[n]o person shall demand or receive any payment, loan, subscription, advance, deposit of money, services or anything of value in return for an agreement not to compete on a public contract."[25]

Washington also prohibits bribes and payments not to compete. In particular, no state employee whose duties performed for the state include advising on or drawing specifications for supplies, equipment, commodities, or services; suggesting or determining vendors to be placed upon a bid list; drawing requisitions for supplies, equipment, commodities, or services; evaluating specifications or bids and suggesting or determining awards; or accepting the receipt of supplies, equipment, and commodities or approving the performance of services or contracts,

> shall accept or receive, directly or indirectly, a personal financial benefit, or accept any gift, token, membership, or service, as a result of a purchase entered into by the state, from any person, firm, or corporation engaged in the sale, lease, or rental of property, material, supplies, equipment, commodities, or services to the state of Washington.[26]

Violation of this prohibition is grounds for firing of the employee, and the contractor must pay out of his or her bond for "all damages sustained by the state."[27] Washington also prohibits anyone from giving something of value "for the purpose of inducing such other person to refrain from submitting any bids upon such purchase or to enter into any agreement, understanding or arrangement whereby full and unrestricted competition for the securing of such public work will be suppressed, prevented, or eliminated."[28]

West Virginia allows the government to cancel a contract if "[t]he vendor has obtained the contract by fraud, collusion, conspiracy, or in conflict with any statutory or constitutional provision of the State of West Virginia."[29] Additionally, "[a]ny person receiving anything of value from a known interested party in awarding a purchase order" is guilty of a crime.[30]

As a final example, Nevada prohibits government employees from accepting gifts, services, favors, employment, economic opportunities, and similar items that would improperly influence them.[31] Nevada proscribes using a public office to secure unwarranted privileges, preferences, exemptions, or advantages.[32] Participating as an agent of government in the negotiation or execution of contracts with a business in which the person has a pecuniary interest is also prohibited, as is accepting a salary or other compensation from a private source for performing public duties.[33] A government employee is barred from using confidential information to further a pecuniary interest or that of others and from suppressing governmental reports or documents that might tend to unfavorably affect a pecuniary interest.[34] Attempting to benefit a personal or financial interest by influencing subordinates and seeking other employment or contracts through the use of the public office is prohibited.[35]

Prohibition against Contingent Fees

prohibited AK/GA restricted Montana

Contingency fee arrangements in the context of government contracts are either prohibited or restricted by the overwhelming majority of state and local governments.[36] A contingency fee is any commission, percentage, brokerage, or other fee that is contingent upon a favorable contract award result. The purpose of the contingency fee prohibition is to avoid the exercise of improper influence on public officials or employees in the performance of their procurement function or role. The 2007 MC PIP § 12-107 states, in pertinent part,

> (1) It shall be a breach of ethical standards for a person to be retained, or to retain a person, to solicit or secure a [Purchasing Agency] contract upon an agreement or understanding for a commission, percentage, brokerage, or contingent fee, except for retention of bona fide employees or bona fide established commercial selling agencies for the purpose of securing business.
> (2) Every person, before being awarded a [Purchasing Agency] contract, shall represent, in writing, that such person has not retained anyone in violation of Subsection (1) of this Section. Failure to do so constitutes a breach of ethical standards.

prof rep v. contingent fee recipient

The commentary to § 12-107 explains that the section is not meant to prohibit professional representation of contractors by attorneys or accountants in the pursuit of professional duties. Accordingly, for example, these professionals can represent contractors in bid protest actions, negotiations, or agency audits; however, these professionals are precluded from engaging in the actual act of soliciting or selling to an agency in exchange for a contingency fee paid by a contractor.

Arkansas legislation illustrates the prohibition on contingency fee arrangements. Specifically, Arkansas law summarily provides that no person engaging in lobbying shall contract to receive or accept compensation that is dependent upon the outcome of an administrative action relating to the solicitation or securing of a procurement contract.[37] Similarly, Georgia law summarily provides that no person, firm, corporation, or association shall retain or employ a lobbyist for compensation contingent, in whole or in part, upon the granting or awarding of any state contract and that no lobbyist shall be employed for compensation contingent, in whole or in part, upon the granting or awarding of any state contract.[38] In comparison, Montana law illustrates a restriction, as opposed to a prohibition, on contingency fee arrangements. According to Montana law, "a principal may not make payments to influence official action by any public official unless that principal files the reports required under this chapter."[39]

Although reversed on grounds that the State Ethics Commission and two respective decisions by the circuit court and the court of special appeals affirmed despite impermissible burden shifting that denied the defendant due process, the Court of Appeals of Maryland, in *Bereano v. State Ethics Commission*,[40] concluded that the Ethics Commission did not retroactively apply a statute that imposed sanctions for contingency fees for lobbying.[41] In *Bereano*, the defendant, a lobbyist, asserted that he did not intend to enter into a contingency fee agreement, and even if the agreement is interpreted as one for contingency, he was not subject to any sanctions because he was "not engaged for lobbying purposes" by his client on the date the legislation took effect.[42] According to Maryland law, "a regulated lobbyist may not be engaged for lobbying purposes for compensation that is dependent in any manner on the outcome of any executive action relating to the solicitation or securing of a procurement contract or any other contingency related to executive action."[43] The contract executed between the defendant and his client stated,

> [t]he nature and scope of my services for the monthly retainer would include and encompass performing lobbying services, giving advice, consultation, strategy and be a resource concerning legislative and political and government matters at both the

State and local levels, attending and participating in all necessary and required meetings, monitoring and watchdogging on behalf of the Company, and providing information to your companies as to matters of concern and importance with its work and relationships with the State of Maryland, as well as any political subdivision in the State and generally performing any and all other such similar and related services and activities as you may request of me. In this regard, I also would register as a lobbyist and fully comply and conform with the State's applicable law.

It is further understood and agreed that in addition to and separate and apart from payment of the aforementioned monthly fee [sic] retainer fee and any further increase thereof, Mercer Ventures will compensate and further pay me one percent (1%) of the first year receivable for continuing representation and services to be performed, provided, and made available when and after each separate facility and/or site or location that is opened in which I was involved in securing and participated in obtaining, and/or any contract and performance of services which is entered into by your company with any government entity, unit or agency in the State of Maryland or any other state or jurisdiction in which I worked on the matter.[44]

The Court of Appeals of Maryland, in applying the substantial evidence test for review of the Commission's fact-finding, held that "the Commission was empowered to resolve conflicts in the evidence, based upon its conclusions concerning its determination of the credibility of the testimony and evidence presented."[45] The court accepted the Commission's findings that the defendant's testimony was less than credible and further found that

[Defendant]'s fee letter . . . recites that he . . . proposes to "represent Mercer Ventures in the State of Maryland" in a "lobbying" capacity relating to the company plans "to develop and obtain contracts and arrangements with various county, municipal, and State government agencies and departments." []. The lobbying services would include "government matters at both the State and local levels" and [defendant] would provide information to the company "as to matters of concern and importance with its work and relationship with the State of Maryland." [Defendant] also indicates that he "would register as a lobbyist." . . . Respondent was being hired to obtain State contracts in Maryland and his testimony that it was not until nine months after the fee agreement that he became aware that [his client] had some existing contracts with State agencies, is not credible.[46]

Accordingly, the Court of Appeals of Maryland agreed with the Commission and the two reviewing courts that the defendant "'engaged in' the lobbying activities for which he was 'engaged []' . . . , making himself available for, and engaging in, lobbying purposes after . . . the effective date of the statute."[47]

Restrictions on Employment of Present and Former Employees

Employment rules applicable to present and former employees are designed to eradicate the temptation to realize personal gain from public employment.[48] The purpose of these rules is to discourage conduct inconsistent with the proper discharge of the employee's duties. State and local governments have followed the federal government's lead in establishing ethical rules for current employees discharging their public duties as well as seeking future employment[49] and former employees engaged in post-employment activities involving their previous government agency employers.[50]

Present Employees

Virtually all state and local governments have a rule prohibiting contemporaneous employment. Florida's prohibition on contemporaneous employment offers a fair representation of other states' laws. Florida's prohibition provides, in pertinent part,

> [n]o public officer or employee of an agency shall have or hold any employment or contractual relationship with any business entity or any agency which is subject to the regulation of, or is doing business with, an agency of which he or she is an

officer or employee, excluding those organizations and their officers who, when acting in their official capacity, enter into or negotiate a collective bargaining contract with the state or any municipality, county, or other political subdivision of the state; nor shall an officer or employee of an agency have or hold any employment or contractual relationship that will create a continuing or frequently recurring conflict between his or her private interests and the performance of his or her public duties or that would impede the full and faithful discharge of his or her public duties.[51]

Similarly, Puerto Rico maintains a general prohibition that provides, in pertinent part,

[n]o public official or employee shall accept employment or maintain contractual business relationships, with a person, business or entity which is regulated by, or does business with the government agency for which he/she works, when the public official or employee participates in institutional decisions of the agency or is empowered to decide or influence the official actions of the agency related to said person, business or entity.[52]

prohibition against contemporaneous employment

Most, if not all, of these rules can be interpreted to include seeking employment with as well as being employed by a person contracting with the governmental body in which the employee participates directly or indirectly in the procurement process.[53] The 2007 MC PIP § 12-108(1) provides the general language that can be found in most state and local government rules related to contemporaneous employment and the benchmark ethical standards applicable to public contracting. § 12-108(1) provides, in pertinent part,

[e]xcept as may be permitted by regulations or rulings of the [Ethics Commission], it shall be a breach of ethical standards for any employee who is participating directly or indirectly in the procurement process to become or be, while such an employee, the employee of any person contracting with the governmental body by whom the employee is employed.

The conduct envisioned by this provision is unqualifiedly prohibited when an employee is participating directly or indirectly in the procurement process and that employee is also an employee or will engage in the process to become an employee of the contractor doing business with the governmental body that employs the employee. The highly publicized case of Darleen Druyun, former Principal Deputy Assistant Secretary of the Air Force for Acquisitions and Management, serves as the classic conflict of interest example involving unlawful employment discussions.[54] Among other admitted violations, Ms. Druyun discussed employment with Boeing while simultaneously negotiating a proposed $20 billion contract with Boeing on behalf of the Air Force.[55]

Fortunately, contemporaneous employment cases are few in number. The question of contemporaneous employment, however, may arise when a person who works for a contractor or who is a consultant performs a governmental function and is considered a public employee as a result. In *Total Benefit Services, Inc. v. City of New Orleans*,[56] the Fourth Circuit Court of Appeals of Louisiana explained that where City documents produced in response to a claim of contract invalidity apparently showed that an agent working on behalf of the City and performing a governmental function also may have been negotiating the same contract on behalf of a private contractor in exchange for a commission, the agent "may have been on both sides" in violation of the public bid law and the ethics code.[57] The court reasoned that "if the evidence confirms this dual capacity, and that the public employee received a commission on the publicly bid contract between the City and [the contractor], then that contract would have been confected in violation of the Code of Governmental Ethics. . . ."[58] No doubt the rule prohibiting contemporaneous employment can point back to a biblical reference where it was said, "[n]o servant can serve two masters, for either he will hate the one and love the other, or he will be devoted to the one and despise the other. You cannot serve God and money."[59]

Former Employees

Personal and Substantial Participation

Most state and local governments' standards of conduct either prohibit or restrict former employees from appearing before the

Representational Prohibitions

executive agency personnel   procurement personnel

governmental agency in which they previously worked in connection with matters in which they personally and substantially participated. State and local government ethics codes may apply general representational prohibitions and restrictions on executive agency personnel while adding further prohibitions and restrictions on procurement personnel. The 2007 MC PIP covers both representation- and procurement-related conflicts of interest. With respect to representational restrictions and former employees who have personally and substantially participated in a matter, the model code prescribes a permanent disqualification that provides,

Rep Personnel (former employees) who personally and substantially participated in a matter are permanently disqualified

> [i]t shall be a breach of ethical standards for any former employee knowingly to act as a principal, or as an agent for anyone other than the [Purchasing Agency], in connection with any: (i) judicial or other proceeding, application, request [for a ruling, or] other determination; (ii) contract; (iii) claim; or (iv) charge or controversy, in which the employee participated personally and substantially through decision, approval, disapproval, recommendation, rendering of advice, investigation, or otherwise while an employee, where the [Purchasing Agency] is a party or has a direct and substantial interest.[60]

elements to be met

The permanent disqualification envisioned by the code is premised upon a showing that the former employee acted with the intent to represent an interest other than that of the former agency employer. As well, before a conflict of interest can be found, there must be a showing that the agency was a party to a proceeding or that the agency had a direct and substantial interest in the matter.

rationale for revolving door rules

The purpose of these prohibitions or restrictions is to minimize the negative impact on the government from those employees who would seek to "cash in" on the knowledge and information obtained while in public service. More objectively, the purpose of the "revolving door" or "switching sides" rules is to "prohibit certain acts by former government employees that might reasonably give the appearance of making unfair use of prior government employment and affiliations."[61]

Whether former employees are prohibited or restricted from appearing before the agency on matters they personally and

substantially participated in when in public service is treated differ-
ently among the jurisdictions. For example, in Alabama, a restriction, ~~two~~
as opposed to the prohibition envisioned by the model code, ~~for two~~ *two year*
years is imposed for appearances in matters that public officials and *restrichon*
employees as well as procurement personnel participated in personally and substantially. Specifically, Alabama's conflict of interest law
relating to post-employment provides,

> [n]o public official, director, assistant director, department or
> division chief, purchasing or procurement agent having the
> authority to make purchases, or any person who participates in
> the negotiation or approval of contracts, grants, or awards or any
> person who negotiates or approves contracts, grants, or awards
> shall enter into, solicit, or negotiate a contract, grant, or award
> with the governmental agency of which the person was a mem-
> ber or employee for a period of two years after he or she leaves
> the membership or employment of such governmental agency.[62]

Alternatively, the law in Massachusetts covering general representational restrictions applies to municipal employees whose bans on
appearances before their former agency employers vary depending
on the specific conflict of interest referenced in the statute. Thus,
according to Massachusetts law,

> [a] former municipal employee who knowingly acts as agent
> or attorney for or receives compensation, directly or indirectly
> from anyone other than the same city or town in connection
> with any particular matter in which the city or town is a party
> or has a direct and substantial interest and in which he par-
> ticipated as a municipal employee while so employed, or (b) a
> former municipal employee who, within one year after his last
> employment has ceased, appears personally before any agency of
> the city or town as agent or attorney for anyone other than the
> city or town in connection with any particular matter in which
> the same city or town is a party or has a direct and substan-
> tial interest and which was under his official responsibility as
> a municipal employee at any time within a period of two years
> prior to the termination of his employment, or (c) a partner of
> a former municipal employee who knowingly engages, during

a period of one year following the termination of the latter's employment by the city or town, in any activity in which the former municipal employee is himself prohibited from engaging by clause (a), or (d) a partner of a municipal employee who knowingly acts as agent or attorney for anyone other than the city or town in connection with any particular matter in which the same city or town is a party or has a direct and substantial interest and in which the municipal employee participates or has participated as a municipal employee or which is the subject of his official responsibility, shall be punished by a fine of not more than $10,000, or by imprisonment in the state prison for not more than 5 years, or in a jail or house of correction for not more than 2 1/2 years, or both.[63]

Official Responsibility

The 2007 MC PIP merely restricts representation-related conflicts of interest when former employees have had official responsibility over a matter where the former agency employer has a direct or substantial interest. Thus, the model code envisions only a temporary disqualification of former employees who once had official responsibilities over matters. Section 12-108(2)(b) provides,

[i]t shall be a breach of ethical standards for any former employee, within one year after cessation of the former employee's official responsibility, knowingly to act as a principal, or as an agent for anyone other than the [Purchasing Agency], in connections with any: (i) judicial or other proceeding, application, request for a ruling, or other determination; (ii) contract; (iii) claim; or (iv) charge or controversy, in matters which were within the former employee's official responsibility, where the [Purchasing Agency] is a party or has a direct [and] substantial interest.

Similar to the permanent disqualification for personal and substantial participation, the model code's temporary restriction for involvement in matters where the former employee had an official responsibility also requires a showing that the former employee acted with the intent to represent an interest other than that of the former agency employer. The model code likely is meant to apply the same direct and substantial interest standard on the part of the agency as is expressed in § 12-108(2)(a).[64] The purpose for a restriction, as opposed to a prohibition, is the need to balance the interests of the government with those of the former employee and the latter's ability to secure employment after leaving government service.

Financial Interest in Business *of an employee triggers permanent disqualification prohibition v. restriction*

Where business can include, among other legal business entities, an individual operating legally, such individual representing his or her business but also having a position as an agency employee can be permanently disqualified from engaging in a matter personally and substantially in which he or she, as the alter ego for his business, has a financial interest. The 2007 MC PIP § 12-108(3) provides,

> [i]t shall be a breach of ethical standards for a business in which an employee has a financial interest knowingly to act as principal, or as an agent for anyone other than the [Purchasing Agency], in connection with any: judicial or other proceeding, application, request for a ruling, or other determination; contract; claim; or charge or controversy, in which the employee either participates personally through decision, approval, disapproval, recommendation, the rendering of advice, investigation, or otherwise, or which is the subject of the employee's official responsibility, where the [Purchasing Agency] is a party or has a direct and substantial interest.[65]

As with the ethical standards dealing with former employees, the conflict of interest rules governing financial interests in business provide for either prohibition or restriction. The model code offers language of prohibition, an approach shared by a number of jurisdictions, including California and Florida. Specifically, California provides,

> Members of the Legislature, state, county, district, judicial district, and city officers and employees shall not be financially

> interested in any contract made by them in their official capac-
> ity, or by anybody or board of which they are members.[66]

The language of § 1090 is broad, and it applies when a public official or employee has either a direct or indirect financial interest in any contract, and as long as the contract is the result of a conflict of interest, the terms of the contract are irrelevant.[67] § 1090 is "intended to protect the public agency's interests and those of its constituency by assuring undivided loyalty and allegiance, removing direct and indirect influence of an interested officer and discouraging dishonesty."[68]

Similarly, Florida provides that employees having businesses with financial interests based upon their personal and substantial participation are subject to permanent disqualification. Specifically, Florida provides,

> [n]o employee of an agency acting in his or her official capacity
> as a purchasing agent, or public officer acting in his or her offi-
> cial capacity, shall either directly or indirectly purchase, rent,
> or lease any realty, goods, or services for his or her own agency
> from any business entity of which the officer or employee or
> the officer's or employee's spouse or child is an officer, partner,
> director, or proprietor or in which such officer or employee or
> the officer's or employee's spouse or child, or any combination
> of them, has a material interest. Nor shall a public officer or
> employee, acting in a private capacity, rent, lease, or sell any
> realty, goods, or services to the officer's or employee's own
> agency, if he or she is a state officer or employee, or to any
> political subdivision or any agency thereof, if he or she is serv-
> ing as an officer or employee of that political subdivision.[69]

Accordingly, a school board may not award a contract to a corporation in which a school board member is the majority shareholder even though the corporation submitted the lowest or best bid under a system of sealed, competitive bidding pursuant to § 112.313(12)(b) and has otherwise complied with all other requirements of the Florida Code of Ethics for Public Officers and Employees.[70] As well, a board of county commissioners may not transact business with a business entity whose officer is serving temporarily as a member of the board.[71]

Other jurisdictions merely restrict conflicts of interest resulting from an employee's financial interests in business. For example, in Puerto Rico,

> [n]o public official or employee who is authorized to contract in the name of the executive agency for which he/she works, shall execute a contract between his agency and an entity or business in which he/she, or any member of his/her family unit, has, or has had, during the last four (4) years before taking office, a direct or indirect pecuniary interest.[72]

This provision does not allow a current financial interest to exist while the employee is in public service, but it does not prevent an employee from engaging in public service if the conflict of interest was remote in time but not less than four years.

Whether a prohibition or restriction, the purpose of conflict of interest rules regarding an employee's financial interests in business is to avoid an employee being pulled in one direction by his or her financial interest and in another direction by his or her official duties, and the conflict of interest is not minimized by the employee's attempt to remain impartial. Where a financial interest in business would prevent a public official or employee from exercising absolute loyalty and undivided allegiance to the governmental entity he or she serves, a conflict of interest must be found and the employee and his or her business should be permanently disqualified or restricted from any further personal and substantial involvement in the matter.

Employee Use of Contractor Confidential Information

Generally, there are two types of information that are considered confidential: (1) nonpublic information that an employee has access to by virtue of his or her government employment and (2) procurement information obtained from contractors. The former relates to non-public information that is only known because of the employee's position while the latter relates to information passed on to public officials or employees by contractors in the form of bid and proposal information. With respect to the latter, contractors routinely entrust public officials and employees with confidential information regarding pricing, cost estimates, business practices, business solutions, and strategies. Most contractors are vigilant about labeling their information proprietary or confidential in order to protect their information, once in government hands, from reaching their competitors. Contractor confidential disclosures to public officials and employees place them in a position of trust with respect to that information and to its owner. To facilitate this trust relationship, the 2007 MC PIP § 12-109 provides,

> [i]t shall be a breach of ethical standards for any employee or former employee knowingly to use confidential information for actual or anticipated personal gain, or for the actual or anticipated personal gain of any other person.

Most state and local governments impose ethical obligations on public officials and employees who have access to confidential information. For example, Kansas legislates, under government ethics, a prohibition against employee disclosure of confidential information for personal gain. The law in Kansas provides, "[n]o state officer or employee shall disclose or use confidential information acquired in the course of his or her official duties in order to further his or her own economic interest or those of any other person."[73] Similarly, Massachusetts prohibits the disclosure of confidential information by public officials and employees under three circumstances. Specifically, Massachusetts's Code of Conduct provides,

> (c) No current or former officer or employee of a state, county or municipal agency may, knowingly or with reason to know:
>
> (1) accept employment or engage in any business or professional activity that will require disclosure of confidential information the employee has gained by reason of his or her position or authority; nor
>
> (2) improperly disclose material or data that are not considered public records, when an employee acquired such information in the course of his or her official duties

nor use such confidential information to further his or her personal interests.[74]

The purpose of this prohibition is to ensure that the playing field for competition is level and that the economic interests of contractors who choose to compete for government work are not harmed as a result of responding to government solicitations.

Conclusion

This chapter canvases the general standards of conduct that apply to public contracting. The purpose of each of these ethical standards is to maintain the public trust and to promote procurement integrity throughout the procurement process. Procuring agencies are not alone in imposing and enforcing ethical standards of conduct. State ethics commissions offer support and guidance to public officials, public employees, and contractors who do work for or on behalf of state and local governments. These commissions should be the first entity to approach when in doubt about conflicts of interest, procurement integrity, or questions related to general ethics, especially as they relate to public contracting.

Notes

1. 65 Pa. C.S.A. § 1103(a).
2. *See* Pennsylvania State Ethics Commission, Ethics: Restricted Activities Under the Act, *available at* http://www.ethics.state.pa.us/portal/server.pt/ community/ethics/8995/restricted_activities_under_the_act/540220 (last visited Jan. 23, 2012).
3. 65 Pa. C.S.A. § 1103(f).
4. Ariz. Rev. Stat. § 38-503 (2011).
5. 186 Cal. App. 4th 1114, 112 Cal. Rptr. 3d 647 (2010).
6. *Id.*, 186 Cal. App. 4th at 1124.
7. *Id.* at 1124–25.
8. *Id.* at 1125.
9. *Id.*; *see* California Housing Finance Agency v. Hanover/California Management and Accounting Center, 148 Cal. App. 4th 682, 56 Cal. Rptr. 3d 92 (2007) (concluding that "an attorney whose official capacity carries the

potential to exert 'considerable' influence over the contracting decisions of a public agency is an 'employee' under section 1090, regardless of whether he or she would be considered an independent contractor under common-law tort principles. . . . Otherwise, the attorney could manipulate the employment relationship to retain 'official capacity' influence, yet avoid liability under section 1090.")

10. 553 N.W.2d 556 (Iowa 1996).

11. *Id.* at 568.

12. *Id.* at 564–65; *see* 48 C.F.R. §§ 9.502(c); 9.504(a)(1)–(2); 9.504(e); 9.505.

13. *Medco*, 553 N.W.2d at 568.

14. *See* National Conference of State Legislators, Links to States' Legislative Ethics and Lobbying Laws, *available at* http://www.ncsl.org/legislatures-elections/ethicshome/states-legislative-ethics-and-lobbying-laws.aspx (last visited Jan. 25, 2012).

15. 392 Mass. 604, 467 N.E.2d 826 (1984).

16. Commonwealth v. Borans, 379 Mass. 117, 393 N.E.2d 911 (1979).

17. *Tobin*, 392 Mass. at 610.

18. *See* Employment: Public Employees and Officials—Bribery and Kickback Statutes, 0060 Surveys 26 (Thomas Reuters/West 2011); *see also* National Conference of State Legislatures, Criminal Penalties for Public Corruption/Violations of State Ethics Laws, *available at* http://www.ncsl.org/legislatures-elections/ethicshome/50-state-chart-criminal-penalties-for-public-corr.aspx (last visited Jan. 22, 2012).

19. ARIZ. REV. STAT. §§ 1-215 (5) and 13-2602 (2011).

20. *Id.* §§ 13-2602(C) and 41-2613.

21. VA. CODE ANN. § 2.2-4371(A) (2011).

22. *Id.* § 2.2-4371(B).

23. *Id.* § 2.2-4372(A).

24. *Id.* (B).

25. *Id.* (C).

26. WASH. REV. CODE § 43.19.1937 (2011).

27. *Id.*

28. *Id.* § 43.19.1939(1).

29. W. VA. CODE R. § 148-1-7.16.1(b) (2009).

30. *Id.* § 148-1-10.3.

31. NEV. REV. STAT. § 281A.400(1) (2011).

32. *Id.* § 281A.400(2).

33. *Id.* § 281A.400(3), (4).

34. *Id.* § 281A.400(5).

35. *Id.* § 281A.400(9).

36. *See* National Conference of State Legislatures, Ethics: Contingency Fees for Lobbyists, *available at* http://www.ncsl.org/legislatures-elections/ethicshome/50-state-chart-contingency-fees.aspx (last visited Jan. 26, 2012). Contrary to NCSL's reporting that the District of Columbia does not address

this prohibition in statute, the District of Columbia does, in fact, address contingency fees. *See* D.C. Stat. Ann. 2-354.16 (2011).

37. Ark. Code § 21-8-607 (2011).
38. O.C.G.A. § 21-5-76 (2011).
39. Mont. Code. § 5-7-209 (2011).
40. 403 Md. 716, 944 A.2d 538 (2008).
41. *Id.*, 403 Md. at 738.
42. *Id.* at 732.
43. *Id.* at 730; *see* Md. Code Ann. §§ 5-706 and 15-405.
44. *Bereano*, 403 Md. at 724–25.
45. *Id.* at 733.
46. *Id.* at 734–35.
47. *Id.* at 738.
48. *See, e.g.*, N.M. Stat. Ann. § 10-16-3 (A)(2011) ("A legislator or public officer or employee shall treat the legislator's or public officer's or employee's government position as a public trust. The legislator or public officer or employee shall use the powers and resources of public office only to advance the public interest and not to obtain personal benefits or pursue private interests.").
49. 18 U.S.C. § 208; 5 C.F.R. § 2635.601.
50. 18 U.S.C. § 207; 5 C.F.R. § 2641; 41 U.S.C. § 423(d) (post-employment provisions within procurement integrity provisions of federal law covering former federal officials and employees who acted as contracting officers or who performed other specified contracting or procurement functions for the agency).
51. Fla. Stat. Ann. § 112.313(7)(a)(2011).
52. 3 L.P.R.A. § 1823(b) (2011).
53. *See e.g.*, M.G.L.A. 268A § 17(c) (2011) ("No municipal employee shall, otherwise than in the proper discharge of his official duties, act as agent or attorney for anyone other than the city or town or municipal agency in prosecuting any claim against the same city or town, or as agent or attorney for anyone in connection with any particular matter in which the same city or town is a party or has a direct and substantial interest.").
54. Darleen Druyun pled guilty to, among other violations, an unlawful conflict of interest in negotiating employment with Boeing. Druyun was sentenced to nine months in federal prison, fined $5,000, and ordered to perform 150 hours of community service. See Project on Government Oversight (POGO) Federal Contractor Misconduct Database, *United States of America v. Darleen A. Druyun, available at* http://www.contractormisconduct.org/index.cfm/1,73,222,html?CaseID=48 (last visited Jan. 26, 2012).
55. *See* Keith R. Szeliga, *Watch Your Step: A Contractor's Guide to Revolving-Door Restrictions*, 36 Pub. Cont. L.J. 519, 521 (2007) (discussion focusing on "understanding and formulating strategies to comply with the statutes and regulations that govern the recruiting, hiring, and employment of current and former executive branch employees").

56.   819 So. 2d 1067 (La. App. 2002).

57.   *See id.* at 1068.

58.   *Id.*

59.   NEW AMERICAN STANDARD BIBLE, Luke 16:13 (1995).

60.   2007 MC PIP § 12-108(2)(a).

61.   5 C.F.R. § 2637.101(c); *see* Jack Maskell, *Post-Employment, "Revolving Door," Laws for Federal Personnel,* CRS Report for Congress, 97-875 (May 12, 2010), *available at* http://www.fas.org/sgp/crs/misc/97-875.pdf (last visited Jan. 30, 2012).

62.   ALA. CODE § 36-25-13 (2011).

63.   M.G.L.A. 268A § 18(a) (2011).

64.   The reference to "direct or substantial interest" in the body of § 12-108(2)(b) of the model code is presumed by this author to be a typographical error, considering that the commentary for the same section references "direct and substantial interest."

65.   2007 MC PIP § 12-108(3).

66.   CAL. GOV'T CODE 1090.

67.   *See* People v. Wong, 186 Cal. App. 4th 1433, 1450, 1113 Cal. Rptr. 3d 384, 397 (2010) (conflict of interest found where commissioner had a financial interest in a contract from which he received $100,000 to influence the city's negotiations with a private contractor).

68.   *See* Chapman v. Superior Court, 130 Cal. App. 4th 261, 29 Cal. Rptr. 3d 852, 855 (2005).

69.   FLA. STAT. § 112.313(3)(2011).

70.   Op. Att'y Gen., 2006-50, 2006 WL 3694848 (Dec. 13, 2006).

71.   Op. Att'y Gen., 073-404 (Nov. 6, 1973); *see also* Op. Att'y Gen., 071-230 (Aug. 9, 1971) (prohibiting the board of county commissioners from granting a garbage franchise to a member of the board).

72.   3 L.P.R.A. § 1823(c) (2011).

73.   KAN. STAT. ANN. § 46-241 (2011).

74.   M.G.L.A. 268A, § 23(c) (2011).

Table of Cases

Table of Statutes and Regulations

Pub. Cont. Code § 100, 19
Pub. Cont. Code §§ 5100
   through 5107, 120n24
Pub. Cont. Code § 12100, 5
Pub. Cont. Code § 12103.5, 172n57
Pub. Cont. Code § 20301(a), 199n54

Colorado
Code Regs. §§ 24-103-202a-
   04(b)(ii–iii), 199n33
Rev. Stat. § 18-8-307, 11
Rev. Stat. §§ 24-30-1401
   through 1408, 123n77
Rev. Stat. § 24-101-101 *et seq.*, 19
Rev. Stat. §§ 24-101 through
   112, 120n22
Rev. Stat. § 24-103-202(6), 86, 199n31
Rev. Stat. § 24-103-204, 58n37
Rev. Stat. § 24-104-205, 57n7
Rev. Stat. § 24-105-201(4), 86, 120n23
Rev. Stat. § 24-109-105,
   273n176, 273n186
Rev. Stat. § 24-109-105(1)(b), 272n158
Rev. Stat. § 24-109-105(2), 273n169
Rev. Stat. § 24-109-203, 273n167
Rev. Stat. § 24-109-204(1), 272n165
Rev. Stat. § 24-109-206(1)(b), 273n168
Rev. Stat. § 24-109-404, 219n30

**Commonwealth of Northern
Marianas Islands**
Code tit. 70, ch. 70-30,
   Subch. 70-30.3, 19

Connecticut
Agencies Regs. §§ 4a-52-1
   through 4a-63-5, 19
Gen. Stat. § 4a-60g(b), 172n40
Gen. Stat. § 4e-16, 174n85
Gen. Stat. ch. 58, §§ 4a–4e, 19

Delaware
Code Ann. tit. 29, ch. 69, 19
Code Ann. tit. 29, § 6904(f), 268n57

Code Ann. tit. 29, § 6932, 57n9
Code Ann. tit. 29, § 6933, 175n133

District of Columbia
Code tit. 2 ch. 3B, 19
Code § 2-308.03(a)(1), 280
Code § 2-308.05(a), 280
Code § 2-309.03(a), 280
Code § 2-351.01 *et seq.*, 19
Code § 2-354.16, 313n36
Mun. Regs., tit. 27-100 *et seq.*, 19

Florida
Stat. § 112.313(3), 314n69
Stat. § 112.313(7)(a), 313n51
Stat. § 112.313(12)(b), 308
Stat. § 120.57(3), 20
Stat. § 120.57(3)(b), 218n4, 218n8
Stat. ch. 255, 20
Stat. § 282.0041(16), 172n51
Stat. § 282.0041(17), 172n52
Stat. ch. 287, 20
Stat. §§ 287.001–287.1345, 20
Stat. §§ 287.14–287.20, 20
Stat. § 287.082, 198n23
Stat. § 287.087, 198n22
Stat. § 337.11, 20

Georgia
Code Ann. § 11-2-314, 270n98
Code Ann. § 11-2-315, 270n98
Code Ann. § 13-10-22, 199n43
Code Ann. § 21-5-76, 313n38
Code Ann. § 36-80-7, 20
Code Ann. §§ 50-5-50 *et seq.*, 20
Code Ann. § 50-5-64, 121n50
Code Ann. §§ 50-5-100 *et seq.*, 20
Code Ann. §§ 50-18-70 *et seq.*, 148
Comp. R. & Regs.
   § 665-2-11-.01, 172n46

Guam
Admin. R. & Regs. tit. 2,
   Div. 4, chs. 1–12, 20

Code Ann. tit. 5, Div. 1, ch. 5,
Arts. 1–13, 20

Hawaii
Code R. §§ 3-120 through 132, 20
Code R. § 3-126-4, 218n9
Code R. §§ 3-140 through 149, 20
Rev. Stat. § 103D, 20
Rev. Stat. § 103D-701(a), 218n9
Rev. Stat. §103D-703, 286n28
Rev. Stat. §§ 103D-1001
through 1004, 170n12
Rev. Stat. § 103D-1001, 170n13
Rev. Stat. § 103D-1001(2), 170n21
Rev. Stat. § 103D-1001.5, 170n15
Rev. Stat. § 103D-1002(a)(1)–
(3)(A–C), 170n16
Rev. Stat. § 103D-1002(c), 170n17
Rev. Stat. § 103D-1002(d), 170n18
Rev. Stat. § 103D-1003, 170n20
Rev. Stat. § 103D-1003(a), 170n22
Rev. Stat. § 103D-
1006, 170n12, 170n19
Rev. Stat. § 103F, 20

Idaho
Admin. Code § 38.05.01, 20
Code Ann. § 40-113(4), 200n60
Code Ann. § 67-5711C(2), 58n19
Code Ann. §§ 67-5714
through 67-5748, 20

Illinois
5 Comp. Stat. § 220/3, 175n132
30 Comp. Stat. § 105/13, 35
30 Comp. Stat. § 500, 20
30 Comp. Stat. § 500/20-20, 58n42
30 Comp. Stat. § 500/20-30,
58n53, 58n56
30 Comp. Stat. § 537/30(a), 200n65
30 Comp. Stat. § 537/30(b), 200n68
65 Comp. Stat. § 5/8-10-1 et seq.,
28n84
65 Comp. Stat. § 5/8-10-16, 28n83

65 Comp. Stat. § 5/8-10-18, 29n85
65 Comp. Stat. §5/8-10-21, 29n87
44 Admin. Code §§ 1.1
through 1.7030, 20
44 Admin. Code § 4.2015, 199n56
Chi. Mun. Code § 2-92-010, 28n83
Chi. Mun. Code § 2-92-050, 29n89

Indiana
Admin. Code Art. 1.1, 21
Code § 4-13.6-6-2, 136n1
Code § 4-13.6-7-6(a), 137n21
Code § 4-13.6-7-7(a), 137n18
Code §§ 5-22-1-1 et seq., 21
Code § 8-23-10, 130
Code § 8-23-10-3, 136n5
Code § 8-23-10-4, 136n6
Code § 8-23-10-6, 136n4
Code § 36-1-12-18, 268n62
Code § 36-9-27-80.5, 268n62

Iowa
Admin. Code tit. 11, ch. 105, 21
Code § 17A.19(1), 218n3
Code § 73A.1, 174n80
Code § 73A.2, 219n32
Code § 331, 21
Code § 362, 21
Code § 364, 21
Code § 384, 21
Code § 473, 21

Kansas
Admin. Regs. Agency 48
and Agency 50, 21
Stat. Ann. § 12-55, 158
Stat. Ann. § 12-5501, 158,
174n81, 174n94
Stat. Ann. § 12-5502, 158, 174n96
Stat. Ann. § 12-5503, 158, 174n97
Stat. Ann. § 12-5504, 158, 174n98
Stat. Ann. § 12-5505, 158, 174n99
Stat. Ann. ch. 46, 158
Stat. Ann. § 46-241, 314n73

Index